WEST OF ARABIA

A JOURNEY HOME

GARY HEATH

CONTENTS

Gary Heath WEST OF ARABIA

A Journey Home

West of Arabia by Gary Heath

Text and map © 2011 Gary Heath

Second Edition, 2021, published by the Caoshan Press of Birchington, Kent, England

ISBN: 978-1-8381577-1-5 (paperback)

ISBN: 978-1-8381577-3-9 (ebook)

www.caoshanpress.com

First published 2011 by Ozaru Books

Cover design by James Nunn

Interior formatting by *Hannah Linder Designs*

Due to the lack of a unique standard for Romanizing Arabic, or other languages encountered on this journey, place names, personal names and other words have been written as they were seen and/or heard at the time.

FOREWORD

Faced with the need to travel from Saudi Arabia to the UK, Gary Heath made the unusual decision to take the overland route. His three principles were to stay on the ground, avoid back-tracking, and do minimal sightseeing.

The ever-changing situation in the Middle East meant that the rules had to be bent on occasion, yet as he travelled across Eritrea, Sudan, Egypt, Libya, Tunisia and Morocco, he succeeded in beating his own path around the tourist traps, gaining unique insights into Arabic culture as he went.

Written just a few months before the Arab Spring of 2011, this book reveals many of the underlying tensions that were to explode onto the world stage just shortly afterwards, and has been updated to reflect the recent changes.

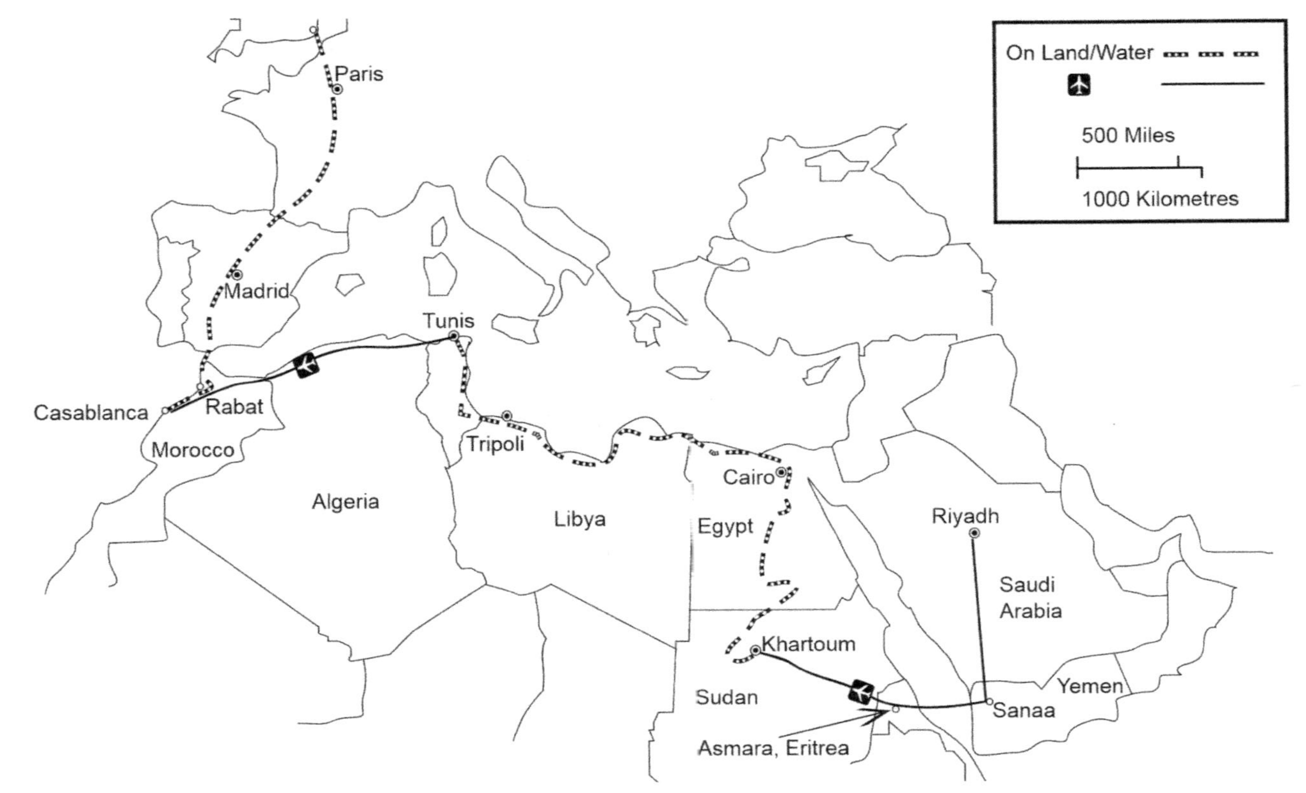

On Land/Water
500 Miles
1000 Kilometres
Paris
Madrid
Casablanca
Rabat
Morocco
Tunis
Algeria
Tripoli
Libya
Cairo
Egypt
Riyadh
Saudi Arabia
Khartoum
Sudan
Asmara, Eritrea
Sanaa
Yemen

PROLOGUE

THE AIRPORT IS ON THE OUTSKIRTS OF A CITY THAT LOOKS, FROM THE snatches of views available out of the plane window, rather decrepit and unkempt, a shanty town almost, embedded into a high plateau of dust and rock. We are approaching from the north, so this impression is probably misleading. The plane, a middling jet, touches down and taxies up to a small building. We passengers duly file off the aircraft and take a short walk over to what looks like a bus station, but is in fact an aircraft terminal. Insects can be heard despite the dryness of the air, and their bothersome presence comes as a novelty to the new arrivals that lately have not had to deal with hostile fauna of any kind. Casting around, one sees a wind sock hanging languidly from a post, a sprinkling of aging passenger aircraft and a small fleet of worn stretch buses. A helicopter buzzes across the aerodrome, more noticeable but less impressive sounding than the insects; it looks like a toy. A glance up to a sign informs visitors where they are, "Sanaa International Airport."

At this moment, we are caught in travel-space time, and this perhaps is the appeal of airports: they take us away from ourselves and our own histories; they are purely functional, modern caravanserais of the mind. The warm afternoon sun shines an intense amber light against the crude, but welcoming, little terminal and we disperse into the hall. Most people are headed for the exit, but the rest of us head to transfers, in effect the right-hand side of the room where smoking is permissible, indeed de rigueur. There is no air-conditioning, another novelty, and the air is mildly stifling, but contains within it a hint of cold nights. A dozen Africans, clearly used to delays, gather together on a pew of plastic seats and wait stoically. It is going to be a long, boring few hours inside the airport and I drop into a reverie and consider all the plans I had laid to visit the country outside, plans necessarily abandoned. The stopover at this airport is as far as I will get in Yemen.

THE ONLY REPUBLIC on the Arabian Peninsula, Yemen, a territory the size of France, is one of the poorest countries in the world, but one that must surely have the proudest citizenry. The population, spread over a rugged and in places very inhospitable terrain, are certainly well armed: it is estimated that 60 million guns are in circulation among a population of 20 million. Guns are the warp and woof of Yemeni society, even more so than in the United States. And then there are all the daggers which Yemeni men of a certain prevalent type would not be seen dead without in public. There is no doubt that Yemenis are in general tough; lacking the pretensions of the Gulf Arabs, they are broad-minded and personable on the whole. The country's problems apparently stem from chronic corruption and from a lack of moral leadership, or so I had been led to believe.

Most recently described as a "failing state" by so many journalists and wannabe analysts, Yemen is nonetheless a complex and, to the romantic-minded, intriguing destination. I desperately wanted to go there, and desperately tried to get a tourist visa organized, but my timing was off. After a bungled terrorist attack by a Nigerian national over Detroit on Christmas day 2009, Yemen was thrown into the spotlight and re-cast as a terrorist haven – the bomber had been trained in Yemen by a well-known group of Islamist militants. Throughout the coming year, a series of terrorist attacks, including an attempt on the British ambassador's life by a suicide bomber, did nothing to improve Yemen's image in the eyes of the world's media. "Is Yemen becoming a Jihadist plotter's paradise", was the title of one of the more considered pieces written by the BBC's Middle East terrorist expert Frank Gardner. The almost successful bombing of one of its planes momentarily caused great consternation in the United States with American politicians more or less intimating that direct military intervention in Yemen was desirable. In the end, the US intervened covertly. The results of this intervention are hard to gauge, but as Frank Gardner pointed out in his article, accidentally slaughtering your friends – an unmanned US drone strike in May 2010 killed the deputy governor of Marib province, for example – is hardly a winning strategy. In June 2010, the White House announced the doubling of humanitarian aid to Yemen; conferences were held, more aid promised. Meanwhile, in an audacious and bloody raid, militants sprung a number of their cohorts from the southern headquarters of the Yemeni government's security apparatus. Sporadic kidnappings of foreigners continued unabated; the tribes still ruled in the lawless mountains. Yemen's central government had trouble in the north, trouble in the south, and trouble on its doorstep and that is not to mention the running out of its oil, gas and even water reserves. The "failing state" label was an all too easy to apply to Yemen in 2010. None of this actually deterred me from wanting to go there, though. I knew there was another Yemen behind the scenes, one filled with beauty and honour, wondrous mountain landscapes, gracious hospitality, great music and colourful ceremony; a place where men were men and to hell with the government. Although the victims of terrorist crimes would surely have begged to differ, I did not think Yemen was quite as bad as some people with ulterior motives made it out to be. Nevertheless, my plans to visit this great country had to be scuppered after the Yemeni government announced, early on in 2010, that tourist visas were only to be issued by the Foreign Affairs Ministry in Sanaa, and no longer on arrival at Sanaa airport, or at the Yemen embassy in the country I was residing in at the time, which made an application ludicrously difficult. Who in their right mind would send their passport to an office in Sanaa? Game over.

After a short while, an airport official ushers us into a semi-air-conditioned transit lounge, which has a coffee bar, and a duty free area that stocks a modest amount of liquor. There is a VIP suite of some kind upstairs. I make a beeline for the latter, only to be beaten back by a rickety stairwell that looks like it will collapse at any moment. The waiting lounge downstairs is charmingly out of date and has space for perhaps 100 passengers. There is a flight in one hour to Jeddah, Saudi Arabia, and a few people sit around in quiet anticipation of it. After buying a coffee with my last Saudi riyals, I take a seat behind a man who busily re-arranges his small, neat suitcase, folding his pyjamas over some new shoes and an assortment of treasured books. He is wearing a western suit and is no doubt headed north to some office job in the oil-rich kingdom. Another airport official keeps up a lively natter with a colleague as he precariously balances a hot beverage on a tape barrier support: it is always tea time in Yemen. Several girls from Saudi Arabia, transferring to I know not where, also talk in an animated way, but individually into their smart phones. They are shy, and keep their veils on in this dangerously open environment. Trying to talk to one of them would be like trying to defuse a bomb: an act fraught with risk. I lower my eyes away from the females and jot down a few notes. It has been a surprisingly long and tiring journey from Riyadh, 1100 kilometres distant, but only a 60-minute flight away. My exhaustion is partly mental and a result of the strain of working a hardship posting. Now I am on my way to North East Africa, a difficult area, via a country I could not secure a visa for, a mangle of circumstances. But this is it: my journey westwards from

Arabia begins here in this airport for better or worse. To stave off the boredom – my onward flight will not leave for another two hours – I pick up an English-language Yemeni newspaper. On page two of this thin newspaper it is reported that tribesman recently held up a UNICEF convoy and got away with $40 000 worth of food and materials, a humanitarian raid so to speak; they say the Lord helps those who help themselves, an idea evidently well understood by Yemeni tribesman.

As I chuckle to myself over the ironies of a raid on an aid convoy, a man sits down next to me. I keep reading, but the paper has nothing else of interest in it and I soon toss it away. The man is dressed in a white Arab long shirt, the national dress of Arabs all over the Peninsula, but he wears it casually and without a headdress, leading me to believe he is not a Saudi. The middle-aged man's boyish face and sparkling eyes speak of psychological security. A pair of spectacles balances off his hook nose and this further gives him a benevolent, professorial appearance; he looks out of place here among the tense escapees and worn migrant workers. He speaks first.

"Hello. Where are you from?" That question again, somewhat inevitably. Coming from this nice man, who has such engaging, innocent eyes, I am happy to answer, and when he finds out I am from the United Kingdom, this is his cue. He is from Aden and doesn't mind telling me British aeroplanes bombed his family's property during the Aden Emergency back in the 1960s. He mentions this like it happened yesterday; and so the Arab mind works, not missing a beat, or forgetting an event.

"Sorry about that." Old boy, I almost add in RAF idiom. But the Yemeni man is delighted at my slightly ironic apology, smiles broadly and slaps my leg amused.

"Haha, not a problem…it was before…Aden was a good place then…good business…ships and people many…good business…" The Aden native is too polite to give me a candid assessment of the British occupation of Aden that lasted 128 years, but he obviously feels a certain nostalgia for the colonial era, despite the violent end to British rule in his home town – a fighting Royal Marines rear-guard were the last to leave Aden in November 1967, no handover ceremony required. The enduring legacy of British rule in southern Yemen, a legacy typical in former colonial territories, was to leave a country divided between those who had been acculturated to British ways under colonial rule, and those who had not. War followed. North and South Yemen re-united in 1990, but the South, essentially Aden, frequently expresses its dissatisfaction with the central government, located in the north. Since I am here with personable Mohammed, I take the chance to quiz him about Yemen's messy politics and north-south relations as the Saudi females bundle through security on their way, I now see, to dangerously open Aden.

"Tell me, Mohammed, the Yemenis I have met seem to be a well-educated and decent bunch, how come you have such a dysfunctional government?" Mohammed, a businessperson in the photographic retail trade, rolls his eyes and replies with typical Arab candidness and directness.

"It is not to do with ideology anymore. Yes, there are radicals everywhere, liberals, too. In the south, we want our rights. All government privileges are given to northerners: they get all the best jobs, all the best positions. We are left with nothing. The country cannot possibly flourish. You see, the guy in charge is not highly educated. He just wants to stay in power and uses every trick to do so. He makes promises to one group, and plays them off against another group, but doesn't keep his promises. That's why people try to get something by force." The guy in charge Mohammed refers to is Yemen's wily president, Ali Abdullah Saleh, who has been the political leader of Yemen since unification. A former soldier, he built a solid power base in the north in the 1960s, and he continues to use this constituency to cling on to the presidency today. Mohammed laments the state of the republic.

"Yemen is the homeland of the Arabs. We have a long history. After the Marib dam collapsed…" The collapse of the Marib dam occurred in the 7th century and heralded the end, many believe, of southern Arabia's golden trade era, trade based on the area's highly-valued frankincense and myrrh. This was the land known in the west as Sheba, as in the Queen of Sheba, and *Felix Arabia* by the Romans. "…our people began to migrate all over Arabia. Some went to Medina where they supported the Prophet Mohammed. To feel proud, we look to this past. The happy days for Yemen are over; the people brood and know this president thinks of nothing other than staying in power, and he will do it by any means. He is tricky at convincing people and has experts in persuasion around him who speak to the people in their own language. The nation is corrupted by bribery from the tiniest cup to the highest judge. Who will reform the country when everyone is corrupted?" Mohammed's glasses repeatedly slip down his nose, and he repeatedly pushes them back up. He has done very well for himself in Saudi Arabia, I discover as our conversation veers onto the personal. After working for a Saudi businessperson for a while, he went into the business as a partner and thrived. He has eight children, all growing up in Jeddah. He has travelled widely in Europe and has a long term plan to migrate to Hungary in order to get EU residency. What is so impressive about Mohammed is the methodical and single-minded way he approaches life, hence his success. He doesn't have time to take pictures because he is so busy making money selling cameras.

Before long, Mohammed gets up, says goodbye to me quickly but warmly, and then heads off with his suited compatriot to board the Jeddah-bound flight. My flight to Asmara, Eritrea, is called soon afterwards. I am glad to be finally leaving the Peninsula because my time in Saudi Arabia had been very trying.

I

ARABIA

1

____

DUST CITY

Whorls of dust beside the road appeared out of nowhere like desert raiders. Whipping up into miniature tornados they seemed to be racing us, perhaps on the orders of a genie, and then suddenly they were gone only to reappear somewhere else soon afterwards before finally disappearing back into the desert. The ground they touched was stirred but not cleaned; dust here was only ever re-arranged. We drove a long way north-westwards out of the city along the main Qassim road, past a camel emporia and a throng of lunatics who were driving their four-wheel drive vehicles up and down sand dunes for amusement. Eventually, we left the main road and followed some tracks across the desert, an escarpment lifting out of the pancake-flat surface to our right. A further few kilometres driving got us to a private aviation club of some kind. In fact, there were no aircraft in sight. The club was also designated a conservation area. What was being conserved out here was hard to imagine, but it is said a surprising amount of life can be found in the desert. Conservation area or no, we charged on slashing across a hard desert floor ideal for driving on, and for a moment I thought of Russian relief trucks driving across frozen Lake Ladoga during the siege of Leningrad. We were on no such important mission, however. We were having fun, Saudi style.

"Ya, you must not take photos. No, no. It's not like England." Hans assumed I was naïve and did not know about the restrictions on photography in Arabia; he wanted me to follow orders. But actually I was always taking photos, basically calibrating myself against authority, and seeing what I could get away with. One had to proceed with the great care when anyone in uniform was around though; police and national guardsmen, often Bedouins, were alert and remarkably observant. One such eagle-eyed police officer at the conservation area post had seen me taking a few snaps from the back of the car. He stopped us and told me in no uncertain terms to cease what I was doing. It was the third time I had been pulled up for taking photographs in one week. On this occasion, because I was with a group of white expatriates, the guardsman let it go.

On we drove, Hans, his wife, a Finnish nurse and I, to rendezvous with some other expatriates for a group walkabout in the desert. It had been a hot day, and what is worse windy, but the afternoon temperature was dropping, and the wind had turned into a pleasant, cooling breeze. We finally arrived at our destination, a dried out valley, or wadi, surrounded by high ground. The area was covered here and there with a splash of green vegetation, a welcome sight. The desert around Riyadh, located on a 600 metre-high plateau, was varied, and threw up all sorts of oddities. In the middle of a totally dry valley, for example, a lone bright translucent green tree might be growing happily, and you wondered just how it survived. Elsewhere, trees and bushes, adapted to the hot climate, clumped together along dry riverbeds somehow drawing sustenance out of the ground. At one time, the whole of Arabia would have been covered in flora of the type we found that day, and lusher, but the sands of time were unstoppable. Now the desiccated landscape, though fascinating in a sort of otherworldly way, was unforgiving. As Wilfred Thesiger discerned, it was a place where "basic truths emerge." Rambling with a group of people somehow prevented one from connecting with the mystery of the desert, but it was safe. The great days of British desert exploration were probably over, and I was in no position, and had no desire, to repeat them. This little jaunt, and a few of more like them, was as close as I would get to the fearsome deserts of Arabia.

Hans, a German who aged thirteen had seen service with a bazooka unit in World War II, meticulously parked his vehicle, which somewhat resembled a tank, next to some others by the dirt track we had been following. An assorted group of 20 to 30 people had rendezvoused and were going through the rituals of introducing themselves. After the introductions, we all went off into the wadi on foot. Two scouts led the way. This area had been chosen for our walk, I came to realize, because it was full of topographical interest: we walked along the vegetated river bed, climbed a steep, crumbling slope, and then hiked along the top of a high escarpment from where one could see other, smaller dried wadis, thousands of years in the making, dropping off the edge of the plateau into an unending abyss of flat nothingness. At one point, I stumbled across blackened, fossilised coral, evidence that this land had emerged from the sea, as most land does in the great drowning and re-birth of continents. I picked the coral up to make sure my eyes were not deceiving me, and they were not: it was unmistakably a marine skeleton. Across the other side of the wadi eroded cliffs looked like a ruined city, but this was just the imagination playing tricks, and on closer inspection the cliffs were revealed as random land formations, but were somehow all the more mysterious for that. We walked on and over what resembled huge slabs of fudge; it was the ridge eroding away, eventually to become dust like everything else, and here indeed was a basic truth right under our feet.

The Finnish nurse walked with me a little way. She was wearing some plastic slip-on half-shoes, hardly suitable footwear for the rugged terrain we found ourselves on, and she had fallen behind the group, my own default position in any herd. She was young and obviously desperate to make friends, the main purpose of going on these weekend expeditions it seemed.

She said, "Do you often come on these walks?" It was my

second time only, but clearly I had a bit more experience of walking than Katarina. What on earth was she thinking wearing those useless green plastic moulds? She struggled along and we chatted about what we were doing in Saudi Arabia, our occupations in other words. I had come to teach English at a local university, a smash and grab essentially. She was a career nurse at a local hospital. Single people in Saudi Arabia are rigorously segregated, so strictly speaking we were breaking the law walking alone together like this out in the desert, not that anyone really cared about us expatriates. If I had been found with a single Saudi woman not related to me by someone in authority, however, it could have landed me in serious trouble. Katarina and I enjoyed our chat, and our breaking of the law, but we both felt the time and place somewhat contrived, or at least I did. Then, as were discussing the cosseted way single women were treated in the kingdom, Katarina told me something that shocked me.

"It is not safe for a woman to take taxis alone here." I asked her why. "Three of my colleagues who went out in a taxi to go shopping in Riyadh together went missing. They never came back and no one knows what happened to them. Despite a search and many enquiries no trace of them has been found. Once a taxi driver took me a long way out into the desert and I realized he was taking me somewhere I did not want to go. I told him to stop, but he wouldn't. Only when I called a friend did he become nervous and took me back into town, where I got out of the taxi. It frightened me."

The three missing women were Philippine nationals, apparently, and the news of their disappearance was kept very quiet. These things did not happen often, I was told, but they did happen, and it is therefore not surprising that elaborate security arrangements are laid on for single expatriate women in Saudi Arabia, because such women are meat to sex-starved men, and to some extent considered fair game if out alone without a male guardian. In general respectful towards women, Arab men, like any men, are capable of gratuitous meanness toward females.

One American woman I knew had had the remains of a take-away meal thrown over by a man from his car window – brave heart that he was – as she walked down a road near her home unveiled. Exactly the same thing happened to a male colleague of mine as he was jogging in his neighbourhood one day, except he was doused with water. Those incidents were but trifles compared to the disappearances. When Katarina told me her story, which to be fair I had no way of confirming, my blood froze because I knew it was something that could happen, especially with so much empty desert around the city inviting wickedness as well as naughtiness.

The walk ended. We re-grouped by the cars, and sipped homemade wine in the quickly gathering dusk. It now felt chilly and it was necessary to put on more clothes to keep warm. Hans' wife had cut her finger on a thorn bush during the safari. I pulled out my small first aid kit and dressed her wound. As I dabbed a little iodine on his wife's finger, Hans, comfortably ensconced in a foldaway chair, shouted, "Ya, you're doing a good job duktor," before turning back to the Finnish nurse with whom he was engrossed in conversation.

"Thank you Hans, and pour me another one won't you," I said, trying to capitalize on the moment, but Hans was not listening, not to me anyway.

The cars left one by one. We lingered a while. Then, after bundling into the car, there was a moment of panic when the engine failed to start – a flat battery. I felt sure a German would have prepared for this moment – Hans probably a spare battery or two fully-charged and ready to go in his boot. But he did not!

"Vere's zee bloody fuckin' spare baattery…" Hans, a lean and energetic man, actually remained calm despite the rather worrying situation. We were stranded in the desert. What were we to do? I looked at blonde-haired Katarina thinking it would only make sense for us to cosy up to one another during the long, cold night ahead. Hans' resourceful wife had other ideas, however. She called the driver of a vehicle, whom she knew, and who had not long departed our camp, and asked him to come

back, which he promptly did. With the aid of a pair of jump
leads, we were then able to get the car running. It was dark by
now and Hans had to rely on the tail lights of the car in front of
us, and on cars on a distant road, for navigation. He was a good
driver though, and our return journey passed off uneventfully.
Soon the tungsten and neon lights of Riyadh welcomed the expatriate singletons and couples back to their somewhat isolated
lives in Dust City – another week of boredom loomed large.

"BUT CHIMPANZEES DO HAVE CULTURE; are you trying to tell me
they don't!! They have tools, and that is culture!! They must
speak to one another!!" My roommate, David, who I had first
met on the long, feelings-of-doom-inducing flight to Riyadh
from London a month previously, had become slightly hysterical. I had been arguing – since this was one of our few available
pastimes – that what differentiated human beings from animals
was language, itself higher consciousness based on the Word.
Chimpanzees are fascinating because their behaviour resembles
human behaviour in so many ways. For example, they patrol
their territories and go to war with their neighbours, just like we
do. However, they do not possess higher consciousness: they
will use a tool if they see it, but they have no word for the tool,
and therefore do not remember its existence when it is out of
sight. I had tried explaining all this to David, a veteran of
teaching English in the Gulf, and sometime poet. The conversation had reached the point where it had to be ended. I was tired
of arguing, and sought another distraction. So, like a chimp, I
went out on patrol.

David and I had been allocated housing in the north-eastern
suburbs of Riyadh not far from the university. The apartments
had not been completed when we arrived and we had to wait
two weeks before moving in. In due course, and after removing a
ton of dust from all surfaces, we settled into our digs. The apartments were not bad in some ways. They were roomy and

furnished to an adequate, if not exactly luxurious standard. But there was very little to do in the neighbourhood, except walk around it to prevent oneself going stir crazy. The neighbourhood was quite weird, which made it sort of interesting. Immediately you walked out the apartment block you faced a building site on the left, and beyond that was open desert, over which birds of prey glided in afternoon thermals. To the right was a large, secure mental hospital; a drug rehabilitation unit of some kind – drug abuse was one of Saudi Arabia's dirty little secrets, and judging by the amount of medical waste dumped outside the hospital, a serious problem in the kingdom. Sometimes, especially in the mornings, passing the hospital I would spot birds in the planted trees just the other side of the perimeter wall. In the winter, a variety of migrating birds made their home here. I had sketched some of these birds in my notebook: one had a black head with a large white spot on its greyish body; another one was all black with an orange beak and long tail. But I never got to identify these birds. The desert falcons did not visit the hospital environs, and these birds seemed safe enough, although I thought it was the ultimate irony for a bird to seek sanctuary in a mental institution. After leaving David, I went on a long walk that took me around this large hospital, and on into a nearby wadi.

The little irrigated valley, surrounded by the building site on one side, and an upmarket neighbourhood of gated villas on the other side, was backed by desert. It was a pleasant place to explore in winter, and this day was perfect for a walk: warm and sunny, but not too hot. The sun warmed my face, and a cool breeze evaporated my sweat, a natural cooling system. The floor of the wadi had been flooded creating a green meadow; I tramped through it getting my feet muddy. Three lugubrious cows stood on the other side of the flooded field, a surreal sight. The wadi had been divided into sections by rows of trees acting as wind breaks. I found an opening through the first line of trees and entered a lemon grove. This place, which I had to myself as I walked, was particularly enchanting: the yellow fruit was abundant on the trees, a peculiar fecundity considering the surrounding dry landscape. But water is everything, and with it comes life; a fat hosepipe hung from a well that stood at the far end of the grove, carrying water to all corners of the wadi. Some household waste water was also being dispersed into drainage channels around the valley, giving off a terrible pong, but also feeding the growth of algae. Pushing on around the wadi, I finally came to a large oasis of tall palm trees, visible in the distance from our apartment. I wandered about the trees, astonished by the greenness and enjoying the pleasant shade and play of light reflected in ground water. Some kind of summer playhouse belonging to a family had been left open, a few children's toys strewn about. In fact, no one would appear either to greet me or shoo me away on this ramble. Only a couple of hired hands, who kept their distance, ghosted the landscape. The magic of the woods eventually wore off, and patrol over I returned to the apartment via a small finger of the wadi that intruded right up to our housing block.

Later on during my time in Riyadh, I would regularly walk around a more established neighbourhood. Also in the northeast of the city, it was still the province of the upper middle classes, impressive villas everywhere. Superficially impressive, it must be said, because the build quality was invariably low, basically a lot of reinforced concrete moulded to some fancy, polyglot design. The most striking thing was that you rarely saw anybody on the roads outside the houses, except at prayer times when men walked to their local mosque, of which there were many in the neighbourhood. Occasionally an Indian migrant worker would ride by on a bicycle. Only once did I ever meet a child, who asked me if I was a Muslim, an odd way to greet somebody – perhaps he had been influenced by some devout adults? The rest of the population seemed to slink about in cars and sports utility vehicles, hardly ever venturing out onto the street. Privacy is everything to a Saudi/Muslim family, most especially in Riyadh, traditionally a Bedouin area after all. Dodging speeding cars down these back streets, I considered it my duty to patrol, to get out there. In the summer, I walked in the evenings, which were stiflingly warm and horribly dusty, but just about bearable if you covered your mouth a cloth. It was on one such hot and dry night, walking back to my apartment along one of Riyadh's principal roads, when I witnessed a new high rise building going up in flames, a veritable towering inferno. A petroleum station stood not 30 metres away from the flaming torchlight, much to the consternation of the local police. This minor disaster – the building was unfinished, unoccupied and, in my opinion, worthless – was a rare bit of excitement during my city walks.

Upon returning to the apartment that autumn day shortly after arriving in Riyadh, I saw David again. He was hunched over his laptop in one of our spare rooms, his highbrow furrowed in concentration. He was trying to write poetry, a hopeless task in Riyadh where we were all practically speaking held captive by our employers and further enslaved by a highly repressive social and political system. At least he was trying, and I respected him for his effort. But the school gig was not for David. He complained about everything, and the day we were instructed to wear neck ties at work was the day he resigned. He left a couple of weeks later, after heroically walking to and from our school, located two kilometres distant from the apartment, every day. Anyone who walked along Riyadh's main roads – as opposed to the side streets, many of which did not have side-walks – was certainly taking a risk. It was David who had taught me the pick-your-moment-and-run road crossing technique. Woe betide you if you slipped on a grease spot, or mistimed your run.

In the 1960s, when slavery was abolished in Saudi Arabia, Riyadh's residents numbered less than 200,000; it was not much more than a provincial town in terms of facilities and infrastructure. The relocation of Saudi Arabia's central govern-ment to Riyadh in 1961, and the 1970s oil and construction boom, led to rapid population growth. Today, about five million people live in the desert city. And Riyadh is fast becoming a mega-city; it has been estimated that the city's population will reach eleven million by 2020. This is astonishing because there are no permanent year-round rivers or lakes near the land-locked capital and most water has to be either extracted from the ground, or piped in from desalination plants. Of course, oil money pays for everything, including Riyadh's relentless urban spread. Divided into quadrants roughly two kilometres square, Riyadh is a large, spread out, low-rise city, and requires a car, hired or otherwise, to get around.

Notwithstanding the dust, Riyadh appeared modern to me: there were large, well-stocked shopping malls and supermarkets in many districts; neat, serviced gas stations could be found everywhere; the arterial roads were extensive and well-main-tained. I found I wanted for nothing in terms of consumer goods, and hiring taxis was cheap, especially if shared. The city had two enormous high-rise towers, located downtown, of unique size and design, very useful for navigation purposes since they could be seen anywhere in the city on a reasonably clear day. Both the Kingdom Tower and Faisiliya Tower had glitzy, clinically clean, shopping malls on their ground and first floors. One of my first experiences in Saudi Arabia was a visit to the Kingdom Tower where I marvelled at the swanky shops and expensive goods available; one store stocked every type luxury watch imaginable, another all the latest IT gadgets, and so on. Strictly speaking, as a single man, I was not entitled to shop there at the same time as single women, but unawares I had turned up on a "family day" and got to eye pretty young girls walking about unveiled. One teenage girl blushed when she saw me staring at her; I had been rather taken by her good looks. Later, I learned not to stare, not because it was dangerous, but because it was a form of self-inflicted torture. One also learned to ignore the hair-raising drag-style driving of many of the locals, although I never became completely inured to the dangers of being on the road, and I personally chose not to drive.

After settling into my teaching job, which was not particularly demanding in the beginning, I set out to discover the "real" Riyadh. Without a guide, and armed with only a little pigeon Arabic, I was never going to get very far with this, and tales of elicit bacchanalian parties remained just tales to me. However, what interested me were the physical aspects of city; the road system, the neighbourhoods and few public amenities. Riyadh resembled a building site: piles of rubble, and unused vacant lots were to be found almost everywhere outside the city centre. In the north-east sector of the city, where I lived for two years, new villas were going up in many of the gaps. There was evidently very little town planning, and the idea seemed to be to buy a plot, get someone to build your house, and then install the necessary amenities, in that order. One neighbourhood I walked through a few times resembled a public housing project in a western country. It had a small sports centre, parks, a mosque and even its own post office. But it was one of a kind, and the rest of the urban landscape had a haphazard quality to it, ordered by the huge, fast roads that carved the city into a grid. An occasional glimpse through a gated villa hinted at austere luxury, small oases of calm and good taste. On one occasion, I accidentally walked into someone's back yard, which actually had a boating pool, complete with glass fibre boats, plonked in the middle of a landscaped lawn. Next to this fantasy creation was the usual vacant lot, covered in scrub and rubble, waiting to be developed into another private mansion. Here and there one would see a closed circuit television hanging off the side of a wall like a gargoyle, but the villas' high walls sent a clear enough message, and caretakers invariably stood guard by the gates. On the rare occasions I met someone in the street during my explorations, I greeted them in Arabic, and was politely greeted in turn. Face to face, I rarely experienced any unpleasantness from strangers anywhere in Arabia.

Other neighbourhoods, located in the southern part of the city mostly, but also in the cracks between the villa-lands, grew more cramped accommodations. Dormitory-style housing, designed for migrant workers, and for professionals working short term contracts, could be found everywhere. These housing developments varied in size and quality, but most were adequate. It was the slums in the south of the city, viewed from the road as you sped past, that I found shocking. In world terms, these areas, mostly inhabited by Pakistanis and Indians, were not that bad, but in comparison to how the Saudi upper middle classes lived, they were awful, as was the infrastructure around them, particularly the sub-standard hospitals and clinics. You had to go to the eastern outskirts of the city, on the road to Dammam, to see some genuine slums. Here even the densest mind could comprehend the concept of social class: just a short distance from one of the richest cities in the world, I saw people living in the most rudimentary of housing with no social amenities at all. Maybe these people were happy with their lot, but I doubt it somehow. Saudi Arabia is ruled by a large family that do not stint on themselves; everyone else gets rewarded according to their position in the pecking order, but incredibly some Saudi citizens find themselves at the bottom of that order.

One downtown area I visited relatively frequently, disdained by middle-class Saudis, was Bahta. This neighbourhood was located near some public gardens, a large mosque, and the National Museum. Bahta was a kind of Chinatown, except instead of Chinese the place was mostly inhabited by sub-continental Indians, including Pakistanis and Bangladeshis, and also Filipinos. On the weekend, Bahta became flooded with these nationalities; they came to shop and to hang out with one another. The buildings of Bahta were dreary 1960s multi-floor concrete boxes, but the place had some life to it, whereas none could be found elsewhere on the streets of the city. Here there were pedestrians aplenty, and all kinds of specialist cheap shops ranging from tailors and tent making businesses to electronics vendors and travel and cargo agents. I enjoyed the bustle of Bahta, and occasionally ate in an Indian or Filipino restaurant there. But, alas, it was the same old problem: this was a homosocial world, and single women and men were not allowed to mix.

In fact, the streets were full of men, and the women, gaggles of Filipino domestic workers, for example, kept to themselves. This was one of the saddest things about Saudi Arabia: people acted as if they were being watched even when they were not.

It was in Bahta, one day during my second year of residence, that I was accosted by a taxi driver, doubling as a Committee for the Promotion of Virtue and Prevention of Vice reservist. He had seen me snapping pictures of the road he had been driving on. What followed was a rare unpleasant interaction with a stranger, but it was *very* unpleasant. The man, dressed in a blue and white striped long shirt, was clearly upset about me taking photos and, after stopping his car by me, tried in an extremely aggressive manner to get me into his vehicle. Naturally, I refused to co-operate, but I couldn't get away from the irate ninny either; every time I tried to do so he became physical. I kept calm, resisting the temptation to punch this moron in the face every time he manhandled me. I had not been photographing a government building or any kind of security point, and I knew I would be okay so long as I did not lose my temper. The goon, with his sloppy dress, bad manners and strong body odour, disgusted me, but he meant business. Fortunately, we were standing by an open road, and after flagging a police car down and explaining the situation to the police officer, the taxi driver was told to back off. He even raised his fingers to his mouth and made a shoosh sound as if pleading with me to not tell the police officer the full story of his abuse. It all ended when I informed the English-speaking cop that I had no intention of pressing charges against the lunatic, thank you and good day. After this incident, Bahta ceased to be my favourite weekend getaway; I had been getting bored with the place anyway.

OTHER AMUSING VENUES were few and far between in Riyadh, but I always enjoyed going to the city's hospitals funnily enough. My local hospital was located downtown, not far from Bahta, and my employee insurance card covered the cost of the visits. Riyadh's hospitals were fascinating. The practise of medicine seemed to enforce a kind of rationality on people absent in the outside world, and the sexes mingled far more freely in those institutions. In one hospital I visited, the best in Riyadh, the staff canteen was arranged so that you could eat in an all-male section, in an all-female section, or in a mixed section, and who could argue with such an arrangement? At my local hospital, which was very modern and bang up to date in every respect, I would pop along early, buy myself a coffee and chat with a nurse or two if I got the chance. Just getting the chance to look at females was rather nice after living and working in the male homosocial world outside week in and week out.

On one occasion, I went to my regular hospital to see a rheumatologist, ostensibly about some back pain I had been having. After registering and waiting an hour or so, I was ushered into the specialist's private office. The doctor, a woman, was culturally Arab, maybe Syrian or Palestinian. About my age, she was a real beauty with shiny black hair, a fulsome body, and chestnut brown eyes. The fact that she was well dressed, confident and impeccably mannered, only added to her allure in my eyes. I muttered something about my complaint to her, at the same time observing photos of children stuck to her X-ray viewing tablet on the wall. She was married, I deduced.

"What can I do for you Meester Heeth?" The doctor's voice, proud and husky, made me shy. She sat still and held eye contact as she spoke. She then gave me a perfunctory examination, uttering words of approval over my apparently good general condition and flexibility; evidently, I was not the worst case she had ever come across, "Yes, oh yes, that's good…"

I played for time. "Do you think I need to have surgery doctor?" The Venus-like rheumatologist was about to wrap up the consultation, and I would not get the chance to talk to another beautiful woman like this for a while. In answer to my question, the doctor, not moving but placing her head slightly to one side, said "Definitely not Meester Heeth. You need take aggressive exercise." She wasn't wrong about that, but the kind of exercise I had in mind, and the kind she was talking about, were probably two different things. "Come back and see me in six weeks," she ordered, writing a prescription for some anti-inflammatory medication, her hand lightly gliding a gold-tipped fountain pen over some paper. The Filipino nurse, who I had barely noticed, but who had been standing in the room throughout this consultation, then brusquely marched me out of the office with the prescription clutched to her clip board.

The National Museum in Riyadh, recommended to me by a colleague, proved to be moderately interesting. Set in some land-scaped gardens near Bahta, I ambled in one warm winter morning and did a quick round of the exhibits that included a large meteorite, reconstructions of the Arabian landscape past and present, model dinosaurs, and the like. What actually impressed me was the way modern science was accepted, and accepted with religious sanction: since God *ultimately* created the world, tectonic plate movements, evolution, and all the rest could easily be incorporated into the world of legitimized knowledge. This seems to me to be a more sensible position than trying to deny the validity of evolution, as a theory, on religious grounds, as some Christians in the United States irrationally persist in doing. The history section of the museum briefly told the story of the Prophet Mohammed, Peace Be Upon Him, and an edited version of the story of Ibn Saud's conquest of Saudi Arabia that focused on his successful raid on Riyadh in 1902, an event that heralded the founding of the modern Saudi state.

Riyadh's Aviation Museum, which I visited during my last days in town, was quite good, too. It featured World War I vintage bi-planes, perhaps used during the Arab Revolt, which had preserved well in the dry desert climate. Ditto, a 1970s jumbo jet, found outdoors, and a British tornado fighter jet, now dated, the latter probably sold to Saudi Arabia in the 1980s when the Saudi government was having problems buying top-drawer fighters from their US allies. But the star exhibit, to my mind, was a vintage Douglas Dakota, the first time I had actually seen one of these venerable planes for real. I climbed up into the exhibit and poked around inside the fuselage. A couple of kids joined me, and that made three of us ready to fly off to break the Berlin Blockade.

WHEN I THINK of my time in Riyadh, I forget about the shopping malls, and strained attempts to socialize on isolated expatriate compounds. What I remember more than anything are the roads and the building sites. One faced them every day, as if facing nature itself, a powerful stimulant to the imagination. To drive on the roads of Riyadh was to step into the pages of J.G. Ballard's novel, *Crash*. There did seem to be a collective death wish out there on those vast, sea-like roads. I noticed some colleagues' personalities change as they acquired cars and joined the great risk taking, becoming ever more aggressive in their driving habits. One had to be aggressive to survive, but aggression was dangerous – a paradox. An article in the *Arab News*, a local English-language paper, which I clipped, reported that 275,000 men, women and children were injured annually in Saudi Arabia as the result of traffic accidents; 6000 of whom died, an average of 500 fatalities monthly, or 16 daily. And that was just the ones recorded, because deaths that occurred in a hospital, and not immediately at the place of accident, were not included in the statistics. On the main road outside my second place of residence, I heard the unmistakable crunch of car metal impacting car metal no less than three times, the third occasion a major collision resulting in the total write off of a taxi. I had my share of near-misses as a passenger, but it was not until two students from the school where I worked drove their vehicle into the taxi I was riding in, fortunately with no serious consequences, that I realized I was living on borrowed time in this city.

2

AN EDUCATION

After the defeat of the Ottoman Empire in World War I, Abdul alAziz, the son of Saud – Ibn Saud for short – saw his chance and began a conquest of the interior of the Arabian Peninsula, a process sanctioned by British colonial authorities who saw in Saud someone with whom they could do business. Ruthlessly, but also prudently, Ibn Saud proceeded to unite a huge territory, a 30-year project. Saud's territorial power base was among the sedentary communities of the Najd region in central Arabia, and his success was dependent on accommo-dating this region's interests. But wily Ibn Saud brought a mix of forces into play in order to achieve his state-building goal, chief among them religion. Coercion was blended in with a revival of Wahhabism, which provided an ideological rationale for the warrior's conquest, and further the basis for a new Islamic moral and political order. Although the Bedouins were important to Ibn Saud militarily, they were never allowed into the central leadership of his movement, and the self-appointed king later turned on them, killing a large number of the religion-inspired *Ikhwan* fighters who were not sufficiently obedient to his command. It has been said that the durability of the Saudi state is exactly because it is based on this overarching Islamic moral and political order, and not on the interests of one tribe, ethnic group or religious faction.

To understand the nature of the modern Saudi state it is necessary to recall that the alliance between the House of Saud and so-called Islamic fundamentalism goes back a long way. Mohammed bin Saud made a pact with the puritanical Islamist Mohammed bin Abdul Wahhab in 1744, and used this alliance to help set up the first Saudi state in central Arabia. This state was attacked and dismantled by the Egyptians in 1818. The second Saudi state, also based in the Najd region, lasted 1824-91, but was finally crushed by the Al-Rashid, a rival clan. It was against this historical background that Ibn Saud rode into Riyadh in 1902 to reclaim his "ancestral rights." But the religious establishment was also necessary to legitimize the House of Saud's rule. Thus the *Mutawaeen*, a kind of religious police force who were given a free rein in the cities to enforce a conservative version of Islamic mores and dress, were born. The *Mutawaeen*, or more precisely their antecedents, were used to control people who were not easily persuaded to accept Saudi leadership. Saudi rule was thus cemented under the guise of "Islamizing" the people of Arabia. It follows from this that there is nothing natural or traditional about Saudi Arabia's "conservatism"; the set-up has always served a specific political purpose: to help keep the Saudi Royal family in power.

Some commentators, among them the British colonial brigade at the time, have openly admired Ibn Saud's statecraft. According to these hard-headed pragmatists, he was the right man for the times, a skilled strategist who pulled a nation together out of many disparate, competing elements: Arabia at the beginning of the 20th century was bandit country, by the end of the century it was a modern state replete with shopping malls to rival the best London and New York had to offer. Previously, the desert Arabs lived in penury, a kind of hardscrabble life that was impossible to break out of, and that encouraged lawlessness. Ibn Saud had a perfect understanding of the Bedouins, and a particular project for them in mind: he would take the errant nomads out of the desert and bring them to a fixed abode, with all the attendant responsibilities that implied. At the time, this project was seen as very progressive. The first major oil well in the newly formed state was discovered in 1938, and within ten years Saudi Arabia would account for five percent of world oil production. Wireless, the motor car, and oil would facilitate Ibn Saud's modernizing programme, and Saudi Arabia was duly transformed; public security was achieved for the first time ever; the Bedouins were pacified.

Ibn Saud consolidated his rule by turning his court into a centre for redistributing the tremendous wealth that oil exports brought. Before he died, Ibn Saud took the momentous decision to throw his lot in with the United States of America as a counterweight to British influence in Arabia, and to further protect his family's rule. It was an astute move, and the US-Saudi alliance, with all its ups and downs, has helped more than anything else to keep the House of Saud in power over the years. There was, however, the problem of how to divide Ibn Saud's patrimony among his descendants – upon his death in 1953, he left behind 44 sons (no one bothered to count the daughters) from 17 partners. What emerged was an oligarchy based on this progeny. The kingship has since been passed between brothers; offspring fill important state offices if they are in any way competent and have the ambition for it. Redundant princes and princesses go abroad to study or for leisure; others remain in their villas amusing themselves however one does amuse oneself in an empty palace. The compliance of the general population with this political fix has been assured by generous public spending: roads, medical care, and education are all provided free to Saudi citizens; the welfare state repays the Saudi people for their passive acceptance of the status quo. The students I taught in Riyadh for instance had their fees paid for by the state, and in addition were paid a small living allowance, a generous arrangement that is now just a memory in modern Britain.

It has been far from plain sailing for the House of Saud, however, and the Saudi government has faced many challenges to its authority over the years, most recently and severely from within the religious fold. The Royal family, who have always held politics in primacy over religion, found themselves being branded hypocrites by radical Islamists. In 1979, radicals occupied the Grand Mosque in Mecca, a truly momentous event and one that shook the Royal family to the core. They responded by paying lip service to religiosity, and by mobilizing their extensive security apparatus. More problems arose in the wake of the First Gulf War when Saudi Arabia served as a base for US-Allied operations – the sight of American females driving on the streets did not rest well with local religious sensibilities, and the US army was politely hurried out of the country on conclusion of the first phase of the war, though substantial US bases remained in-country. It was against these remaining US interests that militants struck in 1996, blowing up the Khobar Towers in Dhahran, the attack killing 19 US service people. Between May 2003 and June 2005, in the wake of the US-Coalition invasion of Iraq, more than 30 major terrorism-related incidents occurred in the kingdom, and for the first time western civilians were targeted: at least 91 foreign nationals were killed in bombings. In addition, there has been significant inter-sect strife over the years, particularly in the south of Saudi Arabia where minority Shiites have been subject to persecution and repression by the majority Sunni government.

The Saudi state therefore has to reckon with many real and perceived threats. Of course, the problem with playing the Islamic card is that you set yourself up to be trumped by someone who will claim to have "authentic" religious authority; the game can only be won by using stick as well as verse. At the heart of the Saudi polity lies a contradiction: on the one hand the state encourages a strict version of Islam, and has financed military Jihad in foreign lands in order to bolster its Islamic credentials, but on the other hand it keeps tight control of official religious discourse and will not allow the religious establishment to become independent. It's a delicate balancing act. Those who opine about the lack of human rights in Saudi Arabia are talking out of context: for their survival the Royal family continues to need to be seen to be religious, and this precludes the development of civil liberties based on secularism. Saudi Arabia is about as far away from being a liberal democracy as Mars is from Earth, i.e. very far away. The third Saudi state, remembering the fate of the first and second Saudi states, is merciless with regard to political dissenters, and there are no leftists in the country to speak of, certainly none above ground. Censorship is widespread and comprehensive and manifests itself in surprising ways: you won't find a copy of the Three Little Pigs in any English-language bookstore, for example, well-stocked with other well-known children's titles though it may be.

Most expatriates who travel to Saudi Arabia don't trouble themselves with the finer nuances Saudi political history, and I have barely scratched the surface of the subject here. US-Saudi relations in particular are complex and multifaceted. But almost every expatriate who does go to the kingdom to work soon abhors the lack of personal freedom they face daily. The heyday for professional expatriates was probably in the 1970s during the oil boom and before the Mecca mosque siege. Since then, salaries have decreased in real terms, and the social scene has become progressively more Islamized. Behind closed doors, everything is permitted. With money, anything can be bought. But no way can you kiss your wife in public, a crime worse than sneaking a photograph of a checkpoint. Though Saudi Arabia is a huge country, and famously more liberal around its extremities, Riyadh remains the conservative political core of the state. Knowing more or less what the place was like, it was with feelings of foreboding that I took up a teaching post in Saudi Arabia. I did so out of desperation – I had spent two years writing my first book for almost no financial return and needed the money. The job was easy for me to get since I hold an advanced degree

in linguistics, and before I knew where I was I had landed in
Dust City.

<hr>

Riyadh University was pioneering a preparatory year
programme where high school students underwent an intensive
course of study in English, maths and computer studies before
starting their academic studies proper – the number of students
being put through universities in Saudi Arabia was rising expo-
nentially due to the high birth rate, and the government had
committed itself to giving access to higher learning to as many
young Saudis as possible, the impetus behind the invention of
the preparatory year. The first time I walked into the preparatory
programme building, however, the wiring was still hanging
down from the ceiling and most of the classroom furniture had
yet to be delivered; this was the brave new Saudi Arabia, where
projects were conceived and rolled out in double time. The
college stood in the corner of a large, sprawling campus that was
empty desert where it was not built on, isolated from the main
cluster of on-campus buildings, like a quarantine outpost. Functionally, the programme was a gateway through which science,
engineering and medical students were sifted and sorted; I have
no idea what happened to students of other subjects – presum-
ably they began their studies directly. The college gradually
slotted into prefab place as we began to teach, and by the end of
the year was complete down to the last swivel chair, personal
computer and closed circuit television camera. The classrooms
varied in size, but most were decent and fairly well equipped.
But, as any educator knows, education is not about the furniture,
a point lost on our British managers who liked to talk up the
supplied smart boards, and other such corporate-style gimmicks,
forgetting that these gadgets actually had to be maintained, or
they might become a liability, one of many obvious technical
problems the genius managers failed to anticipate. The air-condi-

tioning system also left a lot to be desired – sometimes it did not work well enough, and sometimes it worked all too well. During my first class, the students opened a window to let some desert warmth into our over-chilled room.

At first, the preparatory programme trundled along, albeit somewhat chaotically. One pleasant surprise to me was the range and quality of the teaching staff who hailed from Britain, the US, and other countries around the world; others were "local", in the sense that they had lived in Saudi Arabia for many years. There were quite a few British Muslims among us; they were certainly in the right place for the religion. Working on an isolated, all-male campus meant that we all got to know one another quite quickly, and I was afforded a warm welcome by the veteran teachers, and especially by several of the British Muslims, two of whom leant me some money to help me with my initial expenses. Everyone seemed to be happy to have a fairly well paid job. Some people were working for the first time in years – this teaching gig was their big break in life. I, however, saw things for what they were right from the beginning: this was a badly organized and misinformed college programme and we were the flowers in the window; it would all fall apart sooner rather than later. Still, at the time, I was as happy as anyone else to be earning a pay cheque, and if there were no Saudi teachers in sight, then that was not my problem.

From the start, I got along well with my students who, like me, were creative learners. I was quite intrigued by the way they walked in a slow, dignified way, holding their heads up, seemingly having all the time in the world, stopping frequently to greet friends warmly and affectionately, which sometimes included sucking air kisses. The students wore the standard formal dress of Saudi Arabia: a white long shirt, or *thobe*, and a red-chequered headdress held in place with an *iqaal*, a piece of black cord. Seen from behind, the students looked like swarming stingrays. The headdress in particular fascinated me: it could be worn in any number of ways, and the way in which it was worn said a lot about the wearer. A Bedouin, for example, could always be distinguished from a town Arab by the debonair style in which he arranged the one-metre square cloth. Sometimes the headdress, under which is worn a skull cap, can become uncomfortable, and it was not unusual to see some young men dispense with it altogether, though others always wore it as a mark of their dignity, like some men always wear a neck tie to work in the West, even in summer. The students, who had a heavy study programme, were not lazy so much as intelligent and frequently came to class late or missed classes altogether. In the end, the school's management became totally obsessed with this absenteeism, which they saw as a pressing issue. I understood that young men needed freedom, by which I mean some psycho-social space in which to develop, and that to get anything useful done one had to stop hammering on about attendance, but it was no use telling the school's management this. I also understood that the young men needed to be respected, and this precluded making negative comments about them to their face, a point lost on some of my colleagues.

The students liked to talk and were, generally speaking, good verbal communicators. For a language teacher, this trait is something of a blessing, and I never found it difficult to get my class to speak; the problem was to get them to speak in a sustained, relevant way about a given topic. I found it helped if we had something meaningful to talk about and so, in contrast to some other teachers who found the subjects "controversial", I sometimes raised questions related to religion and politics. Such topics needed to be broached in a non-judgemental way. You could not, for example, say anything disparaging about Islam, which was sort of obvious to me, but some people did not get it, and one teacher was actually fired for daring to suggest that a stone relic in the Kaaba was in fact a meteorite fragment. Politics did not seem to exist at the school, and one day a note was posted on the staff room's notice board telling us not to raise political or religious issues in class, a proscription I simply ignored.

One day, Fahd, one of my students, ambled into class and, out of the blue, asked me a very good question: "What is politics Mr Gary?"

"Okay Fahd, lets imagine we have a big cake and there are six of us. Who decides how much of the cake each person gets?" I said. Without thinking about the scenario for very long Fahd said, "The strongest one."

"That, Fahd, is politics."

Well, a simplification. But this is exactly the educators' role: to explain complex, abstract concepts by simplifying them; by making them concrete. To put it another way, learning at school is all about coming to terms with increasingly abstract concepts, until you finally arrive at the big bang. Fahd's naiveté may have been a little shocking, he was only 19 years old after all, but it said a lot about Saudi Arabia that he was clueless about politics: in the kingdom politics were hidden and someone else made all your decisions for you anyway; as Fahd learned from me, so I had learned something from him, and that is education.

Modern and contemporary music, officially banned at the school, was also a topic of conversation in my class. I put our online classroom smart board to good use by showing my students music videos at times when I thought it was safe to do so. In one of my classes, scheduled at the end of a long day, we exclusively watched videos of female artists performing – a double crime, so to speak – including Lady Gaga, Mariam Fares, Susan Boyle, Kate Bush, Siouxsie Sioux, Dana, Avril Lavigne, Marianne Faithful, Oum Kalthoum, Aseel Omran, Janis Joplin, Asalah Nasri, and Sarah Brightman, among others. Plenty to talk about there, and it was the first time I had seen Lady Gaga in action. Of the western artists, the one who held the class spellbound was Joni Mitchell, singing her song *Woodstock* that memorializes the great rock festival held in Bethal, New York, in the summer of 1969. It really touched me when the class burst into spontaneous applause at the end of the video, showing that a real connection between generations and cultures had been achieved, and proof that the meaningful always gets through.

And, of course, it was my privilege to become acquainted with Oum Kalthoum, the inestimable Egyptian singer, loved by Arabs everywhere. However, of all the artists that the students introduced me to, my personal favourite was the Lebanese singer Fairouz – if God has a voice then surely it belongs to her, and so much for trying to ban music! How philistine of the school, and its minions, to think that music was somehow corrupting, a view apparently held by the Wahhabi school of Islam, officially supported in Saudi Arabia. There can be no denying of music, an expression of life itself, and in any case the Arabs are great producers and appreciators of music.

All of my students were interesting, and each had a unique personality. Among the first batch I taught, was Fahd, who asked me the question about politics. He struggled to make his meanings clear in English, but improved rapidly with some instruction. A country bumpkin, he was physically large and unsure of himself at the middle-class university. He had a good sense of humour though – as all the students did – and held himself with great dignity when he wasn't asleep on his desk. One day he kissed me on the head, an expression of affection for an elder in Arab culture, apparently because I had taken the time to personally tutor him a little. Thamer, a town Arab from the north of the country, was another interesting character; he always sat perfectly still, and always wore his headdress. I liked the way he spoke slowly and deliberately, like a sheik, but his shoulders were prematurely hunched: he looked and acted twice his age. Thamer had the slightly annoying habit of announcing break time with the one-liner, "Break time Meester Gary." He intended to speak interrogatively, but spoke in a way that suggested the imperative. Among the young middle class men, Ibrahim was talkative and had a feminine way of subverting any given script: I would ask him to read something, and he would start talking about football or Italy, his two passions. Ibrahim's sidekick, Sultan, was an Iranian national who had been brought up in Saudi Arabia. Sultan wore his hair carefully coiffured, and cultivated long fingernails, like a Confucian gentleman, or Persian satrap. Iran and Saudi Arabia played a soccer match in Tehran during my time in Riyadh, a memorable game that we watched in class. Saudi Arabia won the match. It was noticeable that no one made fun of Sultan over his country's defeat – face had to be maintained. Sultan's modus operandi was typically manipulative; the students were very astute and quickly learned how to get something out of me. Sultan was the first one to say, "We love you Meester Gary." Remarkably, the students, who were experts at reading a person's moods and psychology, had found my weakness, or need, and worked on it to gain an advantage in our relationship. "You're the best Meester Gary," Sultan would say with apparent sincerity, before diving out the door to go for an early lunch, or a smoke. Teaching is like blowing glass, a delicate operation that can be ruined by blowing too hard; conversely, you have to keep working or the learning momentum is lost, perhaps irrevocably. The "professional skills" needed to successfully handle young men like Fahd, Thamer, Ibrahim and Sultan are not easy to describe, but basically one had to be like a sheik: hard and soft in just the right measures.

To anyone who says they are not interested in politics I usually retort that politics, sooner or later, is going to be interested in them whether they like it or not. It was on New Year's Day that Israel launched a ground invasion of Gaza in retaliation for rockets launched into Israel by Hamas, in turn a response to the Israeli blockade of the Gaza Strip. As usual, the Israelis overdid their retaliation. In shock and awe style, they unleashed a furious bombardment against all manner of targets in Gaza, killing over 500 people in a merciless assault. Television images of ambulances rushing civilian casualties to hospitals brought back memories of the 34-day strike against Lebanon in 2006, and of Israel's invasion of Lebanon in 1982. But one had to ask who the real terrorists were in the light of this debauched mess of an assault on Gaza. My Saudi students, and in fact most people I spoke to during this period, had no doubt that it was the Israelis; it was they who were dropping outlawed phosphorous bombs that killed and maimed civilians, including children. Necessary rough justice seemed to be the Israeli line whenever their smooth media spokesman appeared on television, but their punitive action actually achieved little other than stoking up more hatred of Israel throughout the Arab world. One of my students, not exactly the brightest, told me at this time that he admired Hitler for killing Jews. Meanwhile, a Palestinian teacher openly said in conversation that Hitler's only mistake was not to have killed all of the Jews. The student and teacher in question only half meant what they said, and Arabs are not in general racist or anti-Jewish. They spoke out of tremendous anger, and I think they wanted to shock me as they were being shocked. Israel claimed that "dozens" of Hamas fighters had been killed in its operations, but I never saw any evidence of this; there was plenty of evidence of civilian deaths. My students were resentful of Israel; the Saudi government has stood by and watched the Palestinians being bullied for years, only intervening with humanitarian assistance and not involving themselves directly in the conflict – maintaining good relations with the United States had always been their priority. The only thing that surprised me during this whole episode was that the Palestinian cause, after so many direct and brutal assaults against it, was still alive and kicking; Hamas managed to muster a small-scale counter-attack despite the massive pressure being applied against them.

In other ways, it was impossible to keep politics out of the classroom. In fact, the whole order of the school reflected a certain unstated political and philosophical orientation. There was the overarching emphasis on attendance, reflecting an obsession with physical control, for example. In addition, teachers were moved around every semester, effectively breaking the teacher-student relationship. The rationale for this was that teachers were of variable quality and it was good to "expose" learners to different teachers. In fact, the frequent changing of teachers undermined teachers' authority vis-à-vis their students, which was its real purpose. The ridiculous eight-hour day student schedule seemed to reflect a more-is-better philosophy, and ignored the need for quality, joined-up teaching.

The result of asking students to attend classes eight hours a day was fatigue and burnout. Ditto us teachers who were asked to work office hours during my second year at the school, against all common sense; the long hours unnecessarily tiring everyone out. A teacher petition to protest these working hours, on the grounds that they were counterproductive, was ignored: we had no power. In fact, we were blanked by the school, and were merely expected to follow one edict handed down from upon high after another. The institutional culture did not encourage debate, and the result of this was poor communication and, finally, total demoralization. A nascent teachers association was snuffed out before it got off the ground; like the cleaners, we were expected to work out our contracts and disappear after a year or two. Powerless teachers, not much more than skeletons in the classroom, were unable to make any impression on the dean. A large amount of power thus accrued to mid-level managers, who themselves were dispensable, and the quality of whom deteriorated over time. Eventually anyone with any brains came to realize that the job was just to be there – to be the flower in the window – and not to actually achieve anything that might empower the students. A whole panoply of bureaucratic procedures, including utterly pointless teacher observations, were put in place to lend a certain air of "professionalism" to a programme that was actually highly inefficient and very ineffective because of the way it had been set up.

Islam, a religion that maps out an entire way of being and thinking, played an important role in the life of the school's students, who were expected to join prayers held in the school prayer hall daily. In Saudi Arabia, all activity halts during prayer times, which occur at dawn, midday, mid-afternoon, sunset, and about one and a half hours after sunset; my lessons were usually interrupted for prayers twice on any given day. Non-Muslims were not expected to join prayers, and I even noticed one or two Muslim teachers skipping them, but on the whole the students did not miss prayers, and seemed to take them seriously. Interestingly, they were always cheerful after prayers, although this mood could manifest itself in silly behaviour – it was always just after the completion of afternoon prayers that one witnessed young men "drifting", the practice of wildly skidding cars on empty stretches of road. There did not seem to be any Islamic instruction included in the preparatory programme though. Riyadh University's mission statement merely started with the perfunctory preamble, "Based on our Islamic religion and cultural tradition, we uphold the following values...", and then went on to list "quality and excellence, leadership and team work, freedom of inquiry and fairness and integrity", arguably all of which were absent at the college. The mission statement continued with a shopping list of goals, visions, and prescriptive behaviours. It was therefore significant, I think, that prayers were taken seriously: they seemed to provide young men with a spiritual anchor, an ordering of their day which could be quite chaotic in other respects, and committed them to God, as conceptualized by Islam. Religion was also used as a political weapon; it was Islam, after all, that legitimized Saudi rule, and informed the culture of an institution that did not encourage students to speak back: one was to meekly accept one's lot, to *submit* to God, and by inference to the school's authority. One of my students, an ambitious and intelligent Bedouin, had also made the connection between religion and power, and was assiduously memorizing the Koran, the full memorization of which would grant him a high level of authority among his peers.

One afternoon in class, as we did some academic drifting away from the prescribed curriculum, one of my students asked me what I thought of the Koran, a fair enough question.

"Well, I think there is much of value in the Koran," I began, politely, and not insincerely. In fact, I had carefully read the Koran, a Saudi authorized translation of it that I had picked in one of Riyadh's bookstores. Based on this one read, I felt I could at least make some general comments about the book. I proceeded to tell the student that I "heard" different voices in the Koran, a subtle critique since the Koran is considered divine revelation by Muslims, quite literally God's word, and therefore the product of one voice logically speaking. Here we have two different concepts of what a book is, and once you accept the Koran is the word of God, there is no arguing with it, because then you are arguing with God, which is blasphemy. I calmly took on the subject, unruffled by the awareness that I was now sailing in deep waters.

"My problem with the Koran is the emphasis on punishments and rewards. The Koran insists that non-believers will be punished, and seems to use this as a tool to persuade non-believers to recant and submit to God. But I don't believe in rewards and punishments. As an educator, I know they're useless," I said, in a shot across the bow. Othman thought about my comment for a few seconds, and then blurted out that criminals had to be punished and so punishments were necessary. While this may seem a reasonable point of view, it is not one I share. I believe criminals must be reformed through education and moral persuasion – an idealistic point of view, but it is exactly the ideal taught by Christianity, and Islam – we must forgive those who do wrong, and seek to help them find a better way. Punishing people drags all concerned down into an immoral quagmire. We went back and forth around the issue of punishment for a while; I mentioned that the school often threatened students with sanctions if they did not comply with this or that requirement. Again, although this may seem reasonable, it was not. The emphasis on sanctions encouraged a climate of fear, and was a barrier to learning; real education can only be built on mutual respect and mutual consent. All this made a bit more sense to Othman, a bright student, although he remained sceptical about dispensing with punishments altogether. I concluded, "There are no punishments in heaven, and that's what we should be aiming for on earth." Regarding rewards, I said, a bit tongue in cheek, that a pay cheque was the only reward I was looking for in life. But as for those beautiful gardens in heaven awaiting believers, as mentioned frequently in the Koran, that was pie in the sky to me.

There were some other things in the Koran that I did not feel comfortable with, like the idea that believing made you more worthy than non-believers regardless of the latter's merits. But I had said enough for one day, and our discussion petered out as calmly as it had begun. Any kind of discussion about the Koran between non-believers and believers is fraught with difficulty because there are no shared assumptions: the two sides regard the book in a totally mutually exclusive way. It is simply unthinkable that one of my students would openly embrace atheism because there was no room for this in the culture, and a denial of Islam's creed by a Muslim is apostasy, punishable – there we have it again – by death.

Yet there are free thinkers in Saudi Arabia. In his novel *Adama*, the Saudi writer Turki Al-Hamad describes the coming of age of a Saudi youth who, through reading literature, including the study of illicit or banned books, finds himself questioning everything. Hisham, the author's protagonist, immerses himself in Marxist theory as well as world literature, and joins an underground socialist organisation. After a number of twists and turns, which involve the character engaging in very dangerous political activities, such as handing out political pamphlets at school, Hisham tires of the doctrinal authoritarianism of the group he has joined. He is a sceptic regarding pan-Arabism, and also rejects the strictures of the Baathists, eventually disentangling himself from direct political activity. The likeable character remains a sceptic about religion too, and in the final pages of the book agrees with Voltaire that God is a supreme example of the omnipotent father figure, a human like entity that provides in times of need and in times of danger, a comforting fantasy. As Hisham explains to his friends earlier in the story: "The question is how we look at things, not the things themselves...There is no truth *per se*..." This type of thinking, based on reason, is alien to many in Saudi Arabia because there the Koran is perceived to be a self-evident truth, and sadly it comes as no surprise that the author of *Adama* faces four outstanding *fatwas* against him in his homeland. With immense, one might say with typically Arab, dignity and courage Turki

Al-Hamad continues to live in Riyadh, refusing the Saudi state's offer of police protection.

TEACHING English as a Foreign Language (TEFL) is a field of employment that I have been involved with on and off since 1987; essentially it is my day job, work that provides me with an income while I await the Big Break. The TEFL English teacher, it must be said, is generally not taken very seriously or respected. People think if you can speak English, then naturally you can teach English, and so just about anybody could do it, and logically this implies the teacher is an anybody; a nobody. This attitude always perplexed me, but it was in part the result of the job not being structured along professional lines, by which I mean not unionized. If you go to see a doctor, you would expect them to have a proper grounding in medicine, and that is why doctors are respected; why were the same requirements not applied to TEFL teachers? Increasingly, they are, but a flimsy certificate is realistically all you need to get a job in many private sector schools. The TEFL field thus remains amateurish. However, on closer inspection the assumptions and practices of TEFL reveal a particular political agenda that go a long way to explaining the anti-intellectualism of the field, and even of many practising teachers.

The first thing to say about practising English teaching is that it is not a politically neutral activity, you can't "just teach English." "Neutrality" is a code word that means agreeing with the system and being whatever the system requires of us, including the requirement that we be ahistorical. In fact, historically speaking, the role and spread of the English language in the world was a direct result of British and US imperialism. English was used as a Trojan horse to infiltrate elites in non-English speaking countries, a tool for connecting with and developing comprador classes. Every single person born in a colony or ex-colony will know exactly what I am talking about here; the use of language as a tool of control by outsiders. It follows from this that the spread of English language use in the world is not a natural, neutral process, as is often unquestioningly assumed. The idea of language being a "tool for communication" is one I often heard being uttered by uncritical teachers who lean towards the language-as-neutral-tool assumption; but such teachers have been neutered and are not really thinking about what is actually going on. English played a central role in expanding global capitalism, and has also played an important role in the formation of social classes. It is noticeable how different social classes speak differently, reflecting wide differences in underlying political and social assumptions. How can a teacher account for these differences if not by a discussion of class formation and power relations? English grammar, for example, cannot be explained as a set of rules, because language doesn't have rules so much as prevailing patterns that change over time and among different groups of people. If we were to say, correctly I think, that English language teaching has become part of a process whereby political and economic domination has been established by one part of the world (the North) over another part (the South), then we have moved a long way from the idea of English being used solely as a neutral tool of communication. But they don't discuss these issues when you do a TEFL certificate, and this absence is itself very revealing.

In *English and the discourses of Colonialism*, critical theorist Alastair Pennycook does make the connection between the spread of English, colonialism and domination. The story is a complex one but, as Pennycook rightly points out, that should not stop us from trying to understand it, and understanding the influence of colonialism on modern global relations. Interestingly, Pennycook discovers from his research that the (British) colonies were a primary centre for cultural production, and not mere receivers of the metropolitan culture. This is significant because many of the attributes, attitudes and unspoken assumptions of TEFL actually gained force in the colonies. Thus views of racial superiority, the superiority of Eurocentrism, and related ideas about the noble savage, the lazy native etc. all flourished in the colonies and were exported back to the colonial metropolitan centres. In the colonial mindset, those who did not speak English were considered non-peoples with no civilization and no history to speak of; their languages were not worth learning. To put it crudely, if you didn't speak English you were not okay. This emphasis on English has been tremendously distorting. In India, for example, the bureaucracy still uses English as its primary language of communication, even though its use effectively guarantees that Indian bureaucrats become dissociated from the people they are responsible for at the local level, a point well made by V.S. Naipaul in his book *An Area of Darkness*, and by others. Making the study of English literature mandatory for passing the Indian civil service examination was seen as natural in the 19th century, just as "foreign" students today are "naturally" required to study reductive, globalized English language textbooks that focus on subjects like shopping, dating and travel, the current preoccupations of Britain's middle classes. Stuart Hall, the distinguished British cultural theorist, once said that he went to a very good English boarding school in Jamaica that offered a very good education, but where he never learned the names of the plants and animals around him, and never learned anything about local history before the advent of the colonial era.

English teaching then has a role embedded in history and implicated in global economic and political relations. TEFL not only helped facilitate the global expansion of European and North American capitalism over time, but is now considered to be an important business activity in its own right, and is spoken of as such. So, now we hear the catchphrases common to business activity: TEFL is a "service industry"; English is a "tool"; the students are our "clients", and so on. The process began in the 1930s when The British Council for Relations with Other Countries was set up. Ostensibly aimed at increasing "cultural understanding", the British Council has been a key force in the marketization of discourse about English teaching; they pioneered the packaging of teaching English as a business. The

English language thus became a "golden egg" to be exploited for monetary gain. After the retreat from empire, the British Council partly filled the vacuum and helped to promote British interests abroad, via English, and the marketization of discourse served as a camouflage for this hidden political goal. Behind the scenes, the British Council is very much aware of the political and economic purposes of its work, and talks in plain English about them. Publicly, you hear same old guff about "cultural understanding." The Council has cemented its influence by running teaching courses for TEFL teachers that are largely uncritical and focus on a market-orientated, "delivery" style of education, very much in vogue, but which are in practice disempowering because the same old colonial assumptions are at work: you know nothing; this is how we do it.

Everything that was wrong about the preparatory programme at Riyadh University – and much was wrong with it – was linked to this history of colonialism and to the hidden political and cultural assumptions of TEFL that originated in the colonial system. Many teachers complained about the way we were summarily treated by our employer, but they did not have a handle on colonial history, or of the nature of subject relations within a global system of economic domination. We teachers were *deliberately* treated like a subject colonial people who are supposed to accept their subordinate role in the set up, and not complain since we got paid and therefore there was nothing to complain about. Promotion in this system depended on becoming a "team player", i.e. an uncritical follower of the system. The increasing threats of punishment from on high did have a local flavour, but the system of authority; the hierarchical power structure, the assumptions on what was to be taught and how to teach, was straight out of the colonial book. Officially, there was no racism at the school, but non-native English speakers had to work harder to keep their jobs, and could be fired, and indeed some were fired, on a whim by our employer. People who were profoundly uninformed about education were in charge; the school was being run like a factory where teachers were the dispensable workers. My point is that this state of affairs was the result of a system of logic, not an accident or the result of ignorance – there really was no use in complaining. The continuing emphasis on attendance, on bureaucratic procedure, and on paperwork was all part of a massive system of control designed to keep people busy. Proper educational work, which is inter-subjective in nature, and therefore difficult to measure, was never observed. Instead, good teaching was viewed as a kind of performance, and a successful teacher defined by his ability to keep a class under control and focused on a task at all times. It never occurred to our masters that a kind word, a bit of mucking about, or a digression into music, might be, if handled in the right way, of more educational value than the prescribed curriculum.

Every teacher has an obligation to learn, and if you don't learn something from your teaching then it will not be possible to develop a meaningful practise, or praxis. I use the term praxis advisedly, since one must try to make some connection between theory and practice, and it is not enough to rely on folk psychologies, like the belief that a teacher is an authority who is supposed to tell the student what the general case is, or what to believe. Rather, an educator seeks to guide the learner to a better understanding of their own mind. Far from being depressed by the constraining employment conditions of the school I worked at, I felt that my knowledge and insight into the nature of TEFL, such as it was and is, gave me a kind of power. Of course, I had to make compromises in order to fit into the system, but I always did so knowing what the real deal was; within the classroom I always acted in a way consistent with my own principles of equality, dignity and liberation. Within my sphere of influence, I knew that I was a very important and influential role model, and if we teachers were told not to ask the question why, then with my students I made sure to ignore that violent dictate. When a fellow teacher at the university asked me if I was "aware", I would like to have said yes, but we may have been speaking at cross-purposes. I felt I was aware that my students were thinkers, that they were full of latent talents and abilities, that they were intelligent, that we had different beliefs, desires and intentions, but nonetheless we could, and indeed had to build knowledge together, because knowledge is what you make, not something you absorb like a sponge. I was aware, through long experience and through reading the theoretical works of great educators like John Dewey, Myles Horton and Paulo Freire, that the way to learn something was to start and to learn as you go along. As an educator it was essential to start where people were at and not assume that they were empty, deficient or stupid in some way; my students were not receptacles into which I would dump knowledge. My task was to engage the students in meaningful dialogue, through the medium of English, so that they might reflect upon their world in order to transform it: revolution begins with the self. At Riyadh University, I did not respond to the reward and punishment regime; I did exactly what I wanted in the classroom, I fought my corner. However, it is true that no matter how aware and well-intentioned an educator you may be, ultimately you fail if you are unsupported by authority within the institution in which you work because all your positive messages will eventually get drowned out by the institution's subliminal, and sometimes bluntly direct, negative messages.

Whether or not the preparatory year programme at Riyadh University was a failure or not is perhaps a matter of conjecture, but 50% of teachers left at the end of their contracts never to return, an incredible rate of loss of qualified staff. And this is not counting the dropouts: new teachers came and went at an alarming rate. The losses were supposed to happen; it was all part of the corporate strategy that left power firmly in the hands of private contractors and the colonial like school authorities, all part of the "churn." The amazing thing was the way the college carried on as if nothing was wrong – which of course from their point of view was true – and an immense amount of time and energy was put into projecting the school in a positive light. The college had even recruited a propaganda unit to film and photograph teachers in action. Their video productions, slick advertorials, were played on video terminals and screens bolted to the floor and walls of the school's otherwise empty and sterile corridors. It was eerie to see David, my former roommate, pop up in one of these videos one day, long after he and all the former middle management had left, only reinforcing my shocked-survivor feeling.

Day to day, the institution tightened controls, especially when there was an inspection by an outside organization or authority. At other times, they could not care less what was going on. During such loose times, irresponsible behaviour ensued, which was eventually detected, and then there would be another round of threats, purges, and fresh petty bureaucratic procedures to follow. And so it went on in its merry dysfunctional way. Experts were flown in, talked about mission statements, flew out again, and of course the mission statement never materialized, or not one formulated by us teachers anyway. New managers came in full of good intentions and expertise. One of them, I remember, gave a talk in which he admitted that our school-wide tests were not really valid. We all knew this – standardized multiple-choice testing was discredited as long ago as the 1950s. This type of testing is still prevalent only because it serves corporate interests: it is quick, efficient, seen to be fair even though it isn't, and gets easily sifted and quantifiable results. So, what was the genius manager's solution? He talked about Rasch analysis, some mysterious mathematical formulation that re-computes test results to make them fairer. No one asked if the Rasch analysis took into account cheating because we were all asleep, or playing games on our hand phones. "We need to build a test culture", the new manager said, without a trace of irony.

The vice dean of the college once honoured us with a presentation. I forget what he said except for one thing: it was the intention of the university to turn tenured academic staff into contract workers, just like the TEFL teachers. This was interesting because the message was not really meant for us, it had just slipped out. The vice-dean had inadvertently revealed the overall long-term strategic goal of the school, which was the corporatization of the university! Powerful interests were shaping the future of education in Saudi Arabia, and we teachers had about as much influence on that future as the contract cleaners from Bangladesh did, i.e. none at all.

3

DEPARTURE

IMMEDIATELY UPON ARRIVAL IN SAUDI ARABIA, I QUIETLY BEGAN TO plan my escape. One of the first things I did after settling in was take out an atlas to see what the overland travel options back to England were. It seemed to me that my time in the kingdom, apart from anything else, would provide me with a platform from which to launch myself on a journey of exploration through some part of the Arab world, north, east or west of Arabia. Since it would eventually lead me home, and was by far the most adventurous option, I quickly decided on a route that would take me through North Africa and onwards back to the UK via Spain and France. Over time and due to circumstances the exact route would change, but basically it involved travelling to Yemen, Eritrea, and Sudan, and then along the Nile to Cairo before traversing the Maghreb, and then re-entering Europe from Morocco. On paper, it all looked doable. The journey would be a sort of *rihla fi talab al-ilm*: a journey in search of knowledge – a journey for the sake of knowledge may be a better translation – after the medieval Islamic scholars who travelled to distant places as a way of gaining knowledge and insight, particularly as pertaining to their religion. During my time based in Riyadh, I had made some side trips, twice visiting Lebanon to hike in the mountains there, and also to some far flung parts of Saudi

Arabia. I also enjoyed the obligatory booze cruises to nearby Bahrain. But to write about travel you have to be both free when you do a trip, and free when you write about it in retrospect. All the time I was in Saudi Arabia, I was psychologically paralysed and only just managed to keep a diary – like everyone else, I was in a state of shock most of the time from near-miss traffic accidents, and from the tempestuous behaviour of an unpredictable employer. I therefore bided my time, and covertly prepared for what would be a long and challenging journey *west* of Arabia.

AN OPPORTUNITY AROSE for me to teach summer school at the end of my contract, and I applied because the money on offer would pay for my upcoming travel, a neat solution. Summer school was not very demanding, but one had to be there, which was always the job of course, but in the summer one had to deal with the indefatigable and unrelenting heat. Daily daytime afternoon temperatures in Riyadh regularly hit 47-50 Celsius. The Saudi middle classes all left town in July and August, jetting off to foreign countries for holidays much like their British and American counterparts, or retreated to various ranches and oases in the time-honoured manner; schools became ghost towns.

The purpose of the summer school was really unknown, and I came to think of it as a money laundering operation; later I saw it as part of the giant façade of the school. I did not care, and neither did anyone else – we teachers got paid for turning up and there was almost nothing to do as the majority of the students down for the repeat session had fled town with their parents. A rough mental calculation told me the school were paying $50,000 a month to have teachers sit around and drink coffee. Then some students, ones who had apparently failed their end of semester tests and had been threatened with not matriculating if they did not turn up, started to trickle in. Classes were assigned, and I got a class of three young men who had actually passed their exams with flying colours but failed the attendance benchmark. In Kafkaesque fashion, these exemplar students, already ear-marked for the medical college, had to face punishment whilst their lesser-performing but obediently attendant classmates enjoyed the freedom of "going outside," the Saudi expression for going overseas. What was I supposed to do with these three unfortunates?

The three students were cocksure and clever, but passive and not very communicative. They had been burned out by the system. What I disliked about them was the fact they assumed they knew everything, since they had passed their exams, and that nothing but studying a textbook amounted to real education; actually talking to anybody was their interlocutor's great privilege, they suggested in their manner – they were the doctors of the future, the next generation of super scientists. In short, they were takers, not givers, and philosophically stultified. In my experience, students with this kind of mindset are pretty far gone and re-programming them an uphill task. However, an educator never gives up.

I started, according to operating principle number one, with the textbook since that is where the students were at. We ploughed our way around some medical topics, and when a word we all did not know the meaning of turned up I admitted my ignorance, but demonstrated the various ways one could find out the meanings of unfamiliar words. And soon the students were looking up these words by themselves, and so something useful was immediately achieved. The textbook study was a bit dry though, and we soon got bored of it. Medical studies could wait until another day; it was the summer after all. So, what were my charges interested in? Like many of the students at the preparatory school, they were interested in the outside world as seen through the prism of Saudi/US culture; they were particularly interested in cars and movies. Through the Internet, these students knew, in a distorted sort of way, what was going on in the world; they had watched a great deal online including hard core pornography. What could we share though?

"Watch Meester Gary; it's my home town; it's so green."

Jibril, the most insecure of the three young men, was the first to open his world to me, the first to respond to someone being interested in him as a person. It materialized that all three of the students came from the southwest of Saudi Arabia, a mountainous region far away from Riyadh. In these mountains, a popular summer getaway for Riyadh's inhabitants, there were indeed green pastures, farms, and dramatic horizons full of clouds and blue peaks. This is what I saw in the video Jibril had downloaded for me to watch. Jibril also showed me some muscle-men videos, which would not normally have grabbed me, but I patiently watched them, showing an interest in my student's interests. In other classrooms, I overheard teachers ranting about grammar rules, but their classes did not last; their students soon voted with their feet and gave up attending summer school. Meanwhile, next door to the college building, a duplicate preparatory college was being built at a rapid rate of knots. During break time, I watched as Afghan and Indian construction workers toiled away in the fierce heat. And then it was my turn to show the students something.

"...today the parajumpers are picking up a US soldier from a firefight. He's been shot in the face. The bullet has also punctured his lung..." On 29 July, 2010, the British newspaper the Guardian published an extraordinary piece of news video footage from the war in Afghanistan online, and we are listening to the voice-over. The video was shot by Sean Smith, who at the time of filming was embedded with Canadian paramedics in the troubled Afghan province of Helmand, a place the British army had found too hot to handle. The more gung-ho US military replaced the British and took on the job of pacification with typical aggression; but they were paying a high price for seemingly little gain. The title of the video, a 20-minute reality documentary in essence, was "Deadlock in Afghanistan: It's taken a year to move 20 kilometres." Thirty seconds into the video, the wounded soldier in question is hauled into the helicopter by the military paramedics, and what follows is a harrowing half a minute of viewing as the badly wounded man is patched up. I had not seen anything like it since footage of the Vietnam War in the 1970s, scenes that still haunt me. In Afghanistan, history was repeating itself. As the wounded soldier in the video is unloaded from the helicopter, the voice-over resumes.

"An injury like this looks very bad with a great deal of blood loss. But this soldier will survive." Not so another soldier shown in the video: both his legs had been blown off and the shock and blood loss meant he soon died. Sean Smith, with almost reckless bravery, went on to film a battle in progress, following a platoon of Marines as they counterattack a Taliban ambush. The video sequence follows the well-trained, superbly-equipped Americans as they go forward with great courage. But a clear-headed analysis of the video clip reveals that the Americans lost the tactical advantage even before they began engaging the enemy: although the marines eventually "secure" the area, the enemy succeed in wounding some of the US soldiers, effectively taking the initiative away from the counterattacking force. The skirmish represented the proverbial game of cat and mouse, but what impressed most is the way the mice had learned to use the land mine as an offensive weapon, thereby gaining the advantage in an asymmetrical firefight. In a case of role reversal, the Taliban cleverly drew the Marines onto their set traps. At the end of the video, it is particularly poignant to learn that the army corporal who had led this counterattack later lost his life to one of these mines, an improvised explosive device. He was unlucky, but quite a few have been unlucky. My students sat and watched the video. It took a while for them to tune in, to realize they were watching something real and not an action flick.

"They are scared teacher. The Americans are scared." Abdullah, our class's self-appointed class captain, commented. In the video, we saw soldiers under fire, at the moment of maximum battle stress. How they dealt with that stress was very revealing. The US Marines were obviously scared. On the other hand, they fired back. When ordered to, they went forward. In a nutshell, they fought in a professional manner, which is what you would expect of Marines. There were of course moments of panic, when things were not going to plan. "Oh fuck…Oh shit…fuck…" one soldier lets out as incoming bullets thudded into the ground next to him. What on earth was the cameraman doing there? Wasn't *he* scared? The journalist was also just doing his job, like the soldiers, one supposed.

After watching the news video, I asked the students what they thought about it. "We Muslims are not afraid to die. Everyone must die," was Abdullah's trite contribution. Although there was truth in what Abdullah was saying, it was a conceited remark; it is exactly this kind of narcissism that drives suicide bombers on. The other two students had little to say about the video, which had merely been a form of entertainment to them; they could not relate to reality, and they knew nothing about the Taliban, although felt generally sympathetic toward the Afghan resistance, their orthodox Sunni co-religionists. But as to the wider political significance of the war, its strategies and purposes, they were clueless. What was this war really all about? A question I posed to my students, the asking of which led to thought, the start of a generative process.

Italian director Gillo Pontecorvo made the celebrated film *The Battle of Algiers* in 1966. This movie was my next point of departure in our class. Together we watched parts of the drama available through a well-known online video-sharing website. The movie portrayed, in realistic style, the events of the late 1950s and early 1960s in Algiers, which at that time came under attack by urban guerrillas fighting for Algerian independence. It is an extraordinary film, not least because it shows Arab women coolly carrying bombs into public places, something that actually happened. The film is thus an eerie precursor of contemporary times, and was even shown to military officers in the Pentagon during the US occupation of Baghdad. At one point in Pontecorvo's film, one of the insurgents/terrorists/freedom fighters – call them what you will – justifies the methods of the Algerian insurgents by pointing out that there was no difference between delivering a bomb from in an aeroplane, or using an operative to plant one. In both cases, civilians are targeted, innocent people are killed; the result is the same. Since the insurgents did not have advanced aircraft, they used another method to fight back. The logic is difficult to argue with. What did my students think?

Abdullah said, "He's right. If you are fighting, you fight with what you have. People are fighting for dignity."

"They must use any weapon," was Jibril's pragmatic view. But what if a member of their family belonged to a militant Islamist group? Would they support him or her? What if their sister were a bomber?

"No teacher." This was Soheib. He spoke calmly, as Arab men do when talking about something serious. "No. I cannot accept that someone plants a bomb, or threatens to plant a bomb to insist on their point of view. I do not agree to this. We do not agree to this." I was interested to hear Soheib's opinion, though it was a received one; received from the Saudi establishment that has gone to some lengths to condemn the extreme actions of militant Islamists, actions that directly threaten the House of Saud, as well as certain western interests.

As the days of August droned on, we moved on to watching some full-length feature films on the smart board. Usually I chose a movie that would illustrate a point to my students, or give them something to talk about, perhaps a topic that tied in with our developing war/terrorist theme: joined-up teaching, in other words. *Unthinkable*, one of the movies we watched, served this educational purpose very well. The movie, released in 2010, was not particularly realistic, but it did present an interesting moral dilemma, one that is posed to anyone who interviews for a job at the British Foreign Office. The question concerns a scenario: a terrorist/bomber/enemy has planted a bomb. S/he has been captured. The bomb is due to go off in the near future and will kill many innocent people. The captive is refusing to reveal the whereabouts of the bomb. Is torturing the suspect permissible in such circumstances? The film takes the scenario one step further: is it permissible to torture the family/children of such a captive to get information from him/her? In the film, the suspect is put under this pressure, but in the end does not crack. We are left with a view of the bomb, in this film a nuclear bomb, ticking away wondering if it will go off. If they faced this scenario, what would my students do and why?

"I would talk to the man nicely and ask him to co-operate. If he didn't tell me where the bomb was, I would do something," Abdullah said. By something, he meant torture the suspect. The others concurred. They asked me what I would do, looking for the right answer.

"I'm not sure there is a "right answer," I said, "…it is a terrible dilemma. But it seems to me that if intelligence agencies get to the point where they have to torture people to get information from them then they have probably not been doing their job very well." My response was a considered one, but in truth there is no intelligence agency in the world that would not hesitate to rip the teeth out of such a suspect, and this was the cold reality: the film had posed a question that in real life is never asked except in job interviews. It would have been terrible to say this to young men though; as the Arabian proverb goes: "It is good to know the truth, but it is better to speak of palm trees."

Perhaps we had done something useful in class, after all: the students had begun to think for themselves, or at least had begun to proffer opinions about things. I felt it was a start. Noam Chomsky once commented on his brief career as an English language teacher saying that 99% of the problem was finding something interesting to do, and 1% of the problem was deciding how to go about presenting the activity. In other words, content was more important than form, and no amount of lesson planning, research or teaching technique can compensate for not having something real to do or talk about. And, as Paulo Freire once said, it is indispensable that the educator give witness to, and to be an example of, thinking critically.

THE SOUND of a muezzin calling the faithful to prayer woke me up early one morning, and I felt chilled having left the air-conditioning on at night. I took a shower and got ready for my final day at work. I had been sharing an office with several colleagues, and today we would have a coffee party, as we had every day, on this occasion to celebrate various milestones: Mohammed would be leaving to join his family in Egypt; Fahd had successfully completed his TEFL certificate study in the UK, something he was obliged to do in order to defend his position at the school; Meshal, who had gone to extraordinary lengths to help me secure a visitor visa for Sudan, was going to Europe for a short holiday. A couple of my friends had been informed that their contracts would not be renewed: they were nice people and good teachers, but had probably tried too hard, the cardinal sin. It would be our last time to have a get-together.

Fahd and Meshal were both Sudanese nationals, and all the talk was about Sudan, and its ongoing political problems. I had a map of Sudan above my desk. Getting a visa for that country had taken a major effort, but without it I would have had to cancel my proposed trip because in my mind Sudan was the lynchpin between Arabia and North Africa, and therefore the key country in my travel itinerary. Meshal, who was my closest friend at the school, tried to persuade me to stay.

"Won't you join us next year? What will you do in England?" I had told Meshal about my intentions to break out. Meshal had family responsibilities, and he needed his job. I did not. Very deliberately, I had avoided any responsibilities that would tie me down long term. My job in Saudi Arabia was done and dusted, and to stay any longer would have been tantamount to starting a career as a slave.

As we chatted in the office, a flunky from administration popped his head in the door asking for volunteers to invigilate placement testing. We did not exactly jump at the offer: never volunteer was my motto, and the others had become cynical, too. The flunky left, unperturbed by our refusal to volunteer, and we drank the last of the summer coffee before going our different ways.

On the way out of the office I bumped into Phillip, my American pal, a veteran teacher and sometime explorer. He was a little concerned about me, "So, Gary, you begin another odyssey. I hope you take care out there. Isn't it dangerous in those countries?" Phillip had done some travelling in his time, but had become disillusioned by changes he had seen around the world. I replied that if it was a toss-up between driving in Riyadh and exploring some backwater in Sudan, I fancied my luck in the Sudan and on that note left the school building for the last time.

LAST MINUTE COMPLICATIONS – inevitably, last minute complications. At the eleventh hour I discovered I would not be able to travel overland to Yemen as I had planned: getting a visitor visa was next to impossible. Also, the land border between Djibouti and Eritrea was apparently closed making my plan to travel Yemen-Djibouti-Eritrea overland redundant. My original travel concept had three principles: stay on the ground; no back-tracking; minimal sightseeing: just go from A to B to C. Already, my first principle was compromised; in order to get to Africa I would have to fly there. There was an alternative overland route available via Jeddah and Port Sudan, but taking this route would have meant missing Eritrea. I already had a visa for Eritrea, and very much wanted to go there, so I decided to fly. After shopping around, the best I could come up with was a flight out of Riyadh, via Yemen, to Asmara in Eritrea. From there it might be possible to manage the rest of the trip overland, but there was no telling this in advance, one simply had to learn by doing.

Then the Hajji Pilgrimage holiday started, early this year. Due to the religious holiday and overbooked flights, I was obliged to hang about in Riyadh a further ten days before departing. As three million faithful Muslims circumambulated the Kaaba in Mecca, I circumambulated my neighbourhood. However, another incident occurred when I was out photographing a villa, and after this I ceased the chimp patrols. I walked around inside my cavernous apartment instead, checking and double-checking my kit, repeating the process many times. In order to calm myself, I read. Then a roommate returned from his travels, a blessed bit of company. But of course I was going insane. On my last five afternoons in Riyadh, the temperature hit a high of 42, 43, 43, 42 and 43 degrees Celsius. This was during Ramadan when all shops and restaurants were closed during the day. I simply had to get out of Saudi Arabia once and for all; I couldn't stand it any longer. Finally, on the longed-for day of departure, I disposed of a few items in a nearby garbage dumpster and made my way, for the last time, to Riyadh airport.

II

AFRICA

4

ERITREAN KNIGHTS

THE LONG JOURNEY TO MY AFRICAN DESTINATION HAD BEGUN IN
sizzling Riyadh earlier that day, and I was tired on arrival in
Asmara. Tired but somehow energized: although only 500 kilometres due west of Sanaa, and also a city of the highlands,
Asmara had a totally different feel compared to the Arabian
capital I had left but one hour before, the heat and the psychological pressure of Arabia gone; this airport was about the same
size as Sanaa's, but the buzz was quite different: people were
relaxed; their body language open. Most of the flight's passengers were Eritrean migrant workers and Indian traders returning
home, and they were happy to be back in what was for them a
familiar place. But the airport was a bit too relaxed in some
ways, and getting my baggage from the inadequate reclaim area
proved to be a drawn out affair. Then there were the fussy
customs to negotiate, and abstruse currency declaration forms to
fill in. I could not resist purchasing a bottle of duty-free Scotch,
but this meant another long wait, and change for my dollars was
paid in Dutch gift-aid margarine. These inconveniences were
negligible; two other things disturbed me though. The first was
the abusive way a standing immigration official took passports
off arriving passengers, and handed them to an unseen official
behind a desk out of sight. We were made to line up until

formalities had been completed, whereupon our passports were roughly handed back. The second dissonant note was sounded by a clock on the wall of one of the immigration kiosks: it read the wrong time because, for want of a battery, it had stopped working. After changing some money, another time-consuming task, I finally left the airport building, and trundled the short distance to the taxi rank.

A COOL BREEZE wafted through the windows of my room in a downtown pension – the climate in Asmara was a huge improvement on what I had recently been suffering. The average daytime temperature in Asmara at this time of the year was in the low 20s Celsius; mostly dry and sunny, with a low risk of rain. The state-run pension was calm, low-key and running on auto-pilot in the morning. I got up and stretched my legs on the villa's balcony, sticking my chest out like Mussolini and taking a deep draft of the cool, untainted air. Trees only partly obscured the view of a downtown red-brick cathedral. The scene was a pleasant one to behold after having daily faced the glare of Riyadh's desert roads. There was not much to worry about here; it was only after a period of time that you realized there was not much to do either. My arrival, however, had attracted the attention of three young men who sat in an unmarked car in the street. But on that first morning, after a shower and greeting the pension staff, I soon gave these amateurs – maybe they were a road repair crew, after all – the slip and headed out into one of Africa's most intriguing cities.

Eritrea, essentially a mountain province nestled between Ethiopia and Sudan on the north-east coast of Africa, has always, due to its peculiar geography, been somewhat independent. The local people, who are currently divided into nine ethnic groups, including Muslims and Arabic-speakers, fiercely protected their independence from outside influence for a long time, but were thrown onto the back foot by famine and internal discord in recent times. It was Italy, as part of the grab for Africa at the end of the 19th century, which finally conquered Eritrea in a comprehensive way, formally declaring the province a colony in 1890. The Italian colony was relatively successful, and the Italians turned this highland town of Asmara into an impressive, well-planned colonial capital city. By the 1930s, this city was filled with interesting art-deco buildings erected along wide boulevards and leafy avenues; very good infrastructure was put in place; a modern education system was set up; small-scale industries thrived. There was resistance to Italian rule, however, a simmering struggle that was never completely pacified, and the colonial racist colour-bar only added to native resentment. Italian rule did not last, and after a short, bloody campaign, Britain took control of Eritrea in 1941, and held it under a UN mandate for ten years. The British interlude is remembered locally for the looting of industrial hardware, and for the giving up on Eritrean independence: the province was federated with Ethiopia in 1951, but this only led to outright annexation in 1962. War followed; Eritrean rebels demanded full independence from Ethiopia, a goal finally achieved in 1993 after a long and bitter struggle. In the decade that followed tourists arrived in droves, but the tourist boom would not last.

Walking down Harnet Avenue, Asmara's main east-west thoroughfare on my first day in town, I noticed two veteran soldiers in wheelchairs. Dressed in light-coloured "Milano" battle fatigues, they were energetically wheeling themselves along, hailed cheerfully by a soldier standing guard outside the old governor's residence, now the president's office in town. They were not the last maimed men I would see, but it was somehow shocking to see them in this context: right in the middle of the city, right at the start of my walk, right in the line of my sight, as if put there to tell me something. As I walked about the city it appeared to me to be fresh-aired, low-key, and poor. It was also, evidently, battle weary. Overloaded Italian-made buses plied the roads, spewing fumes from their exhausts as they lumbered up and down: ticket prices did not reflect demand for public transportation here. A short jaunt down the avenue to the west soon brought me face to face with one of the art-deco cinemas for which Asmara is famous. The Roma had been renovated sometime in the 1990s and really looked nice; it was a bustling little cinema standing proud with its Romanesque pillars and large golden lettering glittering in the sun. A China-Eritrea film week was showing, but the tickets were free, another misdirected economic decision one felt, and so none were available. I sat down and had a beer at an outdoor café opposite the Roma. This in itself was still a novelty for me at this time, and I enjoyed the frisson of sitting outside quaffing an alcoholic drink. There were a few smartly-dressed patrons having an afternoon coffee there; probably government officials of some kind, a class apart from the majority who wandered the streets with no money and nothing to do.

There were many buildings of minor interest scattered along Harnet Avenue; it was only when you considered them as a group that the Italian era, otherwise absent and gone forever, impressed itself with its curves, windows, large doors and well-proportioned staircases. One of the more original of these colonial structures was the Fiat Tagliero building located at the western end of Harnet. The old petrol station had a wide, winged roof that made it look half-aeroplane, half-ship. The garage was neglected rather than dilapidated, and it looked like it might come back to life again one day, even though it probably won't – gasoline is currently incredibly expensive in Eritrea, and unless some oil is found in-country then private motor cars will remain the preserve of the state elite. After passing by the Fiat garage on this first exploration of the city, I walked out into Asmara's suburbs. Apart from a few high-rise buildings, villas and colonial relics, Asmara started to resemble other African cities: a shanty town of low-rise cobbled-together structures. The colonial infrastructure extended well out of town though: street corners were set square, roads had drains, and the sidewalks were still well paved. The road I took eventually led to a military camp of some sort. Here, at a roadside stall, I bought some bananas and inquired about the camp. Apparently, it was a retirement home for military veterans. A few children played harmlessly in the street as another limbless man hobbled by on crutches. Fresh sheep skins lay in the gutter, the remains of Eritrean Orthodox New Year celebrations; the still soft skins gave off a potent aroma. What would a battlefield full of dead men smell like?

Later on I returned to the café opposite the Roma and, over another beer, tried to sketch the cinema. What interested me more than the building itself were the oversized star-burst Cuban palm trees that graced the centre of the avenue out in front. Out of practice, I was not getting the perspective right in my sketch, which frustrated me. I was just about to have another go at it when a man on crutches sat beside me. He introduced himself; his name was Berhe.

"Oh, you're drawing. Very nice…" Physically challenged, Berhe was used to living off his wits. His well-spoken English and tidy manners attracted me to him, and I bought us drinks. After the usual pleasantries and inquiries about what I was up to in Eritrea, Berhe tried to interest me in a guide book about Keren, and a map of Eritrea that he was selling. Like any good salesperson, he did not pressure me to buy, but suggested this and that while keeping up a charming banter. I did not want to buy these items, but thought to purchase something to help keep him in business. But first, I had a few questions of my own to ask. I wanted to know what, if anything had gone wrong in Eritrea. Over a second beer, Berhe talked.

"…I was born in Ethiopia, but grew up in Eritrea. I learned to speak Italian at school; I learned English from my neighbours. In the 1970s there were still many Italians here; they ran the civil service and held posts in the government under Ethiopian rule. We liked the Italians, although they were racist. Slowly the war of independence got worse. I saw it all, but never got involved. This has been my home all my life and I saw everything happen. The worst years were in the mid-80s. Then the city was under curfew, and the Ethiopian soldiers would shoot on sight. They were frightened. By that time, they were taking heavy losses in the field. Their soldiers had lost heart." Time and a multitude of events telescoped in Berhe's story. He sipped his beer from a whisky tumbler, golden afternoon light refracting through the liquid onto his dark, handsome face. Immensely experienced, but down at heel, he was an expert at keeping up appearances.

Berhe talked more about the recent past. "Eritrean rebels wore a white khaki uniform – *Milanos* – and plastic sandals, called *shedda*. The Ethiopian forces had superior arms and manpower. But the Eritrean fighters always gained the upper hand in battles because they were fighting for liberation, to free their land and people from foreigners." The story of Eritrea's liberation struggle is perhaps not well-known in Europe, but it was the longest armed struggle of Africa's decolonization era. Certainly, I can remember listening to radio and news reports in the late 1970s and early 80s that began, "Today, Eritrean rebels attacked..." Eritrea was a faraway place of which I knew little, but it felt like something real was going on there, and that those Eritrean rebels were not going to go away... Always considering themselves to be Eritrean first and anything else second, the motivation of the Eritrean rebels came from the discriminatory way the Ethiopian government treated the local population of what it considered to be its 14th province. As early as the 1950s, the Ethiopian government banned political parties and trade unions in Eritrea. This was a serious mistake. The Eritreans were in many ways more politically sophisticated than the Ethiopians, the result of an extended period of colonialism that included exposure to British liberalism. Idriss Mohammed Adam, a Muslim leader, founded the Eritrean Liberation Front (ELF) in 1960, which went on to field a small force of mostly Muslim fighters, but which also included embittered working-class Christians among their number. In 1972, the ELF joined forces with the more radical, leftist People's Liberation Forces. The merged entity became known as the Eritrean People's Liberation Front (EPLF), and after a brief but nasty internal struggle, the EPLF came under the firm control of its dominant Marxist faction. It was at this time that Isaias Afewerki, Eritrea's current president, came to prominence emerging as the political leader of the united movement. Early successes brought the EPLF victory in the 1970s, but a new Soviet-backed Marxist regime in Ethiopia was hell-bent on retaking Eritrea. The war was re-ignited, and large-scale Ethiopian offensives pushed the Eritrean fighters out of the main towns and back to lines surrounding the northern town of Nafka. Here the EPLF dug in and held on for several years, before finally counter-attacking. The titanic struggle that ensued involved both guerrilla warfare and major set piece battles. The skill and tenacity with which the EPLF waged this war with the barest of resources are legendary. Eritrean units eschewed military rank and insignia; women and men fought side by side; commanders led from the front. Slowly and inexorably the tide of war turned in the EPLF's favour. The fall of the Soviet Union tolled the death-knell for Ethiopia's Marxist regime, which came tumbling down as its army met one crushing defeat after another in Eritrea. Right to the end, the rebels kept up the pressure, and eventually the remaining cornered Ethiopians in Eritrea surrendered. Ethiopian prisoners of war were well-treated and soon repatriated. After the Eritrean population voted overwhelmingly in favour of independence in a referendum, Eritrea formally became Africa's newest state in May 1993, and Isaias Afewerki became the president of this new state by dint of his leadership role in the revolution, and by popular acclaim. At first, things looked very good for Eritrea, and the new nation bathed in international admiration. Even Ethiopia was pre-disposed to be friendly towards its new neigh-bour. But a costly post-war border conflict between Eritrea and Ethiopia erupted in 1998, re-opening old wounds.

Berhe, who had painted the Eritrean fighters in glowing colours, had nothing but words of scorn for the '98 conflict. "It was a bad war; very bad. Shameful with nothing gained by either side, a complete waste; commanders who had survived 30 years of fighting were cut down on the front lines..." he said, with visible disgust, "...it was a pointless war that led to many bad things. Now the whole male population must go to the army because of the emergency." At the start of the two-year border conflict, in which tens of thousands were killed, the Eritrean government, meaning Isaias Afewerki, suspended Eritrea's new, liberal constitution. Then, in 2001, after a group of senior politicians called for change and the re-introduction of the constitution, among other things, the free press was shut down and the formation of alternate political parties banned. The Eritrean state effectively came under the authoritarian control of the People's Front for Democracy and Justice, headed by Afewerki. Not a few Eritrean politicians disappeared, presumed to be detained by the government. Other people were arrested, too, including many minority-sect Christians. What began so hopefully in 1993 had turned into a nightmare.

Berhe was only half Eritrean, an outsider in Asmara, but there was a limit to what he was going to impart to a stranger over a beer in the street right next to Afewerki's downtown office. We parted company after I finally bought one of his guide books, which was unfortunate because I would not be able to find a map of Eritrea anywhere in Asmara, and the next time I bumped into Berhe he told me he had sold his copy.

THE GAMBIT WAS much gentler than the usual importuning I faced opposite St Joseph's Cathedral on Harnet Avenue, the wide tree-lined boulevard that cut Asmara in half, a street I would walk up and down many times in the coming weeks; "Hi, how are you doing?" I glanced over my shoulder to see a tall, but hunched, aging man wearing a baseball cap and sunglasses, standing hopefully. He smiled at me diffidently, apparently eager to avoid a negative reaction from this tourist. I returned his greeting, and we quickly arranged to do a little black market deal: he was offering three times the official bank rate for my dollars.

I was led down a back alley and into a block of tenement

flats, at the bottom of which the mystery man disappeared into a room. This was a moment of vulnerability: it could have been a trap, and I tried to think of a cover story in case I needed it. But, as is usually the case in countries where a black market flourishes, everything was above board and my contact, who went by the nom de guerre Mikhail, soon reappeared with a wad of cash, which he handed over to me in exchange for 200 greenbacks. Mikhail had dealt through an intermediary, and it was doubtful he made much money on the deal himself, but he seemed satisfied having done an honest day's work, and we were both ready to get something to eat, and so I invited the black marketeer to lunch. My new friend did not hesitate, and off we sauntered to one of his haunts, a hole-in-the-wall bistro just off Harnet Avenue. The restaurant, with its darkened interior, simple furniture, and pay-kiosk by the door, was communist in style, complete with fading 1970s posters of tourist locales in Europe. But there were some really nice landscape oil paintings hung on the walls, done by local artists in the 1990s. One of these paintings featured a lone deer drinking from a watering hole somewhere in the savannah-like Eritrean lowlands against the backdrop of a setting sun; not an especially original idea, but it was nicely done, and made me wonder whether venison was on the menu.

Mikhail, being my elder, took the initiative to order the food after we sat down at a table. There were only two other patrons in the restaurant, happily tucking into huge plates of spaghetti bolognaise, I noticed. My host ordered *injera* for us; large pancake-shaped soft bread made with teff and millet. Our bread came topped with a spicy lamb stew and a portion of greens, which we ate with our hands, rolling the food up in the Arab manner, something Mikhail was more skilled at than I. The food was not bad at all, and probably a lot more satisfying than spaghetti, the only other option available. Mikhail did not speak as he ate, and we bonded naturally over our shared, silent, meal. With his daily work done, well fed, and with little else to do that day, my informer was now happy to talk.

"Well, Mr Gary you see I lived in Italy many years; in the south. I worked in hotels and learned to speak Italian there…" Mikhail's English was just fine, I discovered; Eritreans, a country where all local languages were given equal official recognition after the revolution, were formidable linguists. "I got married to a girl, but she left me, and later I left Italy. I don't know where my child is now. Business is not good Mr Gary…" Mikhail's rambling story had a lot of holes in it, but he was a man who had come down in the world, this much was clear. His hustling, which he conducted with some dignity, was his only means of survival, but he had obviously seen better times. Once a handsome man, he chain-smoked, and this habit had aged him beyond his years; he gave me the impression that he was starting to lose the plot; he had spent too much time alone and the conversation became unsatisfying to me. I paid for the meal, and we then went outside where Mikhail became animated once more, suggesting places to go and things to do, but I decided to part company with him, leaving the door for future black market deals open.

THE EUROPEANS who populated Asmara in the middle of the 20th century built their houses with gusto, and planned a city that would last. You saw evidence of this confidence everywhere in Asmara, which was really haunting. Indeed, a hotel named after the surrounding area, one of several near my pension, was built something like a haunted house: it had a high ceilings and a tall spire with birds living in it. Another nearby hotel, popular with expatriates, was more redolent of the 1960s. In the evenings, the bar at this establishment became crowded with locals who enjoyed quaffing beers, of which there was only one local brand available, in groups. It was observable that there was not much else to do in Asmara. Those who couldn't afford a beer ambled along the streets chatting with one another, or nursed a coffee in one of the numerous cafés downtown. On the weekend, some of

these cafés became quite lively – rumours of a starving population were not true, at least not here in Asmara. Going to the
movies was the only other entertainment available in town. Not
all of the nine cinemas in Asmara were as in as good shape as the
Roma, but most were at least operational.

At the Cinema Impero, on Harnet Avenue, I went to see a
movie entitled *Salem*, directed by Ghirmay Ghebreab. The ticket
was cheap, and the large cinema full of punters. After entering, I
sat down and tried to follow the movie's storyline, which was
difficult, not because of the language barrier – although Salem
was a Tigrinyan-language film, it was shown with English subti-
tles – but because the drama was so long-winded and laboured
in its presentation. The production was, nonetheless, of some
sociological interest: the heroine of the film, Salem, is an
orphaned child of the revolution. She has been brought up by
relatives in a village, and has now come of age. The girl is pretty
and attracts the attention of several suitors. These male characters represent certain archetypes: there is the good-hearted
redneck, a stubborn traditionalist, and a sophisticated Eritrean
expatriate who has come back to Eritrea to look for a wife. Salem
is intelligent as well as pretty, and seeks to delay her marriage in
favour of pursuing further education in the big city. Various
complicated interludes and twists in the plot ensue, with Salem
eventually running away to Asmara where, unaccountably, she
enrols in the air force academy. Meanwhile, her male suitors are
all falling over themselves jockeying for position. The expatriate
male ditches his arranged match and, at the end of the film, gets
hitched to Salem, who by this time has become an air force pilot.
I found *Salem* a bit convoluted; it was poorly filmed and not
exactly logical, but it was topical and the audience loved it, actually cheering out loud when Salem ran away from her village
rather than be married off in an arranged wedding. Moreover,
the story raised important social issues, relevant to Eritrea, such
as the generation gap, women's rights, and the aspirations of
young people who yearn for a modern life. These issues were
foregrounded against the traditional culture with its emphasis

on male patriarchal clan values. Rather contrived, the most didactic scene in the film was one where the competing males sit down in a traditional difference-settling meeting and come to agree that they should act in Salem's interests, and let her decide her own future, a position put forth by a wise elder. The men agree, and there are reconciliatory hugs all round.

Outside on the street, meanwhile, there were many real life Salems trying to get by in an economy that had not been able to take off. The pretty girls worked in cafés and bars, apparently on the lookout for a pick up if I read their body language right. Savvy and well-educated, the girls oozed sassiness. On the weekends, the city's cafés and bars swelled as young men flowed into town from the surrounding countryside, but traditional rules, and economic realities, meant that many male-female relationships were conducted on a commercial basis, a commerce stoked by visitors from the even more socially conservative Arab Gulf states. Young men mostly socialized with their peers, sipping coffees and smoking, although in one café I saw a young man reading a book, something I had never seen during my time in Saudi Arabia. Above this layer of youth, there was a city bourgeoisie; those who ran the state-owned hotels and enterprises. One wondered how these citizens attained their positions, and how those who lived in the former colonial villas got allocated such salubrious accommodations. The one social group missing in the city seemed to be men of working age; of course, there were some of these, but not as many as one would expect. The deficit could only be accounted for by the fact that Eritrea kept a big standing army relative to the size of its population, and that the country's economy was still largely an agricultural one. Sophisticated in look and feel, Asmara was not much more than a market town, functionally speaking.

One morning, I set out to explore Asmara's environs more fully. Starting early, I walked eastwards along some mud-road suburbs thinking to get the sun behind me for the rest of the day. This walk took me past yet more period buildings such as the Red Sea Building and the old American and British Tobacco headquarters, the latter a 1920s gem of curvaceous concrete. In the morning's cool mist old ladies dressed in white shawls milled about. A man was also dressed in the traditional white robes of the Tigrinya people; he was an Orthodox priest I later learned. Down a back street I bumped into one of those pretty Eritrean women on her way to work. She hailed me and spoke in English asking me to get her a job in England. Fat chance of that, but I took her details so as not to disappoint her. The sun struggled to come out from behind some clouds, and the resulting diffused light was ideal for taking photographs of the various churches and related buildings I found in the eastern part of the city. No one seemed to care about my picture taking; I was mostly politely ignored wherever I went. At the modernistic Nda Mariam Orthodox Church, a small crowd of white robed women were busy with their private religious rituals. I had no idea what was going on, but there appeared to be an Orthodox New Year ceremony taking place inside the church.

"Cristo…cristo…cristo…" went a refrain from a voice broadcast around the compound on a public address system. Curious, I went into the church, dedicated to St Mary, only to find a packed congregation listening to a priest talking from a lectern. The church's interior was decorated with murals from floor to ceiling; the air was enveloped in clouds of incense.

"Cristo…cristo…cristo…" Oh, of course, *Christ*.

From the church I meandered down some roads into the poorer southern part of the city. Here itinerant workers, who had obviously come in to the city looking for work, huddled together in cheap pensions and crowded tenements. It was on this side of town that the city bus station and a POW-like prison were located. When I passed by the prison, a whole bunch of young men with their heads shaved were being delivered to the gulag for who knows what offences – one could get locked up in a shipping container indefinitely for being a practising Pentecostal Christian in Eritrea; the men I saw were probably minor criminals, and therefore got better treatment. Lurching buses exited the bus station, a place about as well organized as the airport, which was not very well organized at all. Roadside hawkers sold prickly pear fruits, oranges and bread, but there was not much else for sale; agricultural goods brought into the city by pickup truck and camel had been sold earlier in the day. I came across some unexpected surprises: an interesting modernistic building here, a nice art-deco villa there. One store sold upmarket Italian racing bicycles and related accessories. And then there were the ubiquitous cafés with their puff pastries, flam cakes and dusted crêpes.

It is undeniably true that the general conditions at a university reveal a great deal about a country. Without wanting to be too condescending, it must be said that Asmara University came as something of a let-down. I found the school I was looking for in the southern outskirts of the city, but it was a gated community and it took a while for me to find the entrance. Once inside I discovered the main buildings which looked like those of a high school. There was not much going on here; no classes were in progress. No one approached me, even though I must have seemed like an exotic bird wandering about, but then neither did anyone bother me. Rather, I was ignored. There were no restaurants or cafés on the campus, and I couldn't find a library. It then dawned on me that it was not term time, and so I was probably wasting my time there anyway.

Further south one had to climb up a steep road to get out of the city into the highland countryside. My hike up this road afforded me another view of the town, which looked a lot poorer from this angle than it did from my pension window on the north side of town. Instead of villas, fir trees and a cathedral, all one could see from this vantage point were grubby lines of ill-kept housing, the occasional goat, and some old factories that manufactured basic goods. One metal scrap yard looked positively Dickensian, blackened and ramshackle as it was. Meanwhile, out on the breezy road the people I met were friendly without being familiar; they had a certain native reserve emphasized in their dress and body language. I continued on up and over the hill which took me onto a plateau. Here wheat was being manually harvested by some workers; a white-robed woman worked a plot of vegetables in the distance. A football pitch lay dormant and unused. Scattered here and there were some modern villas, generously spaced but poorly designed, the homes of more prosperous farmers perhaps, or of government officials. The open grassy views on the plateau were a relief after the confinement of the city, but with nothing to do there I soon left. On the return leg of my walk I once more passed by the city prison. A guard standing in a watchtower, obviously bored out of his mind, waved to me as he cradled his assault rifle.

Back in town I got caught out in a seasonal thunderstorm. It was an impressive downpour; I had completely forgotten just how intense African rain near the equator can be. A few heavy drops heralded the deluge. I took shelter in the bus station along with many stranded passengers. Rain and hailstones then pelted down. Unlike in England, where a thunderstorm soon comes to an end, this African storm would not let up. High winds blew rain sideways into the bus shelter, forcing everyone to move closer together. Soon the street started to flood, and then the main street literally turned into a river. An aging gas tanker stoically ploughed through this raging torrent, its driver undeterred by the conditions. A man stood on his donkey-cart and drove his chariot up the road cracking a whip as he went. These people were clearly used to the sudden storms and were unfazed by the flooding, which logically had to run off the streets quickly since the city stood at an altitude of 2000 metres. Hopping over pools of water, I managed to get out of the bus station during a lull in the storm and get to a café. But when I asked for a beer there I was told they didn't serve alcohol: the people running the café were Muslims. Subdued, I sipped a coffee until the rain abated, and then made my way back to the northern suburbs.

The staff at the pension seemed disappointed in me. Either I would wander about the city in the morning and spend the afternoon sipping whisky on the pension balcony, or I would spend the morning in bed reading and sipping whisky, and then stroll around town for an hour or two before taking dinner at the hotel down the road. In other words, I was not acting like the ideal guest who gets up in the morning, disappears all day, and then returns conveniently late after the cleaning has been done. My rhythms were irregular; I was unpredictable; I did not spend much money. Eritrea was proving to be a difficult nut to crack; the people were really quite nice, but did not open up to outsiders, and what I learned only came in drips and drabs. But running around the place like a headless chicken photographing colonial architecture was not going to give me any more insight into the country than hanging around the hotels; in fact, the latter places, with their surly staff and poor service, were really quite revealing of what had gone wrong in Eritrea. But when I announced my intention to visit Massawa, Eritrea's principal port on the Red Sea coast, there were whoops of approval from the women who ran the pension. They were delighted that I had at last come to my senses and was starting to act like a real tourist. Through Mikhail's good offices, I rented a bicycle with the intention of riding it to the coast, about 100 kilometres east of the highland capital. That was quite an ambitious distance to attempt on a bicycle in an African country, but I knew it would be downhill all the way, and that the road was in good shape. In addition, there were no security problems to speak of – the government had firm control of its territory through its extensive military presence in the countryside, and through a system of travel passes and road blocks. To leave Asmara and travel to the coast, I had to apply for a travel permit from the tourist office, and formalities proved to be fairly straightforward.

The Tigrinya ladies of the pension gathered to wave me off on the morning of my departure. In the spirit of the *tegadelti* – Eritrean fighters – I carried very little: my camera, a few necessities, and a bottle of water. By this time, I knew my way around town, and had even scouted the route out east the day before, so I had no trouble finding the highway. On the way out of town I passed a small group of army recruits on guard duty. A friendly wave from me deflected their attentions. The prickly pear bush-lined road then snaked its way up and out of the city, quiet save for the occasional overloaded long distance bus or truck; there were few private cars on Eritrea's roads.

Before long, I arrived at the British Commonwealth Asmara War Cemetery, which lay just a few metres away from the road in a wooded patch of land. I stopped, got off the bike, and took a look around. During the war, the Italians led by General Orlando Lorenzini, put up stiff resistance to the British offensive of February 1941. Keren eventually fell to the British forces, opening the road to Asmara, but at a cost over 400 British dead, perhaps half of whom were later buried in the cemetery I walked around. The site, like all Commonwealth cemeteries, was digni-fied and well-tended. The soldiers buried here found equality in death: there was no distinction based on rank. Rather the men were buried next to their regimental comrades, in neat lines and with identical grave stones. The first grave stone I studied read, "Captain M.W.C. Tutton, B.A. General List 12th November 1941." Another head stone belonged to Sergeant E.F. Hannan of the East Kent Regiment, a unit colloquially known as "The Buffs." Where had this soldier been born I wondered, Canterbury? Faversham? Thanet? At the age of 25, Hannan's life ended in Eritrea, and he lies among the prickly cacti and thin trees of the Hamasen high-lands; a corner of a foreign field that is for ever England.

Over the hill and past a church, I found myself cycling in open country, a beautiful and picturesque landscape of acacia trees, euphorbia and other shrubs. The cacti, with their big flap-ping ear-like branches, looked like tropical plants, and seemed to be invaders in this mountain country. The land was only exten-sively cultivated, and I did not see too many farmers; only a scat-tering of dwellings indicating a human presence. Birds, resembling buzzards but smaller, flocked in the wide skies above the rolling hills, attracted, I later discovered, to a landfill. The road finally began its long descent to the coast, and on this side of the mountain there was plenty of evidence of a long history of settlement: the hills were terraced for many miles about; the roofs of distant villages reflected the sun's rays giving them away. By a church, children stood begging for water and money, though more for something to do than out of desperation. The track of the famous narrow gauge Eritrean railway line, built by the Italians, coursed its way through this landscape and I caught glimpses of its tunnels and track as I freewheeled down the road in the warm sunshine. The railway had been rebuilt in the 1990s and is now a tourist attraction, running on a chartered basis. By all accounts, a ride on this train was a marvellous experience, the mountain line almost impossibly romantic, but the train wasn't running on this day. The sight of a camel nonchalantly grazing on a hilltop reminded me that it was this animal that was still the most important method of transport in the wide and inaccessible Eritrean highlands.

Nefasit was the first village I passed through as the road levelled out on the first of several small plateaus. The ambience of a village is always deceptive because the population will ebb and flow according to the season and time of day, but Nefasit appeared to be empty. The landscape was full of bush and small trees but dry, almost desert-like, and one wondered what anyone would do in this place in any case. Extensive terracing proved that farming had been going on for a long time though, and the landscape had undoubtedly been a lot greener at one time; desertification was well underway in the mountains. On the way through Nefasit, I passed an abandoned factory. Only the façade with *Fonte Acqua Termo Minerale* chiselled into it remained standing, along with some forgotten flower beds bordered by neat rows of stones. A few boy herders shouted in English at me as I peddled by, asking for money. They were just having fun really. Around the corner a small caravan of loaded camels loomed on the other side of the road, their owner diplomatically greeting me in a friendly manner.

The next dozen kilometres were the best of the trip: the weather was sunny, but cool, and I glided my way comfortably through a land where even the stones burned in summer, or so it was said. Then disaster struck. My bicycle's bottom bracket worked loose. It had been foolish of me to attempt this long ride on a wonky machine, and I was now obliged to walk the rest of the way to Ghinda, another village en route to Massawa. It was a downhill all the way, so pushing the bike along was not too taxing. At Ghinda I got a local blacksmith to do some repairs, and his bodged effort was good enough to allow me to continue riding. But by that time it was late in the day and so I repaired myself to a little guest house in the village. This inn's only saving grace was that it served cold beer. And so after settling in to my crummy room at the mosquito-infested inn, I went out to get dinner up the road, finally eating at a local bistro that served bread, beans and surprisingly good prickly pear smoothies. The food was simple, but tasty and nutritious, and I saw no evidence of anyone starving at Ghinda despite the limited menu options. The village came alive at night, the locals enjoying some Eritrean shoulder-shuffle dance music that blared from speakers hanging from doorways. A couple of people tried speaking to me in Italian, which was interesting. Others I felt sure spoke English, but they kept to themselves.

The next day, I walked back through the village in search of breakfast, finding a café where I enjoyed a cup of tea delivered with a squeeze of fresh lime in it. A large, open dirt space opposite the village's main street was already filling up with cars and minibuses. Behind these buses a market had formed up with simple makeshift stalls; fruits, vegetables and some basic clothes were put on display. I sipped my tea and observed the unfolding morning scene. The market was big enough to suggest that not a few people still lived in the highland countryside; a hobbled camel lay in the sun, awaiting the return journey to some distant hamlet or dwelling. Children played acrobats nearby the beast, ignoring it as if it was a weed. A consignment of water melons had just arrived in a pickup and were being unloaded just as luggage and bundles were uploaded onto the tops of the minibuses. Circling in the sky above a bird of prey searched for breakfast. What interested me most about this scene was the kaleidoscope of clothing styles worn – some dressed as Muslims with head scarves and veils, others wore bright Indian-style saris, yet others donned western dress, or Arab long shirts and Sudanese style turbans; the village was a meeting point of styles and cultures as well as a centre for transactions, and Eritrea's cultural diversity was on full show.

Breakfast over, I mounted up and peddled out of the village, riding uphill for a short distance, and then downhill again towards the lowlands. Although downhill, the gradient was much gentler than the day before and in fact almost non-existent in places. And as the day warmed up so the ride became more toilsome. Then another breakdown, a punctured tyre, gave me the excuse to retire from the ride altogether. I flagged down a bus which stopped. My bicycle was loaded on the top rack, and a space was made for me inside the bus, all done without any fuss. The driver then continued on his slow, methodical way. From my elevated seat above the gear box, I got a good view of the landscape out of the bus window, which became progressively drier and more desert-like the closer to the coast we got. As we rolled along we passed a battalion of Eritrean soldiers on the march. I could see the men clearly, and vice-versa. To say they were an impressive sight would be an understatement; marching at a smart pace, they carried little but their personal weapons; they were clearly strong and inured to the hardships of a tough military life. One of the soldiers, carrying a heavy mortar tripod, had the spare energy to wave to me. The unit walked in single file on both sides of the road to some unknown destination. These men were experienced, and this movement along the road was not a training exercise but a troop redeployment of some kind. It spoke volumes about Eritrea that this manoeuvre was taking place on foot, fuel too precious to use transporting men to a new posting. The bus soon came up alongside the battalion vanguard led by a grey-haired veteran who merely carried a swagger stick and map board. The commander set the pace walking briskly, but not over-energetically, while his subordinates, the brilliant and unflappable knights of Africa, brought up the rear.

———

AFTER SWERVING about the hot lowlands, and stopping at a checkpoint on the outskirts of town, the bus eventually arrived at the Port of Massawa. The bus station was located a couple of kilometres inland. I got off the bus and dived into the nearest restaurant for a cold beer while a roadside mechanic patched up my bike's flat tyre, and then rode off towards the port in the sweltering heat once the repair was done. Massawa was quite nondescript, a mixture of public housing and shanty dwellings. When I stopped to photograph some of the modern buildings, however, I was accosted by a security guard who quickly informed me I had been photographing a military base. He insisted I delete my digital photographs on the spot, an annoyance, but I did what I was told to do to save an argument, or worse. There had been absolutely no indication that the housing was military, and I really felt this individual was being overly officious, if not totally paranoid.

Massawa's old town and cargo port were located on an island linked to the mainland by a causeway. I crossed this causeway slowly, innocently photographing estuary birds and flowers as I went. The security official had been aggressive and he had upset me; photographing the birds helped calm me down. Another bird, a shot down Soviet transport plane from the 1980s, had been parked on one side of the causeway, a trophy from the war of independence – until 1990, the Soviet Union had been a vigorous supporter of the Ethiopian Marxist regime, known as The Derg. The collapse of the Soviet Union marked the end of Ethiopia's attempt to re-occupy Eritrea. More evidence of the war could be found at the end of the causeway where three captured tanks had been put on plinths, a war memorial. Shot-up buildings in the old port dated from the 1998-2000 conflict when a regrouped, and rearmed, Ethiopian military made a determined assault on Eritrea, attacking by land, sea and air. One large Romanesque villa showed evidence of having been machine gunned, shelled and aerially bombed. Elsewhere, the port was poor and neglected where it was not new, but largely empty. The Italians evidently helped to build a modern hotel in the harbour, completed in 2006, but it was not in use. Another large state-run hotel was virtually empty, an air-conditioner unnecessarily keeping the foyer cooled. Completing a meandering ride past these sites in the old town, I went back to the bus station and booked in at the motel there for the night. The window in the en suite bathroom of my room was missing, which made it a perfect hide from which to photograph birds, downed jets, and neighbours hoeing their fields at dusk.

The trip to Massawa had all been about getting there, and I was not going to spend any time along Eritrea's Red Sea coast. Tourists came here in the 1990s to enjoy snorkel and scuba diving around the Dahlak Islands. But I knew very well that the main island of the Dahlak group hosted a secret prison full of political detainees; it was unthinkable to go there for leisure purposes, and indeed the tourist industry in Eritrea seems to have dwindled to almost nothing in recent years due to the country's political repression. From Massawa, I took the bus directly back to Asmara the next day, once again slinging my bicycle on the roof rack, and paying for two tickets so as to give myself a decent bit of room inside the vehicle. The trip back, unrushed and comfortable, gave me a chance to take a leisurely look at the countryside as we gradually ascended to the highlands. We stopped at a military post where a perfunctory check of our travel documents was done, and then motored on and up past quiet villages and remote abandoned mountaintop monasteries. It was not until we arrived back in Asmara that it felt cool enough to put a sweater on again, a slap of rain welcoming us back.

REGRETTABLY, modern Eritrea has an appalling human rights record. Since 2003, large numbers of people have been imprisoned for political and religious reasons; many have died in detention. The exact whereabouts of other prisoners is unknown as they are held incommunicado. There is no free press in Eritrea, and no alternate political parties are allowed. Isaias Afewerki long ago crossed a line and has become a ruthless and utterly paranoid, authoritarian leader. His descent into a Macbeth-like hell is disguised by a carefully cultivated public image; his large physical size cuts an imposing figure at rallies, and he is a convincing public speaker. The fact that he is also somewhat mad has not been not lost on the people who have known him, however, and he is directly responsible for the morbid atmosphere that has descended on a country that had everything going for it at its inception. In Asmara, this depression was at first hard to detect; Eritreans' natural reserve made them hard to read. But the unmistakable signs were there: people avoided eye contact, they were tired and demoralized, and there was an undertow of fear and loathing on the streets. Almost no one dared to talk to me in the Eritrean capital, except my black marketeer buddy.

Mikhail would stop by the pension for a drink in the morning and to see if I wanted anything. Usually I did not, but we often went on a walkabout together and invariably ended up having a meal in one of Harnet Avenue's cafés. Not long before I left Asmara, Mikhail and I sat in the Rosie Bianca bar for a lunchtime drink. We fancied cakes and beer – I had suffered a nasty bout of food poisoning, and was just on the mend again. One of the waitresses in the bar flirted with me, her hand lingering on my shoulder as I ordered our refreshments. The bar was quite noisy, with both music playing and a television on. The allmale clientele watched the soccer game; I tried to listen to the music. It was then time to ask Mikhail some direct questions about the political situation in Eritrea; I wanted to know his opinion.

Mikhail said, "In the 1990s business was good. I made a lot of money. The Ethiopians were still here then; many of them owned businesses. There were a lot of harlots, too. I had a good time then. But things went bad after 2003. Many people were arrested, maybe 3000. Others were shot. I saw it happen myself in a square in town where they publicly executed several politicals."

I asked Mikhail what he thought of Afewerki. "He was a good man; a fighter. But he arrested a lot of people. Some of them had wanted to betray our country to Ethiopia." That was the official story concerning a group of senior officials, known as the G-15 group, who were arrested in May 2001; they had written an open letter to party members criticizing the government for acting in an "illegal and unconstitutional" manner, effectively signing their own arrest warrants. Afewerki had been running amok ever since and tolerated no criticism of his rule or policies. I had observed the Eritrean president on television. In one interview he gave to an Australian journalist, he point-blank denied knowing the whereabouts of a well-known Eritrean revolutionary, or even knowing him at all, which could only have been a lie. In a cabinet meeting called to deal with agricultural policy, the president lorded it over all present, and although the officials at the table remained calm and dignified they were also clearly afraid of Afewerki, whose manner would change from jovial host to bullying schoolmaster and back again within the space of half a minute. A good actor, Afewerki was clearly a dangerous man. What did Mikhail *really* think of him?

"Afewerki has depressed a lot of people. He doesn't let anyone disagree with him. Before he didn't care what anybody thought about him, but now he goes out and asks people how they are and what they want. He is afraid of losing their support." Mikhail had described Afewerki's transformation from hard-headed revolutionary into a popular authoritarian leader. I had also seen the president on television working a crowd, and he was actually very charismatic, although his holding of an overly-enthusiastic young soldier in an arm-lock did not look very presidential.

"We are depressed. There is no business here. Everyone has gone." Mikhail was right. You cannot lock up your best people and pretend everything is hunky-dory. My friend was not an intellectual, and it was difficult to draw him out. It occurred to me that what was missing in Asmara was a free and active intellectual life: the place was braindead. Despite some nice paintings, including a magnificent portrayal of two fighters receiving water from a villager on the wall at the Asmara Post Office, life was empty here because you could not breathe the fresh air of ideas; no one could state a contrary point of view. The revolution had been betrayed.

Mikhail sucked on his cigarette, and we had another round of drinks. The flirty waitress had forgotten about me and by now was engrossed in a conversation with her girlfriend.

"Mr Gary, if you want to understand Eritrea, we are a quiet people, and we don't talk so much about ourselves, but a lot was sacrificed for our revolution. Many people were killed. They expected it and died willingly. They thought it was for a good cause. We all thought that way. Now we don't know what is happening, but we know that we paid a high price. The struggle was bitter and hard, but the people were fighting for freedom. Now we are disappointed; no one wants to come here." Mikhail took a long drag on his cigarette and then lapsed into a coughing fit. His health was not all it might have been, and he was a man who knew his fate; he was depressed and unable to articulate his feelings fully.

The next day Mikhail helped me carry my luggage to the airport. We waited a long time for the bus. Fortunately, I had time to spare, and reflected on the breaking of my no-fly rule again – I would be leaving Asmara on a flight bound for Khartoum. There was no other way of getting to Sudan as the land border was not open to foreigners.

Several days before, I had gone out to the Ministry of Tourism to try to get permission to make the crossing overland. However, the border was closed because it was not secure: many refugees tried to escape Eritrea via Sudan, and bandits preyed on them, and so, although I had been politely received at the ministry, the answer had been a firm no.

The bus eventually came and we journeyed the few kilometres to Asmara airport for a pittance. On the way a cycling squad on a training ride passed us by, a sign of apparent normality. At the small air terminal Mikhail helped me with my bags and then got us macchiato coffees, our last, while I waited for the security check to get into the building: ironically, the airport was a fortress within a fortress. And then my turn came, and I disappeared into the system to be frisked, scanned and interrogated as Mikhail, back hunched, quietly slipped away.

5

FLIGHT

DEPARTING ERITREA WAS TIME-CONSUMING AND FULL OF bureaucratic procedure. First, I had to prove I had changed money at government approved outlets. This I could do because I had in fact exchanged a certain amount of money at banks, only changing a portion of my cash reserve on the black market. Then there was the rigmarole at customs whose officers were intent on checking the money I was carrying, which obliged me to pull banknotes out of various concealed places on my person. One of these officials decided to make a very thorough search of one of my bags, completely missing the false bottom where I kept stationery but which could easily have concealed a gun or a kilo of heroin. When he found and confiscated a small pair of craft scissors from my transparent pencil case I sarcastically congratulated him on his diligence, "Well done, you found something!", and he took the jibe well, immediately allowing me to proceed to immigration without any further hassle. At a final desk, I faced an immigration official at last. He checked to see if I had a Sudanese visa, and then banged a horrible inky exit stamp over the exquisitely designed Eritrean visa in my passport, ruining the latter.

By now I had resigned myself to flying again. There was only one way out of Eritrea for me: on a flight booked at the sole

Sudanese Airlines representative office in Asmara. Incredibly, I had been required to pay for a return ticket, as per Sudanese regulations, even though I would not be coming back. The whole arrangement was bizarre, and the ticket was not exactly cheap either considering Sudanese Airlines has a terrible safety record. After going through contortions of angst, I had eventually caved in and bought the ticket. Now that I had actually got through security, customs and immigration at the airport, I relaxed and waited for my flight as I drank a cup of heavily sugared tea. It was actually a huge relief to be leaving Eritrea; I was starting to starve there, not because there wasn't any food, but because there had been such a poor choice of dishes and no decent meat or fish to be had. The departure lounge in the airport had a shop selling leather goods, but what I wanted was a beefsteak, not tanned skins. Neat lines of shiny gin and whisky bottles caught my attention in the small duty free store, but alas I could not risk taking a bottle into Sudan, a country that had embraced Sharia law.

As I waited for my flight, the only scheduled departure for that day, I sat down and read Tayeb Salih's classic novel *Season of Migration to the North*. The book had been a gift to me from Meshal, who had inscribed the inside cover as follows, "I have never believed in East is East and West is West, but lots of work needs to be done to convince people of this universe that we are one…" I completely agreed with these sentiments. Tayeb Salih's complex, clever and powerful story was the ideal antidote to the bad taste left in my mouth by a month of hanging around Sudan's awful embassy in Riyadh in 40-degree heat in pursuit of a visa. *Season of Migration to the North* has famously been described as the *Heart of Darkness* in reverse, where an African protagonist travels to London where he exploits and destroys the women he befriends. But it became apparent to me, reading this masterpiece, albeit in English translation, that Tayeb Salih had created something more fantastical than Conrad had done in his highly original, arguably flawed, novel. Salih plays with temporal linearity, jumping back and forth between Knightsbridge and a small but socially rich Sudanese village on the banks of the river Nile; the identity of the narrator changes, a common device in Arabic literature; the climax to the story is brilliantly hinted at throughout the book, and previewed in a false, or dual, climax, a horrible love murder. *Season* really bowled me over, and it absorbed me from the moment I started reading it; the peripheral details, descriptions and detours interested me as much as the main plot, which was an unlikely though fascinating concoction. There is a memorable description of an English District Commissioner: "[he]...*was a god who had a free hand over an area larger than the whole of the British Isles...*" But there is no resentment of the British in Salih's tale; resentment is saved for the Sudanese comprador class, referred to as "nonentities" and "nobodies." An examination of the complex East-West relationship, an artificial construct, lies at the core of the book, and simple, sweeping judgments are not held by any of the characters. Reading *Season of Migration to the North* took me on a journey into the psychologically complex, fraught, and deeply emotionally intertwined relationship between colonizer and colonized.

A helicopter buzzed about outside near some hangers, a scene reminiscent of Sanaa airport, I noticed as I glanced up from the book. The sun was now coming straight through the terminal windows, blinding me, and I put my reading material away. The flight was due to depart at any moment, in theory. Then suddenly, out of the blue yonder, a perky Fokker 50 darted into view like a hawk. It quickly closed in on the aerodrome, making a surprisingly loud noise for a small aircraft. I scanned the machine that would take me to Khartoum through my binoculars as it made a confident landing and taxied to within 50 metres of the terminal, no stretch buses required. It was the regular Khartoum-Asmara-Khartoum service, but the aircraft had little to do here, and I did not see it refuel. The point seemed to be to get in, drop off one load of passengers, collect another batch of customers, and then get out as soon as possible. When we were called to the flight I did not hesitate, almost running to the aircraft.

As flights go this one, which was almost full, was of above average interest. The take-off was stomach-churning, as is often the case in a small aircraft, but then we settled down into a steady flight westwards across the highlands into the drier Eritrean western lowlands. I had planned to traverse these lowlands overland, but that was not to be, so all I could do was try to view them from the air as best I could. From an altitude of 20,000 feet the land looked stark and dusty, not quite what I had imagined it to be. There was plenty of evidence of ground water, but most of the rivers seemed to have dried up, and I could not see any people or dwellings in the dust. Contrast this with the landscape of England as seen through Tayeb Salih's protagonist's eyes in *Season of Migration*. Mustafa Saeed, from Sudan, is astonished by how much water there is in the English landscape, how green it is, and how well ordered, adding, "The smell of the place is strange, like that of Mrs Robinson's body..." In the plane, I only smelt the male flight attendant's after-shave, and mechanical lubricant, the smells of the landscape below completely cut off from me. An excellent lunch of cold fish, beef, bread and a nice sweet was served on board, even though our journey would only take an hour and 40 minutes, which left me wondering where they had managed to procure the fish. Meanwhile, we continued to race above dried river beds that streaked across the ground beneath us like Nazca geoglyphs. Originally thinking to travel through this territory by bus, I had carefully studied the land border area between Eritrea and Sudan on maps, but I now saw for myself how remote and rugged the place was; Meshal had warned me about its inaccessibility and the potential dangers of bandits. I had not taken him seriously because I knew he would never have found this African landscape interesting. He was Sudanese and, like Mustafa Saeed, he yearned for "the North and the ice." But Meshal had been right; the landscape below was unforgiving, a lethal maze, and any kind of travel there would have been dangerous without the assistance of a reliable guide.

Sudan and Eritrea had been buddying up to one another in the months before my visit. Both states had become pariahs in the eyes of the international community; Omar Hassan Ahmed al-Bashir, the president of Sudan, like Isaias Afewerki, had received opprobrium for oppressing groups of people within his sphere of influence. In October 2004, the International Criminal Court issued a warrant for Bashir's arrest, a warrant still outstanding, for crimes against humanity committed in Darfur. Genocide was added to the charge list in 2010. Although the president was re-elected in Sudan's first national elections in April 2010, it is widely believed this election was rigged. Bashir had been directly responsible for the ruination of Sudan, and the country was on the brink of separating into two halves, but he still tenaciously clung on to power. Sudan's modern history is complex, but the country has almost never been at peace since independence. Culturally very different, the Muslim north of the country and the Christian south never really gelled. Perhaps it was unrealistic ever to have expected them to get along, but Bashir certainly made things worse and not better. After coming to power in a coup in 1989, he instituted, together with the National Islamic Front (NIF), a reign of terror banning parties and newspapers; Islamization proceeded apace with Arabic becoming the official language of governance, and Sharia law strictly applied, at least in the northern Sudan. Bashir eventually turned on the Islamists though, and in 1998 implemented a new constitution with himself as leader of the National Congress Party. Sudan had effectively become a one-party state. The war with the south was halted in 2004, but this only triggered a new, vicious conflict in Darfur, a war Bashir did nothing to stop. The nature of these conflicts is complex and Bashir is not solely to blame for them by any means, but his insistence on Arabism and

Islamism was at complete odds with Sudan's cultural diversity; the state's new institutional framework effectively excluded the majority of the population, including non-fundamentalist Muslims and women as well as Christians and numerous ethnic groups.

The military coup of June 1989 was a major turning point in Sudan's modern political history. Previously there had been coups, civil strife and serious conflict in the country, but no systematic terror and a liberal and secular ethos had prevailed. With the coming to power of Bashir that all changed, and numerous new religious edicts were proclaimed. Not just political parties, but even mixed-gender wedding parties were banned. There were serious purges of the police and military, and those active liberals not arrested sought refuge in foreign countries. Famously, the new Sudanese regime sponsored an assassination attempt on Egypt's president, Hosni Mubarak in 1996, and also sponsored militant Islamist groups, the latter prompting the US missile strike of 1998, the opening shot in a contest that would lead to the 9/11 atrocity. The attempt to impose Arabization and Islamization in Sudan's southern provinces was plain stupid and never going to work. In essence, three competing visions of the country – NIF Sudan, Old Sudan and New Sudan – became locked in competition with one another. After using the NIF to win power, Bashir came to represent New Sudan, a clique that controlled power through a monopoly on religious authority and secular instruments such as the constitution, the police and the courts; he has kept himself in power by clever manoeuvring, by working his constituency in the north, and by ruthless thuggery. Old Sudan left the country. Meshal, who at the time had been a student at Khartoum University and a socialist, had been a victim of one round-up, finding himself incarcerated in a makeshift prison along with dozens of other activists. Meshal survived, but a number of politicians and activists were killed or tortured in custody at this time. The terror represented the triumph of religious-backed political opportunism over reason. Like many Sudanese, Meshal later migrated to Saudi Arabia to work, and to avoid re-arrest. Internally, Sudan has not recovered from the shocking events of the 1990s, or the Darfur conflict, as I was to discover.

As a narrator in *Season of Migration to the North* says, "Everyone starts at the beginning of the road, and the world is in an endless state of childhood." The beginning of the road westwards for me began in Khartoum where infantile politicians bickered and bungled. There had to be more to it than that though, and after landing I jumped out of the Fokker with more alacrity than normal after a flight. Although no one was smiling, it was immediately apparent that Khartoum was a much livelier place than Asmara; the airport had a comforting modern feel to it. Formalities proved to be relatively straightforward, too. I appeared to be the only foreign-passport arrival, and at immigration the green-suited, slovenly and casual official queried me needlessly about where I was going to be staying. I had no idea. "But which hotel are you staying at?" he kept on. "The first one I find," I replied. The idea of just going somewhere without lining up accommodation or a host in advance seemed incomprehensible to this fellow, but he soon let me through, the easiest course of action.

As I wandered out into arrivals I noticed the terminal had a distinct East Asian flavour about it: the furnishings, Wi-Fi hotspot, and café were all redolent of Hong Kong, Seoul, and Beijing. Oil money had bought these new facilities, and Khartoum was prepared for a rush of visitors, even though there was no rush at that moment. I sat down in the arrivals café and had a cup of tea to gather myself for new explorations – I had no idea at all where I was in relation to downtown; these things one should really look up in advance, but these days I cannot be bothered with guide books and prefer a more spontaneous on-the-spot approach to orienteering. Sure enough, I was soon able to procure a map of town from an information desk in the airport, which was all I needed. It was hot in the terminal, and I sweated profusely. As I mopped my brow for the umpteenth time I noticed a couple of UN-Rwandan soldiers wandering about the building. Superficially impressive with their big physiques and smart combat fatigues the soldiers looked like movie extras. A young Sudanese woman, dressed in a near-see through yellow sari style dress, also caught my attention. The woman was stunningly pretty and her dress showed off her figure to good effect; she fidgeted in a restless way, and did a few twirls in front of me displaying her massed gold jewellery and hennaed high-heeled shod feet. Being used to the restrained body language of Arabian and Eritrean women in public, this peacock display aroused me, and I restlessly fidgeted in my seat. I tried to concentrate on the map I was reading, but found my eyes wandering back to the woman's ample body. She had a male guardian, a servant of some kind, and a pile of fancy luggage, and was basically unapproachable, but still she held me spellbound. Then, in a flourish, she got up and left the terminal picking her nose as she glided by me, an action that instantly broke the spell. Not long afterwards, after changing some money, I also left the airport, braving the heat of another high-temperature city.

6

KHARTOUM IN AUTUMN

MY FIRST IMPRESSIONS OF KHARTOUM WERE MIXED. ON THE ONE hand, the place had some energy; something was clearly going on here, unlike in sleepwalking Eritrea. The energy again reminded me of freewheeling East Asia, although here the commercial spirit was expressed differently both spatially and culturally. There were plenty of cars on the roads, but the roads were not really built for the amount of traffic on them and it was slow going getting over to the main government and tourist area located by the Blue Nile River. I noticed some new Chinese-made buses on the roads, which looked very neat and did not have faces pressed against the windows. The neighbourhoods we passed through were messy and unkempt but not really poor as such; most people were adequately if not well dressed. As we approached the Nile the traffic got worse. I was still more or less lost, not knowing where we were going, other than it was to a part of town where most tourists congregated. The taxi driver was quite nice and tolerated both my haggling over price and demands to stop and start as I checked hotels, most of which were fearfully expensive compared to Eritrea. Attempts to knock down the price at one hotel failed because I was not a) UN personnel, or b) a honeymooning couple. Eventually, I found a large room in a hotel down a back street for a reasonable price; it had air-conditioning, a bathroom and a refrigerator.

The room also had a television and I flicked through the satellite channels after checking in, relieved to have got out of the busy, dusty streets and into a new, temporary base. Khartoum was hard to pin down. The name was so romantic and resonated so strongly in my mind with colonial/historical associations, yet the city itself was disappointing. Neither wholly of Africa nor Arabia, it lacked a distinct identity; it was conflicted. Surprisingly, it was also a lot less intense than I thought it would be, too, but this was because the city was so spread out. The downtown area was full of poorly constructed hotels that offered overpriced, poorly-designed accommodation to UN personnel, Gulf Arabs, and unwitting tourists; the urban infrastructure was bursting at the seams where it was not falling apart. The pool of rainwater in a pothole immediately outside the hotel was typical. Why hadn't this road been fixed? Where had all the oil money gone? Downtown was only a few kilometres from open, dusty land, and keeping Khartoum's streets free of sand and dust is a never-ending task. But the holes in the road could at least have been filled in, I thought, and perhaps some of the drifting dirt removed. The food served in a local canteen, which was fresh, simple, and satisfying, was a treat though – a bright spot.

The next day, after a good night's rest, I travelled in the hotel's dodgy elevator up to the sixth floor to take breakfast. The restaurant was just an empty room, like one might find in any office block, without hunting trophies or any other kind of adornment. A continental style buffet breakfast had been laid out that included bread, jam, boiled eggs, cake and tea. I ate alone as no one in Sudan eats breakfast much before eleven, and I was therefore the early bird getting the pick of the boiled eggs. This breakfast would be the first, and probably the best, of many similar morning meals across North Africa where boiled eggs and bread were the only alternative to Egyptian-style *foul mudammas*, a fava bean purée made with garlic and herbs. My internal body clock would always remain out of sync with the local people in this region, whose daily habits meant they ate and slept late; a Spaniard would have had no problem with this late schedule, but at times the lack of activity first thing in the morning infuriated me. At least this hotel was making an effort, or so I thought. Alas, the breakfast rapidly deteriorated. The next day there was no cake; the day after no orange squash, and the jam soon disappeared. No wonder no one bothered getting up early.

All foreign visitors arriving in Sudan, regardless of the purpose of their visit, are required to register at the Alien Registration Office, and pay an outrageous fee for the privilege of doing so. To save money, I decided to register in person, a big mistake as it turned out; one which led to me on a long and frustrating safari around the suburbs of Khartoum. I started my walk on Al-Hurriya Street, one of the main north-south thoroughfares set perpendicular to the south bank of the Blue Nile. The road, not much wider than a suburban street in London, had been built during the colonial era, and it was still tree-lined. The morning rush hour was in progress and lots of people were striding about purposefully, another Londonesque touch. However, street hawkers and small stores selling necessities and bananas placed the scene in Africa. One man dressed in an Arab-style long shirt hailed me in a friendly manner, but mostly people hurried on their way in that mad dash common to large cities. Tiring of the walk along the dusty street, I hopped on one of the green China-made buses and continued south. Communication with the locals was something of a problem; surprisingly almost no one spoke English. One man did speak English, and seemed to have some idea of where I wanted to go, which apparently involved getting off at an intersection in the middle of nowhere. An Indian-style tuk-tuk, another colonial legacy, picked me up, but I promptly got out when I realized the driver had not understood where I wanted to go. Then a minibus came along. The driver of the bus understood "police." But instead of taking me to the registration office, he took me to the nearest local police station, outside of which a truck full of rounded up illegal aliens sat glumly – evidently, the north of Sudan was rich enough to attract large numbers of unofficial migrant workers. Fortunately, one officer at the police station spoke fairly good English, and with no further ado I was taken to the registration office that was not far away.

The Alien Registration Office depressed me on sight: the large, school-like building, which also therefore resembled a prison, was bound to be a swamp of inefficiency. And so it was. One had to first report to the compound gatekeeper before getting anywhere near the relevant registration desk. Waved through, I then found myself in one of the large rooms of the building that was arranged something like a bank with a long counter. The officials here, dressed in hideous blue uniforms, were bored and slovenly. I queued up at the counter marked "Registration foreign nationals", and waited to be dealt with. My turn came. I shoved my passport under the counter with a filled-out form and some money. They took part of the money for an application stamp, a postage stamp, which was stuck onto the paperwork. But then I was told I also needed a letter from the hotel stating that I was a guest there. Oh God, no! What was this? I had a tourist visa in my passport for goodness sakes, what was the problem? Of course, I hadn't followed the drill, and failure was the result. It was no use arguing using reason, and being British did not count for anything in this grotesque office either, a carbon copy of so many Gulf Arab government hell-holes where you wait, then fill out a form, and are then made to come back next day, usually only to have to repeat the process. After returning to my hotel in a taxi, I did what I should have done in the first place: I paid for a gofer to register me while I got on with my life.

In the coming few days I went on my usual walkabouts. By far the most atmospheric part of Khartoum was Nile Street, the road that ran parallel to the Blue Nile, the latter a green streak across a brown landscape. The river was a powerful, life-giving presence, and its waters cooled a city that was still hot in autumn. Along this main street were a number of government buildings such as the renovated Grand Hotel, where Winston Churchill, among others, had once stayed, and the Ministry of the Interior, where political prisoners were being held even as I walked past it. A James-Bond like raid to liberate those detainees was out of the question – there were plenty of well-fed and well-armed paramilitary police around the ministry. Arabization was apparent everywhere; it was expressed in the arrogance of those paramilitaries, in the unhelpful attitude of the officials at the airport and at the Alien Registration Office, and also in the creep of Arabiconly signs around the city. Most women wore the veil, and the mosques in town were very active. This religiosity seemed a bit hysterical in character, but it was very much a feature of northern Sudan; it was even more prevalent in the smaller towns I would later visit.

The National Museum, also found on Nile Street, had not had a makeover since the socialist 70s. In the museum one found a few statues hewn out of granite, plus the usual pots, hair clips and vases from antiquity. Upstairs a number of frescos from the Christian era in Sudan had bravely been put on display, albeit in a darkened space. It is easy to forget that for most of its history Sudan did not know Islam, and that this all-encompassing religion was actually a relatively new phenomenon, a point that Muslims explain away by simply dismissing the pre-Islam period as *al-Jahiliyah*, or the Days of Ignorance. Outside the museum's main building, in a compound, parts of some temples had been reconstructed, temples of a religion whose values were difficult to reconstruct. I nonetheless felt respect for this ancient religion, as it was connected to the world in an earthy way that I could somehow relate to. Before leaving, one of the museum's staff tried to sell me an archaeological brochure, probably seeking funds for a slap up breakfast. I declined the offer, whereupon he launched into a running commentary about the museum's exhibits, and there I had to cut him short – it was a warm day and I really could not face listening to his script; I was in Khartoum for the first-hand impressions only.

The museum was located near the confluence of the Blue and

White Nile tributaries, a geographical landmark and a metaphor in my mind for the Anglo-Sudan relationship. From the museum I headed straight to this landmark. To reach it I had to walk through a charming, but dilapidated, children's funfair, at the very end of which was the last of the "island" land between the two rivers. At its confluence, the Nile was astonishing, a writhing silver and burgundy two-tone anaconda. Incongruously, a man sat on the mud flat patiently fishing with the simplest of lines and hook, as if by some mountain creek, and not by an oceanic-sized discharge. Meanwhile, a teacher had brought some children to play in the park, and it was delightful to hear their screams as they played in an uninhibited manner: the park was pure magic to them, in the same way that the river was magic to me. Over the White Nile a bridge hurtled towards Omdurman, scene of Britain's revenge on the Mahdists of Sudan, and I stood a while staring at the great river, its mangroves, and the setting sun.

THE BATTLE of Omdurman actually took place eleven kilometres north of Khartoum's western satellite town, near the village of Kerreri, on 2 September 1898. I was staring at a picture depicting this momentous clash in the Khalifa's former residence, now a museum in Omdurman, on almost the same date 112 years later, brought there by Tareq, a friend of Meshal's whom I had hooked up with in Khartoum. In Sudan, no one has forgotten Omdurman, a battle distinguished by its unevenness: the final death toll of the native Mahdists was 200 times that of the British; a number increased by Lord Kitchener's order to finish off the enemy's wounded at the end of the day, an unnecessary measure (to be fair, the Mahdists did not spare their enemies). The painting showed the British brigades, backed up by a large Egyptian force, facing off against the more numerous, but hopelessly ill-equipped, local rebels. One could see that the British were more organized and disciplined than their opponents, their officers coolly prancing about on horseback viewing the battle through binoculars. The Khalifa's – Khalifa Abdullahi Ben Mohammed Taashi, who led the Mahdists after the death of the Mahdi, Mohammed Ahmed, in 1885 – house contained aging artefacts of the era including an old Maxim gun, muskets, rifles, spears and shields, cases of medals, the Khalifa's personal weapons, and money issued during the Siege of Khartoum that took place 13 years before Omdurman. There were also newspaper cuttings from the London Times on display, which reported on the battle in vulgar, self-congratulatory tones. By far the most affecting exhibit in the house, I felt, was a photograph of a Mahdist lying dying on the field of battle, his bloodied long shirt forming a holy shroud of glory.

Tareq and I went outside and had our photograph taken together in the courtyard by the museum's obliging curator. My friend's friend was a professor of chemistry at Khartoum University. He had only just got his job back after the years of purges – the government of Sudan had suddenly realized it needed its educated people, and had invited Tareq to come back to his native land. Although he never said so, I knew he had been a communist sympathiser along with Meshal. The communists were actually very strong in Sudan in the 1950s and 60s, dominating several powerful trade unions; they had even attempted a coup against the civilian government in 1971. The mercurial Gaafar Nimeiry, president of Sudan from 1969 to 1985, weathered that storm and later turned on the Sudanese communists, executing their Secretary General, whose house we passed on the way back to Khartoum after leaving the Khalifa's house. There had been little else to see in the huge sprawling suburb of Omdurman, its richness to be found solely in the people who lived there. As one of the narrators in *Season of Migration to the North* notes, "By the standards of the European industrial world we are poor peasants, but when I embrace my grandfather I experience a sense of richness as though I am a note in the heartbeats of the very universe." That was Sudan: it was all about human relationships. Without Tareq's company and assistance, I would never have gone to the Khalifa's house.

TAREQ, the same age as me but paunchy and patrician-like, invited me to his house for dinner one night. He also invited a male singleton, one of his PhD students; the only doctoral student in the chemistry department, in fact. The previous day, I had visited the run-down but cheerful Khartoum University, formerly known as the Gordon Memorial College. Strolling through the leafy campus, a young Islamist, who was giving an impromptu speech to a crowd of listless students, denounced me as a CIA spy as we walked past, or so Tareq told me. We both had a good laugh about that. Tareq recalled this silly episode at the dinner table in his modest university-owned apartment as his beautiful and unveiled wife heaped food onto our plates. He then related the story of how he was denounced as a leftist and hauled off to prison from the very same school all those years ago, a story he told in some detail as we ate our cold buffet.

"I was a good student, an A-student at school. I liked maths, and sciences, and especially languages. I applied to do a Bachelor of Science degree at Khartoum University, a five-year programme. In those days the school was very good, and we had many foreign instructors who taught us very diligently. But even before going to college, I was active socially and politically. This is quite normal in Sudan; it's said that every Sudanese is a politician. I had some problems. I experienced some difficulties in secondary school; I failed the entry tests for university, perhaps because of my political involvement. I missed two years, and repeated the entrance examination twice. The problem was I tried to enter through the humanities department, but actually my aptitude was for science. When I changed section, I succeeded. I then went to university." I asked Tareq when he had joined the college, and he said in 1987, although he should have joined in 1985.

Tareq continued, "Two years later trouble started. I missed another year due to political problems. The university had to close for many months. We enjoyed only two years of democracy after Nimeiry was ousted, and then this military coup occurred. The military took power on the 30th of June 1989. At that time I had finished my second year at university. After the coup, the university was never stable. I was detained while still a student for two months. We were taken to a military court in a "ghost house." These makeshift prisons were built by the military government and they were unknown by anybody; they were hidden in secret places. But they were all located downtown. The cells were built in government houses. The house I was sent to was actually the residence of the Chief Commander of the army. The cells were built in the garden. I remember there were exactly 18 cells, but some prisoners were detained in the main house. The prisoners were all politicals. Meshal was there, too." What year was this, I asked, and Tareq said 1992. "I was actually taken from my bed at the university accommodation. At that time I was very active; we were boycotting the examinations because the government had stopped the system of free accommodation and free food for all students; some of the food was produced by university-owned farms. The university was fantastic; it was a place where you learnt everything, including politics and culture, and prepared yourself to be useful in society. All this was damaged by the new regime. I didn't feel easy about the boycott. By then I was a member of the Democratic Front, an alliance between democrats and communists; I was known as a leftist. On the day of a committee meeting I was warned not to sleep in my room, but in the evening I went there to get something and took a nap on the bed as I was very tired. Unfortunately, I fell asleep and just before dawn prayers the security forces came, guided by pro-government students. One of the officers came and asked me if I was Tareq and I said yes, he told me to go with him. I got into a truck and was forced to put my head between my knees. When I was taken I did not know who was arrested with me, but later I found there were 20 of us, all student leaders, in the ghost house. It was winter, and we were cold. The cold was used against us as a kind of torture; we were forced to recite the Koran in the yard even though we were not prepared for the low temperature."

"The cells were only one metre by two; it was better to be in a group cell. The guards insulted us continuously, and would hit us from behind so you did not know who the attacker was. One of them hit me, but I recognized him by his voice. They used false names, but we knew some of their real identities. In Sudan, relations between people are very tight. You can't hide by pseudonyms or anything else." The closely-knit nature of Sudanese society explains why these students were not more severely abused; their captors feared retribution.

How did Tareq get out of detention? "I had an uncle who was a cousin of my father. He even belonged to the regime to some extent. He came with about ten people and got me released. That's it: *wasta*." This Arabic word literally means influence, although it is a concept that encompasses other ideas such as power, connections, family relations, and so on. "Actually this was my first detention. The investigation was nonsense. I went home to my aunt's house in Khartoum, and then I went to my home town. Of course, I had lost two months of classes. My family suffered a lot during my detention; the reputation of the government was very bad and they knew that this government was very cruel and very savage. This was just the beginning of the terror. In fact, people were murdered by this government and everyone knew it. The regime was like a pack of lions, absolutely savage."

After his first detention, and after graduating from Khartoum University, Tareq went back to his home town in the Blue Nile River State and took a teaching job at the local secondary school. But politics followed him, and suspected of organizing a student demonstration he was re-arrested by the local authorities, who would have easily been able to check his background out via the central security apparatus.

"The government used excessive force during the [student]

demonstration. One female student, a friend of my family, was shot dead. She was in first intermediate school and was about eleven or twelve years old. It was very, very strange. They were just young students. About six or seven of them were injured. We went to the funeral of the girl. On the third day after the funeral the police came to my house at three in the morning. They were armed; two men in civilian clothes carried Kalashnikovs. When they came to the house I was awake writing a poem honouring the girl, and I heard them coming. My brother, who was in the police, had warned me away, but I felt I had to stay in town. It was a rash decision. I opened the main gate of the yard when they came, and they told me to go with them. I woke my father and told him security agents had come for me. To the end of my life I will never forget the horror I saw in his eyes when I told him this. He spoke humbly to the police asking them not to take me away; he was also a police officer and knew the business of these national security men." Tareq paused and refilled our glasses with fruit juice. His two young children played in the sitting room as he finished his story, the doctoral student and I listening intently.

"This time I was no longer a student. It was more serious; I was considered to be a professional politician. This time I felt I was really causing my family problems. I myself was frightened, not for my own fate – I had my own principals, my cause – but how my situation was affecting my father. On the same night they took others from the town, including men in their fifties and sixties, not just me. After my arrest, I was taken back to the ghost house in Khartoum and put in the No. 4 cell. I was detained for four months. I was there from March through to August, 1996. The cell was designed in such a way there was no ventilation, and I was sweating all the time. We only went outside at prayer times, and sometimes even prayed in the cell. I was not interrogated until the third month, and was asked about my connections to the Communist Party. I denied everything, and then after the fourth month I was released. But I had lost the chance to take my master's degree. I never intended to work abroad. I worked as a teaching assistant in a college for girls in Khartoum, but in 1996 the government took control of college appointments and my family advised me to go to Saudi Arabia. I was not willing to go, but then I went and buried myself alive there for 13 years."

Tareq taught English in Saudi Arabia, a waste of his talents. Then the "amnesty" came, and an offer of work at his old school. He had returned to help build up the department, which was struggling after years of neglect. We talked over some other topics. Tareq's wife asked me where I would travel to next, and when I told her she rolled her eyes; "No fun actually," her verdict. I was headed north to Egypt, but south was where Sudan's best scenery was to be found she insisted. No doubt true, but south was not en route for me. Later, I thanked my hosts for a nice evening, and Tareq accompanied me a short way back to the bus stop by the Nile, wearing a traditional conical hat in my honour. The hat made him look like a wizard – Chemical Tareq. As we walked, I asked the Khartoum University professor what he thought Sudan's future was. "War," he said, "Not immediately, but after a couple of years. The northern regime cannot survive without oil, which is found mainly in the south."

AT KHARTOUM UNIVERSITY the next day I sat in the chemistry department's office and watched the comings and goings. Tareq held court like a sheik as his students drifted in and out of his barely furnished office. The school, a nice Victorian style red-brick building, had suffered greatly under Bashir's rule. Different forms of knowledge, specifically Arabic and the Koran, had come to be foregrounded, English and the modern academy being seen as a fifth columnists, which they were actually, just as Arabic and the Koran were: the two languages and two kinds of knowledge inevitably associated their learners with the interests of imperialist power. Arab imperialism was cultural more than military, but it was imperialism nonetheless and west of Arabia had originally been conquered by force of arms; the assault on Darfur had been extremely violent. The British interlude in Sudan had been much shorter lived, and its long term effects shallower than the Arab conquest, a conquest that had brought with it Islam. Girls at Khartoum University wore head scarves rather than veils and were quite relaxed about mixing with men, but sex segregation was the norm in classes, and in the antiquated library where no book under 30 years old could be found.

Tareq was, like many modern-educated Sudanese, an Anglophile. In Sudan, perhaps to a greater degree than in many of their other former colonies, and certainly more so than in Egypt, the British are remembered with fondness and respect. The British colonial class were of course carefully selected for their role; and studying classics was the ideal preparation for life as a colonial official because such study inculcated broad-mind edness and fair-mindedness. Tareq showed me a volume on Sudanese anthropology published by one such official, a dedicated and interested man. Meshal's friend suggested the British should come back and rule Sudan, and he was only half joking. The British in Sudan had acted as an honest broker between the many competing ethnic groups, and had kept good order. Such peace has eluded Sudan since independence; there has been at least one conflict raging in this vast country every year since independence. But, as I pointed out to Tareq, this colonial order was kept by separating the north and the south; travel between the two zones was severely curtailed by the British authorities. Although this helped to prevent conflict and slave trafficking, it set up a future problem, much like that in Yemen where north and south also struggled to meet accord.

As Tareq left the office on an errand I spoke to one of his former students who now worked as a chemistry teacher in Qatar. Like many Sudanese men, he had gone to seek his fortune in the resource-rich Gulf, but probably regretted the lost years. He was still young though. Did he not want to come back to Sudan and help build up the country? He smiled at my naïve question; he knew peace was not around the corner, and probably another major war was.

"We are waiting to see what will happen…" he ventured tentatively. I said that it was no use waiting to see what would happen and that he had to act; he had to author history rather than be a passive object in someone else's history. He thought about my comment for a moment, his gold wrist watch flashing against his dark arm. He went on to say that the best solution for Sudan was federation, but this was not going to happen, and he would return to the Gulf to work. He was cagey and evasive in general and seemed discomfited by my questions. He asked me what I was doing in Sudan, and I told him exactly what I was doing there: passing through and making some observations along the way. When I told him of my intention to travel across North Africa he was surprised. Wasn't I afraid of militant Islamists? A lot less afraid than he was, I could tell.

THERE WAS of course the problem of how to get from Khartoum to Egypt, where I would begin my trek westwards. The following day I headed to the local tourist office to make some enquires. The office was small and relaxed, the main room simply filled with some school desks, one computer and a few artefacts including a shield and a couple of spears. As usual, nothing was going on first thing in the morning. I was invited in without fanfare by one of the staff and offered a seat in an armchair. Knowing exactly what to do, I sat in silence like a contented Buddha, the polite way to behave in Sudan. Having asked for nothing, and having made no demands, I thus succeeded in making a good impression. Next came some relationship building. I asked another staffer, a large southerner who sat at the computer, what he was doing.

"Reading," he replied. This was followed by a silent pause.

"Why don't you ask me what I'm reading?" He was doing the talking now.

I said, "Because that's a political question." He burst out laughing at this, and everything went very smoothly thereafter. I was introduced to all the staff. A late breakfast was ordered and we all ate together. That was followed by coffee and then tea. I almost forgot why I was there. And then remembered: trains. When the department head came in I knew I had the right man: so, how did one get to the northern border by train? That was not possible, I was told. Okay. But wasn't there a railway line that went directly north to Wadi Halfa? Yes, the director confirmed this, but there was no longer a passenger service on this route. One could only travel as far as Abu Hamed by train; you then had to switch to local trains that followed the Nile in its great meander, or take buses. An alternative option, recommended to me by the director, was to take the direct coach bus from Khartoum to Wadi Halfa. This was, apparently, how everyone travelled north these days. But the direct bus would whisk me through northern Sudan too quickly; there had to be another way of doing this. After a friendly send-off by the tourist ministry's staff, I made my way to the railway station to further investigate my travel options.

Any kind of trip around Khartoum was something of an adventure, and the trip out to the railway station, located in the northern suburb of Bahri, was no exception. The first taxi driver I spoke to took me for a fool, but I soon struck a deal with the next taxi that came along, driven by a dashing northerner who was impeccably mannered; I felt like I should have been driving him around. We motored off in the direction of the Blue Nile Bridge, a steel span masterpiece. It was noticeable how the air cooled over the river, the horizon to the south shimmering in a heat haze. Before long, we arrived at the station via some old residential streets. I got out of the taxi and walked into the station's main hall. There were no passengers about, and a quick reconnaissance of the platform area revealed there were no trains about either: this was a ghost of a railway station. On the wall was a poster of Bashir's turbaned head next to an image of a train, an ironic association: the Islamist regime had neglected the railways in the same way they had neglected Khartoum University. It had been the military regime's policy to promote road travel partly because of the discovery of oil in Sudan, and partly as a means of reducing the power of the railway union, once one of the most radical political forces in the country. Khartoum's railway station had been reduced to an administration centre and cargo hub. There was, however, a ticket office there.

As it turned out, the ticket office also acted as an agent for the ferry that shuttled between Wadi Halfa and Aswan in Egypt. I resolved to book the ferry to Egypt while I was at it. But the passenger train to Abu Hamed left at night, and one wouldn't be able to see anything out of the window. So, I decided to make the journey by local buses in stages buying tickets along the way as needed. Having decided all this it only remained to buy the boat ticket. The ferry left weekly. I chose a target date and got into line along with a few others who were there to purchase a ticket. We waited and waited. From inside the agent's office a fat officer came out and tried to hustle me to the front of the line. This was nice of him, but it only led to an argument with the men in front of me, who had reasonably refused to allow me to push in. The agent was furious, his honour had been besmirched, and it took some time for him to back off. I watched all this in amazement. This small incident was interesting in two respects: firstly, the legacy of colonialism whereby it was assumed a white man should get preferential treatment over a local. The second interesting thing about the altercation was the way it blew up because the agent felt he had lost face. Over such trifling arguments, serious conflicts started in Sudan. It all starts with an argument, with finger waving. Then someone gets killed. The next thing you know, a large skirmish breaks out, which in turn escalates. On this occasion the agent, who seemed to be suffering from high blood pressure, did calm himself down. I was invited into his office where I waited patiently for my booking to be made. People came and left. One young couple were trying to book a honeymoon somewhere. Another man, a railway worker, entered, sat down, and talked with the agent awhile, swigging honey from a two litre plastic container full of the nectar as he did so. I kept smiling. Finally, my ticket was issued: cabin No. 1, port side.

Back at the hotel, I whiled away my time sipping sodas in between sallies out into town. By now I had become a regular at the Red Sea Restaurant where they served wonderful fresh food including excellent fried Nile fish. In the restaurant one day I picked up the *Sudan Vision*, an English-language newspaper. The governor of the Central Bank had announced measures to shore up the Sudanese pound, which had been slipping in value on fears of a partition war. Another feature article bemoaned the imminent break-up of the country, claiming the south simply did not have the ability or the institutions for effective self-rule, classic colonial propaganda: it came as no surprise that the article quoted directly from an IMF report. A smaller piece tucked away in the paper described how Acholi mobs had assaulted members of the Madi community in Iyii (Kit) in Eastern Equatoria, one of Sudan's southern states. This was the daily reality in Sudan: argument/fight/war; the first assault invariably led to escalation. But the process was reversible. Indeed, it was Bashir who had negotiated the end to north-south hostilities in 2004. Elsewhere in the paper was an advertisement tendering a catering contract for all the UN personnel who were about to descend on the country to help monitor the independence referendum. There was no doubt in my mind that the contract should have been awarded to the Red Sea Restaurant, because there was no competition.

On my last day in Khartoum, I sought out the bucolic solitude on Tuti Island, a large land mass found at the confluence of the Blue Nile and the White Nile. The island was accessible by bridge, and I took a taxi there asking to be dropped off on the island farthest away from the bridge, thinking to walk back at sunset. It had been another hot afternoon, the temperature reaching a high of 40 degrees Celsius, and it was a relief to get out of the city. Tuti only had one major settlement on it and was mostly covered in grass and fields. After being dropped off, I walked along the river bank on the southern side of the island, a tranquil setting. The only noise was the chugging of a water pump, which at first I imagined to be the engine of a British gun boat, like those used during the Siege of Khartoum. The other sounds came from chickens, goats, birds and humming insects. The water of the Nile made this rural scene possible, and the river water tasted sweet: you could scoop it up with your hands and drink it no problem; the island was also a clean place. Presently, an aging goat herder came along the path and shook my hand warmly after I took a candid photograph of him. What a difference in reaction from what one typically got in Saudi Arabia! The difference was that this man, although "humble," had confidence in himself, and felt complimented that I had taken an interest in him.

The island was bigger than I had expected, and before long I flagged down a tuk-tuk that was wobbling along the track, to get me along. The ride in the three-wheeler, which was sort of fun, got me to the island's village. Here I sat and watched young men playing soccer seriously on a patch of dirt in the late afternoon sun. It was a great scene, full of colour and enthusiasm. At dusk, I rented a skiff and took a joy ride out to the river confluence, this time viewing the Blue and White Nile rivers simultaneously and at high speed as we did a couple of circuits over the start of the merged river, an energizing experience. There was no way to dismount from the boat in Khartoum, or so the boatman made me believe, and so we returned to the island and I walked the remaining distance to the bridge, finally crossing it on foot back into town. Down below one could just about make out British-era river boat winding gear, and a number of small pleasure craft, unused and falling into disrepair.

7

LIFE BY THE NILE

A PRETTY, BLOND-HAIRED YOUNG WOMAN STRODE UP AND confidently introduced herself with "Hi, I'm Stef", in a dust-hole settlement downriver from Khartoum. My only thought, as we had finally got underway from the chaotic bus station in Khartoum, was how much more pleasant it would have been to have travelled north by train. On the bus, which was at least air-conditioned, it was difficult to see properly out of the curtained windows, and besides there was not much to see: mud-brick dwellings by the roadside, scant vegetation and, in one spot, a stranded tuk-tuk that sat in a ditch like a dead fish. Still, it had been my first real burst of travelling on the ground that had actually taken me forwards toward my final destination, and now there was no turning back. In Shendi I had hooked up with Omar, who was head of English at the local university, affiliated to Khartoum University. He had been briefed to take care of me, and after a delay picked me up from where I had been dumped by the bus. A sandstorm of sorts was in progress as we stumbled into a lamb kebab joint looking for something to eat, and that's when the young woman made her move. It was shocking to have been approached by a European woman here in the middle of nowhere.

Stefanie was wearing jeans, a chequered lumberjack shirt,

and an Africa Corps-style cap. At first, I didn't know what to say, the situation was so novel. Then I introduced myself and invited Stef, who was at something of a loose end in Shendi, to eat with us. She was an Austrian national travelling alone through Africa after a two-year stint working as a volunteer on an agricultural project in Malawi. She had entered Sudan via Ethiopia, a place that offered tourists better value for money than expensive Sudan, but that, according to her, was decidedly less friendly than its northern neighbour. She wanted to visit Port Sudan, and then cross the Nubian Desert by camel, an almost ludicrous ambition that she had dreamt up after reading one of those popular, but in some ways silly, travel guidebooks. Our food arrived, and I plonked a leg of chicken on her plate. "Oh, I didn't expect to be fed", she said. Stef was all beans and flirted with Omar, my benefactor, and I watched as his defences quickly crumbled. He ended up inviting her back to the school's dormitory, where I was scheduled to stay the night. I was not unhappy with the arrangement, although by local standards it was irregular for two single people of the opposite sex to stay in the same guesthouse. I was given a room; and Stefanie roughed it on one of the couches, but she actually got the better of it because the room's bed was uncomfortable.

Stef, I had already discovered, could be very charming; she was active in a tomboyish way, had a ready smile, and talked freely. She asked me what I did. It is a question I always find difficult to answer, but Stef was interested to hear my story, which I delivered edited to cloak the fact that I was a writer; in general, I dislike telling people I'm a writer because if I do they invariably proceed to tell me what I should write about, which can be very irritating. Stef had some stories to tell about her time in Malawi, a posting she had found trying. She evidently had a low opinion of the locals who "just don't listen," or so she claimed. The time spent in Malawi had obviously taken its toll on this young woman, and now she wanted to have some fun. Used to unwanted male attention, she was quite adept at manipulating such attention to her advantage, and I had also been drawn in. It was now me and Stefanie going to Meroe, a local archaeological site. Omar had arranged the trip, and we would go there the next day with a couple of students from the archaeology department. It seemed to be the thing to do in Shendi. Although I had made no plans to visit these sites, it had been assumed that I was interested in them. What else was there to do around Shendi? I had no idea. Meanwhile, Stefanie was all in favour of Omar's arrangements; it was her modus operandi to visit these types of historical sites, which she had read about in her gushing guidebook.

According to Stefanie, whom I sat and chatted with the next morning, Omar had made some kind of half-hearted pass at her the previous evening. The two of them had gone off to a late-night market the night before, after dinner. So what? It was to be expected, and Stefanie knew it. The dormitory lounge was comfortable and spacious and we enjoyed our drinks in peace. Then a man came in uninvited. Stefanie was all friendly with this stranger as usual; I rather resented his presence. He did not speak English, and it was never clear who he was. He sat and drank tea with us, not saying a word. I knew very well he had come to gawk at the white woman. A cleaning lady came by, not cleaning so much as checking the scene out. It was one of those slow mornings, and I started to get fidgety. Stefanie, however, was more attuned to the slow pace; it seemed to be her normal practice to dawdle a morning away drinking coffee, smoking and talking.

Later that morning we found ourselves in Omar's small office located in a building off a courtyard. The sandstorm had abated, and it was a nice warm and clear day outside. The departmental head's office was modest and barely furnished, like most offices in Sudan. We sat down and met Salem and Hala, the two graduate students who would take us out to Meroe. But Omar was absent: he still hadn't got out of bed. Either that or he was plugging away on some archaeological opus. We sat and waited for him, chatting to our escorts. Salem was a youngish Bedouin man, very handsome and full of ambition to enter the field of archaeology. He spoke good English, and quizzed me by way of trying to establish our relative social status. Very smart, he was also a bit of a bore, and in the end I gave him something to read just to shut him up; Stefanie was not interested in him at all, and chatted in a desultory way with Hala, a female graduate student who generally kept quiet in front of us, two males. There was a bottle of "Desert Stud" perfume on Omar's desk, along with a copy of *A History of Archaeological Thought*, and a few old Pelican titles. I picked up the book on archaeology and flicked through its pages. The location around Shendi was actually called "The Island" in Arabic, a tongue of land between the Nile and Atbara rivers, a kingdom in ancient times. The area was apparently famous, and the ancient city of Meroe a draw for international archaeologists. Then, just as I was nodding off with boredom, Omar suddenly arrived. He dashingly placed a few phone calls, and then sent us off with Salem and Hala, all smiles and hugs.

Our chauffeur drove us out of the college campus, still completely quiet as the academic year had not yet begun. The school's buildings were rudimentary red-brick structures, which at a distance could have passed for a factory or a farmhouse. But actually every single building looked like this in northern Sudan, and I would not learn to see any significant differences between them. The private car ride came to an end at the outskirts of the dusty market town where we transferred to a minibus that would take us down the road. When we were told how much our tickets would cost, Stefanie threw her first tantrum.

"No, no, no! No vay! No way is zee ticket that much!" Now it was a fact that we were probably paying a little extra being rich foreign tourists with baggage, and may well have being subsidising our hosts to some extent, but still what we were asked to pay amounted to peanuts. Stefanie, however, saw the situation from a different scale of values entirely. She had been a volunteer worker and had earned almost nothing in two years; she was used to the low prices of Ethiopia; she wasn't going to be taken for a ride, figuratively speaking. Eventually, I got to calm her down, but the outburst had been embarrassing; we were with hosts that had shown us hospitality. Her sudden, very public, display of hostility towards Salem was, by the standards of Arab culture, extremely ill mannered. Fortunately, Salem was a level-headed fellow and took this barrage from Stefanie as if he were dealing with a quarrelsome younger sibling. In this respect, you have to hand it to the Arabs – they can be very patient, especially with family and guests. Stef's huffing and puffing over, we got in the minibus and journeyed along the main highway north-wards for half an hour or so. The bus took us across a semi-desert landscape dotted with villages. Gay, uniformed children returning home after school added innocence to the scene. And then, after following a track through scrubland, we found ourselves outside the archaeological site. The bus had made this detour for our benefit, stopping at the gate of the Meroe Royal City.

Salem carried some tools for a small dig in a carrier bag; Stefanie and I, however, were carrying somewhat more baggage, which needed to be deposited at the gatehouse. A small group of people had been expecting us, and then another match was put to the powder keg of the woman I was travelling with.

"Twenty dollars? Twenty dollars?! No way! What are you talking about?" They wanted US $20 from each of us. This was the entrance fee. I looked up at a rusted metal sign that read "Ministry of Environment and Tourism National Corp. for Antiquities & Museums Royal City." Behind the sign were a few brick dwellings and a scattering of acacia trees. It did not look promising. I don't know what I had been expecting, but Meroe was not exactly Karnak. I would never have gone along on this wild goose chase had I known I would have to pay to enter the site. The fact though was that we were there, we had gone there willingly and indeed in Stefanie's case enthusiastically, and all foreign tourists were expected to cough up.

"But we were told we wouldn't have to pay!" Omar had made some noises about us not having to pay at this or that site. I had taken no notice of him myself; in Arab society you don't necessarily take promises at face value. Stefanie, less culturally assimilated, continued to complain and argue. Eventually we bargained a two-for-one price, and I paid for my ticket, a compromise to keep the peace.

As we walked into the compound, which exactly resembled the open country we had just travelled through on the other side of the gate, sweating all the while in the warm sun, Stefanie once more returned to her charming, vivacious self. Apart from not wanting to pay for anything, she was the ideal tourist, and kept asking Salem all sorts of intelligent questions. Hala had remained at the gate house, and I wished I had stayed with her, because the warm day had turned into a hot day and the heat was becoming oppressive. Stefanie was having a ball though.

"Ya, so here was the temple…ya, over there, oh I see…and where was the voof?" The roof of the temple had collapsed about 2000 years ago, and there was not a lot left of the main structure. The wall around my family's house in England was more substantial than some of the remaining walls of this royal city. There were, however, a few notable pillars, carvings and ram statues scattered about, which were actually city-like. And besides, it was sort of fun being there by ourselves in amongst the acacia trees that were filled with twittering heat-resistant birds. Pausing under a tree on the way back to the gate house, Salem took a moment to explain the ticket and transport pricing to me, which was polite of him. I had no complaint, but I was seen to be Stefanie's male guardian and so Salem spoke to me, and not to her. In reply to his reasonable explanations I muttered something along the lines of "Quite, quite…quite…yes…yes…of course, of course…" and hoped that would be the end of it.

It wasn't the end of it. "What?! Are you joking…are you joking…no vay!" Thus began Stef's third outburst in the space of less than two hours. A taxi had been called to give us a ride over to some nearby pyramids. I must confess, I had little interest in going there, unlike Stefanie, who definitely wanted to go there but didn't want to pay the going rate for the taxi. It's true that the wily taxi driver was charging us over the odds, but again it was not, in absolute terms, a huge amount of money. I did understand why Stefanie felt it was a ripoff, but her reaction in front of our hosts, and the site staff, was extraordinary. She made no attempt to bargain the price down diplomatically; she was next to hysterical. Essentially, she was throwing a tantrum, and everyone present knew it, and everyone present remained calm. The taxi driver was not budging on price. I averted my gaze and drank some water from a clay pot placed under a thatched shelter. The water was delicious.

"Is that water okay?" Stefanie was surprised to see me drinking from a communal pot and momentarily stopped her ranting. Then she calmed down realizing the situation had become a stalemate. During this lull in the storm I put in an offer for the taxi ride a bit less than the driver was asking, knowing he would accept the face-saving deal. The driver duly accepted my offer. Stefanie's reaction: "He's a good man. I won't pay this…no vay!" I told Stefanie to shut up and get in the car and then paid the driver, thus ending it. Salem and Hala would do some excavations at the site and then return to Shendi, and so we left them at Meroe. On our way at last, I waved out of the window of the car as the driver gunned the engine and drove off in the direction of the ancient burial grounds. Hala was having a good laugh under her head scarf as she waved us off.

After passing by some small-scale pyramids that looked like tents we arrived at the main pyramidal structures. The taxi driver left, all smiles, while we went up a sandbank towards the site office. Here another argument ensued about whether or not we should pay for admission. I did not get involved this time, and Stefanie won the battle on her own after a call was put through to Omar – more of my *wasta* used up. We left the office and walked up a steep sand dune onto a desert field filled with medium-sized pyramids that were in pretty good shape considering they had been there three or four thousand years. They looked like giant upended ice cream cones. We enjoyed the site to ourselves; Stefanie was as happy as a child in a playground, and so was I.

The main road north passed nearby the pyramids, and after our sightseeing we went over to it and tried to flag down a north-bound bus. There were almost no buses on the road, however, and the few that passed us did not stop. It was a ridiculous situation, and some measure of just how much Omar really thought of us that I now found myself hitch-hiking in the middle of the desert with three large bags and an unstable woman in tow. Still, having an attractive female hitchhiking partner was no bad thing, I reasoned to myself, and we waited for the magic ride to come along. A donkey sat on its haunches on the opposite side of the road conserving its energy, and stared at us like an aging and knowing schoolmaster. Another bus whooshed past: no luck. There is a knack to hitch-hiking, which involves looking like you want to go somewhere, and I swung into action adopting purposeful body language. The next vehicle that came along, a long transporter truck, stopped and we scrambled up into the cab, which was high off the ground giving us a grandstand view of the desert as we headed north again.

Sudan is enormous, and several hours of driving through the desert hardly got us anywhere on the map. We were relieved to have got a ride though; otherwise, we might have ended up lying by the road side considerably less active than the donkey we had seen. The desert was hot, and as we drove along even the driver needed to take constant sips from a water bottle to stay hydrated. The Nile was not too far to the west of us – occasional glimpses of palm trees gave it away. The road cut through red and black rock, and then ploughed through yellow and orange sand dunes. The colours changed with the light, and the desert was surprisingly varied topographically. Stefanie was her usual bubbly, non-confrontational self in the cab and we had a long, friendly talk, putting the morning's stress behind us. She was an agriculturalist and sought to work as a manager for an aid agency, which seemed like a good ambition. We then started to work on our Arabic. Stefanie did have a gift for communication, and was saying a surprising amount with the few words of Arabic she had learnt. We ran through The Arabic numbers again, the driver smiling at us approvingly as we did so. *Tamaaniya*, "eight," pronounced tha-maa-nia, was the number Stefanie kept forgetting.

We presently stopped at a rest station in the desert. The place was full of big trucks, their drivers sleeping on string beds in the shade of the road side cafés. Stefanie and I sat at one of the restaurants; a simple shelter with an awning over it in, but it had everything one might want. Stefanie even ordered up a hookah pipe and puffed on it as the Sudanese men stared in astonishment at the sight of a young white woman openly smoking in front of men. Our driver did some repairs to his vehicle and then took a rest by himself before rallying us for the next leg of the journey. An hour and a half later, we arrived in Atbara, and got out of the truck after thanking the driver for his kindness. Stefanie wondered if we should give him a tip. She was feeling generous.

"No", I said, "he'll get his reward in heaven."

From the side of the road on the outskirts of the River Nile State's railway junction town, I made a call to one of Omar's contacts on my hand phone, and a car was presently sent out to pick us up. Stefanie was impressed by this. The two men were officials from the local tourist office, and treated us like VIP guests. We were taken back to their office and given a warm welcome by the head honcho there. The director of the tourist office turned out to be a youngish, well-educated man. He informed us there were three classes of hotel in town: standard, cheap, and dirt cheap. After a little tête-à-tête we went off in the car with the junior staffers and reconnoitred all the available accommodation options. But even dirt cheap was not cheap enough for Stefanie, who once again embarrassed me by arguing the toss over price with a patient hotelier. Eventually, we took a room built on the top of a flop house for a discount. Our bemused hosts left us and we settled in. It was not what I had been expecting, but the arrangement was okay with me. I enjoyed being a backpacker. And like backpackers, we later went off to scavenge a cheap meal at the local night market. In a canteen-style restaurant there, we ate eggs, tomatoes, beans and bread. It was a simple, tasty meal. Stefanie made the mistake of ordering a special dish, a salad, which was not on the menu. This slowed down the delivery of the food, and naturally the extra dish came in at a small premium. How much was the total cost of the meal? I forget now, but it wasn't more than a few dollars. I was about to pay for both of us when Stefanie, again referring to Ethiopian prices, had one of her most explosive outbursts to date.

"No!...no vay! It cannot be that much. What, just for eggs and a few beans? Are you joking?" The people who worked at the canteen were embarrassed at first. The manager, or headman, patiently tried to explain to Stefanie that the meal's price was precisely what any local person would pay, which may or may not have been true. Any difference was negligible to me. In any case, Sudan was a relatively expensive African country, the result of the oil boom. I tried explaining all this to Stef, but she was really on the offensive in more ways than one. She screamed at the headman, a dignified gentleman, "You're crazy!" He didn't like that at all, and retorted that she was the crazy one. By now, everyone in the canteen was watching the scene, and I was mortally embarrassed. I insisted on paying and quickly got Stefanie out of the restaurant. By the standards of the local culture, it had been a really appalling, unforgivable, outburst. Back at our slum accommodation I had a talk with Stefanie about how to handle bargaining more diplomatically. In my younger days, I had certainly been guilty of price-rage when travelling in foreign countries, but had learned over the years not to get into heated arguments with Orientals or Africans because such arguments led to a loss of face, and this was something to be avoided at all costs. It was always better to gain the moral high ground by arguing in a token way, and then giving in to some extent. This way, everyone kept face.

Stefanie groaned from under her sheet sleeping bag, "Ya, you're right", soon falling asleep after a little sulk. A mosquito buzzed through the window, a final annoyance.

In the morning we waited for one of the tourist officials to pick us up, as had been promised, but no one showed up. In this small town, word would almost certainly have got around about the previous evening's escapade. As we sat having a tea outside the hotel, served by a woman who brewed it on a small charcoal fire, one of the merchants next door smiled at us, and winked at me, and then I knew we were the gossip of the town. Oblivious to the ripples, Stefanie puffed on a cigarette and drank strong black tea, charming a local man as she did so. I was wondering what she would do next. Next, she went off to buy herself some trinkets at the local market. Meanwhile, I waited on our hosts, the most junior one of whom eventually came by on a moped. What was there to see in Atbara? From where I was standing, a dusty street full of three-storey concrete blocks. The road was filled with pickups and donkey carts. The place was actually quite lively at midday with everyone having a late breakfast, but apart from the local railway museum, which was closed, I could see no reason not to move on. And so when Stefanie came back, all aglow with some market junk, we gathered our things and left for the bus station. We soon managed to get out of town on a minibus that would take us, in a short cut across the Bayuda Desert, to Karima, a town located on the Nile's long south-flowing meander. The tourist official shook our hands before darting off on his bike, clearly relieved to be rid of us.

At a road block on the outskirts of Atbara, Stefanie, getting all the attention once more, charmed a police officer into giving her his sunglasses. I angrily took them off her and gave them back to the cop like a disapproving parent. It was no use. She got the sunglasses given to her again through the window of the vehicle as we headed off, formalities done. Stefanie seemed to be fascinated by the desert. She constantly took photos of it out of the bus window. The Bayuda was a vast area of almost nothing, although in places there was enough vegetation to support a small population, and a clump of mud-brick houses stood here and there. Such a desert should properly be called semi-desert, I pointed out to Stefanie, who started an argument with me over the definition.

"What is this desert or *semi-desert*? It's a *desert* to me!"

Stefanie persuaded one of the females on the bus to exchange her ring for one of Stef's cheap market trinkets; I hid my face. Half way to Karima, in the middle of a stretch of sand desert, we stopped at an isolated way station where we lounged about under a shaded enclosure and sipped sodas, pulled out of a large cool box by the owner of the makeshift café. Being there was like starring in an episode of a dislocated dream, but it was fun. Further up the highway another road block and some greenery announced the outskirts of Karima, where I called another contact. The contact, a professor, basically informed me that he could not arrange accommodation for a single man travelling together with a single woman: that was it, the end of the line of my *wasta*, and from now on my fate was entwined with that of Stefanie's.

We had been travelling together since Shendi, and now Stef and I roomed together in a grotty guest house in Karima, another dust bowl of a town considerably less glamorous than Atbara. For me, it was just another stop en route to the west. Stefanie, however, wanted to visit some temple by a giant rock outcrop, and several nearby tombs. Over a meal of fish at a local restaurant, staffed by Egyptians – they must have been really desperate to seek employment this far upriver – I coolly informed Stefanie that I would be following my own schedule the next day, and she could likewise do her own thing. She dropped into a severe sulk when I told her this, refused to eat, and texted her faraway mother feverishly. The room at the guest house was a horrible concrete box; Stefanie sensibly slept outside during the night, later complaining to me that she had been harassed by a male, and that I was not much use. Not much use? I was paying half the price of the room, which was actually of great use to her, the bloody skinflint. By now we had started to see one another as a liability, only remaining together out of convenience.

In the morning, I felt pathetically reconciliatory and gallantly offered to go with Stefanie to the rock, the temple, and the nearby tombs – since it was a Sunday and I had nothing else to do. Stefanie consented, but she was still in a bad mood; I had upset her the previous evening. We went off to a local hotel, where proper tourists roomed in air-conditioned chalets. What were we doing there? Stefanie wanted to ask directions on how to get to the rock, but the latter was clearly visible from the road. It seemed to me she was trying to pick up a juicier contact; a bit lazy, unenthusiastic, and no longer having any helpful contacts, I had ceased to be of much use to Stef. After smooching with some well-heeled British guests for a short while in the designer hotel, we left for the rock, which overlooked the Nile and the town. There was a museum, a ruined temple, and a couple of pyramids spread out around the foot of the huge outcrop. Stefanie, who strode off ahead of me not appreciating my wonderful company at all, made the mistake of chatting to a local woman and her child. This alerted the park – the rock was a national monument – officials, one of whom trotted out of the museum to tap us for an admission fee, US $20 each. Twenty bucks to climb a rock. It did seem exorbitant, even if entry to the museum was included in the ticket price.

Stefanie went berserk. "What...are you joking...no way!" I braced myself for the coming verbal combat. The park official was Stefanie's match though; politely and firmly he insisted we pay up. After the opening round of argumentation, Stefanie was invited to make her case to the museum staff who were at that moment having tea under an oak like tree next to the museum.

Tears welled up in Stefanie's eyes as she spoke before the assembled power structure. "But please, please, this is my one chance to see this place. Please, no ticket..." The handful of men heard her out respectfully; they sought to listen and to understand before making a final decision on this village dispute. But it was Stefanie who was doing all the disputing. What country did she come from, asked one of the wise men, in perfect English. When Stefanie informed them she came from Austria, they all mistakenly thought she had said Australia, which was Eldorado in their minds. Waiving the park's entry fee was out of the question. At that moment Stefanie's case was put on hold as a small Sudanese tour group tramped into the park; greetings had to be attended to. None of the group paid for a ticket, I noticed.

"But please...I'm just a poor volunteer worker...," Stefanie soon resumed, unconvincingly. I then intervened and told the male council I would pay for my ticket if they let Stefanie go in for free, a face-saving solution that had worked before. That would be fine they said, glad to have been gifted a way out of the impasse – Stefanie had been wearing them out. I paid, and we then started for the rock.

"Your mistake, Stefanie, was to draw attention to yourself by talking to that woman. They would not have noticed us if you had kept a low profile." Stefanie did not like this analysis of recent events and rounded on me viciously.

"Really Gerard" – she had apparently forgotten my name – "That's not very helpful. It's not very helpful to say this *arftavards*." She had a point, the little ingrate. Then she shot off in a huff. I scrambled around by the temple's ruins, and up the rock, alone. "Hmm, nice pillars...I like the expressions on those reliefs...Oh, and here is a nice wall to sit on...gosh it's hot." I talked to myself like this all the while. I did not bother with the pyramids, and only got halfway up the rock where I stood and stared at the desert horizon, resigned to having been dumped. My mobile phone suddenly rang. It was Tareq, full of concern for me.

"Gary, how are you? Where are you?" Tareq had no idea what I had got myself into travelling with a woman, and I felt guilty at having completely forgotten about him. Yes, I was fine, having a wonderful time, I assured him.

A MAN STOOD in the shade of a Baobab tree unravelling a small net. Around the flood plain mop-top palm trees broke up a flat horizon; cows grazed lazily beneath them. Haystacks dried in the sun as egrets pecked at loose grains around them, the air redolent with the smells of irrigated soil, cut grass and manure. A family tended to their smallholding farm, one of them ploughing the ground with a crude wooden plough pulled by an ox. If the agricultural implement looked rudimentary, it was getting the job done. Someone was teaching a youngster to ride a donkey, and before long a whole troop of children on donkeys went trotting past in a cavalry-like flourish. In the cooling afternoon, there was moderate activity going on all around as assorted individuals dressed in long white shirts and wearing skull caps came out to check on their livestock, hoe a bit of land, or just sit by the river to enjoy the sensation of being outdoors. Never far away was the chug chugging of a water pump, one of which was pouring a continuous discharge into an irrigation channel. People here owned very little, but it was enough to subsist on. As the afternoon progressed, so small groups of people gathered for a tea, or just to be together, their homes simple dwellings with few utensils, and bare beds the only furniture. Over all was a sense of peace and belonging, a way of being that had lasted millennia and could be still found down by the Nile.

After shaking off Stefanie, or after she had shaken me off, I had left Karima in a speeding minibus early one morning. The rapid, no-nonsense journey had taken me 200 kilometres in a straight line across the Nubia Desert to Dongola, capital of Sudan's Northern State. The short cut meant that I had missed a throng of Nile-side villages, but asthe-crow-flies seemed right at the time, and if any of those other villages were anything like Karima then I had not missed much. We charged over the desert on a newly-built road, one of Bashir's projects, and the going was good. The Nubia Desert was utterly brutal: hot, sandy and with almost no vegetation to speak of or cover from the sun. Anyone who wanted to travel through such a landscape by camel needed their head examining. One of the most memorable scenes in David Lean's great film, *Lawrence of Arabia*, is when Faisal eloquently explains to Lawrence that Arabs did not in fact like the desert; what they liked were green trees, gardens and fountains; it was only Europeans who yearned to traverse the desert's great wastes, *out of a sense of adventure.* There is nothing romantic about the desert, as any Arab would agree; the desert is simply an extremely hostile natural environment which punishes the unprepared mercilessly, and the Nubia Desert was no exception. The indefatigable, relentless and unremitting sun fell down on our minibus like a military bombardment, and we huddled in our seats as if in trenches, the air-conditioning barely making a dent on the high temperature. Seeing trees again was deliverance.

The ferry to Egypt was not scheduled to leave Wadi Halfa for a couple of days, and I therefore delayed my onward journey. Dongola was a lively but parochial provincial town. The first thing I noticed was the religiosity of the place: local mosques blared away at prayer times, and communal prayers took place in the street, right in front of restaurants. Posters of local politicians, the remains of April's presidential election in Sudan, were still plastered all over the place, most of the candidates touting religion. Girls wandered about unaccompanied, often wearing the full veil, which was their perfect right, only it seemed uncomfortable garb to wear in the heat. After arriving in town, I found a cheap guest house to put up in. At night, this guest house filled with poor people; they would turn up for a bed after dark, and disappear early the next day. The owner of the hotel, a swarthy Nubian, spoke good English and was very friendly. He tried to point me in the direction of some ruins, but I was more interested in the Nile, and the town. The town was hopeless: when I went to the national bank to change money, for example, they told me to go to another bank because they did not offer this service. As for the local post office, it took hours to find, tucked away out of sight as it was. Service at local restaurants was patchy; the local tuk-tuk drivers were sharks, and so on. A walk around the town's suburbs brought me into a neighbourhood where poor people camped out in the open. Here children came after me like zombies clawing for money. Later, in a tale of two social classes, a couple of girls dressed in school uniforms came up, said hello, and shook hands with me.

After two days, I left Dongola, a place that had at least provided me with a swathe of land by the Nile to study, the sort of place that had been Tayeb Salih's lifetime inspiration. A tuk-tuk took me to the bus station, a sprawling ramshackle dirt yard. I unloaded my luggage, tipped the driver correctly but not lavishly, and then sat in a small, open concrete waiting room sheltering myself from dust that drifted outside in the street like snow. Minibuses came and went, but I awaited the big, beautiful bus, which I was assured would arrive at midday. I waited a long time, and then finally it came, a Chinese swan of a bus. When I got on, I discovered the bus was almost empty. I sat at the back of the plush coach, next to a peasant returning home to some distant village. To my surprise, this man spoke some English and tried to communicate with me as we glided out of Dongola into the outer space of the desert. On the outskirts of town some plainclothes security officials checked our papers, and then we were off, warp speed 9. The landscape was once again desolate, though more rocky than in the south. Here and there, outcrops of rock had been weathered into slag heaps of loose material. Strangely, as we moved northwards, the flora became more varied in colour, but smaller in stature; it remained concentrated in the Nile vortex. It was while cruising through this landscape that I noticed the mountains resembled pyramids, no doubt the inspiration for the ancient engineers, who knows. About halfway to Wadi Halfa the bus stopped and the peasant got off and walked into a mud-brick village, his home. I waved to him from the bus window, feeling sort of sorry for the guy – he had been unnecessarily singled out by checkpoint police for a thorough search. The rest of the journey was uneventful, and two hours later we arrived at Wadi Halfa.

THE UPPERMOST TIP of Lake Nasser reaches Wadi Halfa. When I went down to the lake, shortly after arriving in town, I noticed that the water level had fallen in recent weeks, but not by much: plenty of ancient Nubian culture lay submerged under its large silvery expanse. The huge lake looked incongruous here because Wadi Halfa was little more than a desert way station. There were no pleasure boats or leisure activities to be had on the water and all who came to Wadi Halfa were either arriving from Egypt, or departing Sudan. The ferry was not a tourist boat so much as a genuine means to cross the border – there was almost no other way to get into Egypt from Sudan unless you flew from Khartoum. Finally, I had got myself into position to make this lake crossing, and I was excited. I had arrived early, wanting to explore a bit, and stayed two nights at a big guesthouse that had a veranda and ceiling fans. Here I flopped about on the easy chairs and read during the daytime, leaving neighbourhood exploration until the cooler evening. There were a surprising number of transients in Wadi Halfa, who like me appeared at dusk, and empty shipping containers hinted at a lively cargo trade on the lake. A welcome breeze blew at night, flowing in and out of the guesthouses, and many slept in the open by their vehicles.

The ferry arrived mid-morning one day before my scheduled departure, at a distance of some two kilometres from the guesthouse area. Climbing up a nearby hill, I could just about make out the ferry in the distance. Soon, new arrivals turned up at the guesthouse: a couple of Finns touring Africa in a German-made camper van; a throng of Danes doing likewise on huge motorbikes. The Europeans' vehicles were being transported separately on a barge, and so they were also obliged to wait in Wadi Halfa. We sat around and chatted on the veranda. According to the Finns, Sudan was a lot more laid-back than Egypt. It was certainly less densely populated, as would soon become apparent to me. Other traders and merchants melted into the desert, taken away on minibuses, tuk-tuks and even on donkey-pulled carts. It was while watching this general dispersion that I noticed Wadi Halfa had a residential district over yonder from the guesthouse, complete with gated villas and ordered streets. It seemed incredible, because all around was a sea of sand and rock; what was the basis of this settlement's economy? The owner of the guesthouse, who was a fan of president Bashir, later informed me that the Egyptian government had paid for this housing as part of the deal to re-settle the Nubian population, which lost its land to the flood waters.

The next day I scooted out to the ferry terminal in an old Land Rover. We soon hit an asphalt road and it was then only a matter of minutes before we reached the crowded terminal. Inside the building, a couple of hundred people were milling about carrying bundles, bags, suitcases, boxes and just about everything short of live chickens. A tall Egyptian, dressed in a smart shirt, took it upon himself to help me out, pointing me in the direction of immigration and customs. The previous day I had registered – my umpteenth registration in Sudan – to leave the country at Wadi Halfa's police station. But the system in operation at the terminal required you to surrender your passport and wait for your name to be called out. I ignored this protocol and went straight to customs where I was made to fill out three separate forms with exactly the same information, and then had my passport checked on the spot, by three different people – a nice job creation scheme. Finally, after being asked if I was carrying any guns, I was allowed to make my way to the ferry, a task that involved walking 100 metres along the quayside in the sweltering heat. Despite being the No. 1 cabin port side passenger, I was then made to wait some time before embarkation.

THE TARDIS-LIKE FERRY absorbed a large number of passengers with all their baggage, and it did not seem overcrowded at all; one of the ship's officers, an Egyptian, told me the boat was under-subscribed and usually there were even more people on board. I made my way to the cabin, dumped my luggage, and then went for a stroll around. On the upper deck I became acquainted with a Dutchman who had been kept on board because he had left his passport in his motorbike. The bike was being transported on a separate barge, and this meant that both he and his bike would have to return to Aswan to rendezvous again: he was very frustrated at being kept on board, and desperately wanted to get off the boat. As we stood chatting, Stefanie walked past in her rapid, confident manner.

"Where have you been Garee?" Stef uttered casually, addressing me. I was touched that she had got my name right, but her presence disturbed me: she might have an outburst on the ferry, an environment where I had no way of getting away from her. I smiled, mumbled something about sitting around in Wadi Halfa, and then returned my attention to the depressed Dutchman, who was threatening to jump ship, something we managed to talk him out of, Stefanie turning on her charm again.

In the end, the Dutchman stayed on board to suffer another traverse of the lake, his third in a row. The trip had a *Heart of Darkness* air about it; there was something suspenseful about the journey, and I expected natives dressed in war paint to come alongside in canoes at any moment, their ghost-like presence a reprimand from the other world, the real world. In fact, after departing from Wadi Halfa, we saw no signs of life along the lake's scorpion-infested shores for many kilometres. The ferry was sort of cosy, and I enjoyed the frisson of the adventurous lake crossing in this aging boat, a smallish but powerful vessel. We cruised at a steady rate of knots on the lake's placid surface, the sun setting over the desert and a cool breeze lifting as the evening wore on. Stefanie busied herself chatting to some European backpackers on the top deck, and I left her to it, almost expecting to hear screams at any moment. The evening's meal was later served for cabin class passengers, a decent chicken and beans dish, and after this I returned to the top deck to await our passage past the Abu Simbel temples. Unfortunately, we did not pass this monument until after dark, and so there was not much to see. I then sat with the Dutchman and listened to his motorbike travel tales for a while before retiring to my cabin for some privacy and a good night's rest. The cabin may not have been luxurious, but it was a big improvement on sleeping out on the top deck next to the ship's noisy funnels.

Sixteen hours later, like magic, we approached the Aswan Dam from the lake side. The ferry eased its way past the almost four kilometre long high dam and then moored at a quayside next to the "Sunrise African Dream" river boat, one of a large number of tourist boats, most of which were concentrated on the north side of the massive concrete barrier. Everyone was smiles as we disembarked, after a long delay – Egyptian officials were no more efficient than their Sudanese counterparts, and the ship's passenger list had to be checked carefully for likely asylum-seekers. Finally, the all-clear was given, and we stumbled out of the ferry and walked up a concrete screen toward immigration following a sign that read, "To Arrival Hole".

* * *

At Aswan, I met the rest of the world. After settling in at a well-appointed little hotel, I spent some time exploring the back streets of this strange town. The place was weird in appearance because it faced hilltops on the opposite shore, and this gave the riverside an unnatural, model-like appearance. A towering five-star hotel, also on the desert west bank, dwarfed all the *feluccas*, the traditional Egyptian sailing boats, that criss-crossed the narrow waterway in a stately regatta. Along the riverside, many oblong-shaped tourist river boats were moored; they acted as both transport and accommodation for their mostly European occupants. The boats typically had a swimming pool on the top deck, and I was staggered to see young women sunbathing in bikinis by these pools. I suppose it was the kind of shock the average British person might feel seeing, for the first time, a woman dressed in a *burqa* walking down Oxford Street in

London. It is not that I objected in any way to seeing women in bikinis, but that I was seeing them on this occasion from a Muslim's perspective; I interpreted their appearance as a cultural provocation. What interested me about Egypt was the way Islamic rules had been suspended for non-Muslims, obviously in the interests of maintaining the valuable tourist industry. Although my shock wore off, I never quite got used to seeing skimpily dressed Europeans wandering about Aswan's street markets; they somehow looked indecent.

Tourism was everything in Aswan, and the local economy entirely revolved around it. There was something worn and predictable about the routines though, and I would not be surprised if most tourists, like me, were not a little disappointed by the town, and perhaps by the whole River Nile experience. In Aswan, horses and carriages drove up and down the riverside *corniche* road, almost in a parody of tourism, sometimes with occupants, more often not, and the desperate coachman would importune anyone walking up and down the street.

"Ride, Meester…Meester?" The poor horses looked like they were dying, as in fact some of them were. The local market ran the full length of Aswan parallel to the riverside road, and was full of junk. Why on earth anyone would want to buy the useless trinkets and T-shirts on offer in this market I could not fathom, but probably the tourists went there as much for the atmosphere as for the goods, an entirely phony atmosphere as anyone who had been around the Middle East would know. The Egyptian merchants were quite adept at drawing customers into their stores, and charming them into buying something; they knew exactly who was a soft touch, and who was not. And that was Aswan in its entirety. In the evening, the local population came out to play, and a surprising number of people walked the streets at this time. But Egypt had a population far exceeding its ability to feed such numbers, and unemployment was obviously a serious problem. One only had to go down Aswan's back streets in the morning to see what modern Egypt was all about: unfinished and poorly constructed housing was the norm; there was a total lack of public amenities and a poor range of food available. The new and very large mosque built on high ground overlooking the town was even more revealing. In the face of widespread corruption and a sinking economy, Egyptian Muslims had turned to religion to give themselves moral purpose. Meanwhile, privileged tourists sipped cocktails on grotesque river boats that spewed clouds of pollution into the air as soon as they lumbered into action.

Many a boatman tried to persuade me to go for a *felucca* trip on the Nile, a not unreasonable proposition. The sailing boats certainly looked like a civilized way of getting about, but I was not in the mood for it. I did, however, visit the new and modern Nubian museum not far from the famous Old Cataract Hotel, the latter being redeveloped by an oil company at the time of my visit. The museum had everything one would expect: the very best intact artefacts and statues, models, photographs and multi-media presentations. It was the photographs taken by archaeologists in the Nubian region just before the Aswan dam was built that caught my attention. They showed the original positions of the Philae, Kalabsha, Qertassi, and Dakka temples, all of which were dismantled and moved, along with Abu Simbel, prior to the area's flooding, an extraordinary effort. The busts of ancient Nubian dignitaries were also fascinating, but overall the museum said more about the modern fetish for exotic archaeology than it did about Nubian culture. Where was the connection to Egypt's modern Nubians? What about the communities who were re-located because of the dam project? Why no pictures of these people?

In Aswan I could only be a tourist, and it was not long before I embarked on the next leg of my journey, choosing the most direct method to get to Cairo. I booked my train ticket at Aswan's Soviet-era station, a regular second-class ticket departing in the morning; most tourists left on the overnight train, but I wanted a train ride with a view, and I had no plans to stop in Luxor. It was a straightforward purchase. Relieved to have got a ticket out of town, I left the station and walked back

to my hotel. On the way back I bumped into the intrepid Dutchman. He was awaiting the return of his German-made motorbike
and passport from Wadi Halfa, and then he would attempt to
cross over into Sudan once more. Meanwhile, he had befriended
Stefanie and spent a day with her, but he seemed disenchanted.
In an exasperated voice, he told me she had argued vehemently
with the owner of a *felucca* over the cost of a ride, proceeded to
ignore him after they arrived at the Philae Temple together, and
then almost got into serious trouble after attempting to steal an
apple from a fruit stall rather than pay the asking price.

ON THE DAY of my departure from Aswan, I turned up early at
the station not wanting to miss the train. As standard, nothing
was going on first thing in the morning. The platform café
assistant was asleep on a bench when I strolled in and asked for
a tea. He was displeased to have been woken up, attempted to
overcharge me for the cup of tea, and then, when he realized I
knew he was trying to rip me off, gave it to me for free. Egypt
was full of amateurish chancers like this poorly paid state
employee. As the train's departure time came round, people
started to fill the platform, their timing much better than mine.
Then the train arrived, a sturdy Russian model dating from
Egypt's pro-Soviet era. I boarded my carriage, and was relieved
to find I had two seats to myself; it seemed second class was not
especially popular, but it was perfectly okay and air-conditioned,
and I could not see how anyone would have wanted a first-class
ticket. At least I didn't at this stage.

The train slowly pulled out of the station. We passed several
dozy security officers who sat slumped behind armoured shields
on the platform. There were a large number of such armed
guards all over Egypt, a response to the Islamist terrorist
campaign that had attempted to cripple Egypt's tourist industry,
a campaign that peaked in 1997 with the dreadful Luxor attack
in which 62 holidaymakers were murdered by lunatics wielding

automatic weapons. Despite security being stepped up every-where, small-scale terrorist incidents still occurred all over the country. It's the reason I felt uncomfortable about women wearing bikinis; I knew that that kind of cultural insensitivity was feeding religious fanaticism which ultimately led to violence. Egypt, like the other Arabic-speaking countries of North Africa, had been going through an identity crisis since the early 1990s, and the Islamist challenge, itself complex and multifaceted, was a major protagonist in this crisis.

The train had left on time, and I settled in for a long session of viewing out of the window, really quite thrilled at the prospect; this was more like the romantic vision of travel I had envisaged when planning my trip, and now it was a reality. And I was not disappointed: the day's journey would prove to be remarkable both for its length and because the train, apart from a half-hour delay, kept moving. As we moved out of Aswan one got the usual glimpses of back yards. Satellite dishes sprouted from the roofs of squat dwellings like mushrooms. But no laundry was on view – Muslim propriety demanded that it be kept out of sight. The train weaved beautifully down the lush east bank of the Nile; at first there was nothing but dry sand and rock on the west side of the river. The morning light turned the Nile, a magnificent, serene presence, into a mirror that reflected the green river bank, a total contrast to the unforgiving, desic-cated land found to the west. Occasionally one saw a peasant in a field heading home after a bit of early morning labour, but mostly the landscape was empty.

Empty until we came to the first of a series of cities. These urban centres were all located right next to the Nile in a sequence that stretched from Aswan to Cairo; and they got bigger as time went by. The capacity of the Nile to support so many cities, and to have done so since antiquity, was its great mystery and wonder. It was never really clear which city we passed at any given moment as the stations were not well marked, but we must have passed through Kom Ombo and El Nasr early on. These cities resembled Aswan: motley agglomerations of brick houses and concrete tenement blocks with only a mosque's minaret breaking up the monotonous cityscape. The pattern of farming changed as we travelled north, however. In Sudan, and around Aswan, farming was family-based and extensive, but further north agriculture was pursued intensively; fields became well-ordered and one could see tractors dotted about asphalted access roads. With a population of well over 80 million, Egypt had been obliged to apply science to its agricultural sector, an ongoing effort.

A waiter walked up and down the train's aisle carrying glasses of tea on a tray with some panache, an anachronism in this age of trolleys. I ordered a tea, and sat back sipping it happily as the world went by outside. Our direction, which I had been carefully monitoring with my compass, changed several times as we followed the meandering river, crossing a couple of impressive bridges along the way. Each time we crossed a bridge, I saw the Nile getting bigger and stronger like a rapidly growing wild animal. It was somewhere near Nag Hammadi where I saw a train in a siding which looked dirty and disused. Only at the last minute did I notice some bullet holes in several of its windows, a disconcerting sight. We rolled on and on, ever nearer to our final destination. Another city passed by, then another stretch of riverside farmland, followed by another city, and so the pattern repeated itself. In the late afternoon, the train started to fill up and I no longer enjoyed two seats to myself. Hawkers came by between stops desperately trying to sell chewing gum, or some similar small item. Their technique was to give you what they were selling, and then return later to see if you wanted to buy it, an annoying imposition I felt, but no one seemed to mind. Everyone understood the hawkers were trying to support their families.

The sun set over the Western Desert, and this meant I had been on the train twelve hours. By now I was tired and rather fed up with the journey, the lack of movement discomforting me; walking about the train was no longer very easy. Everyone seemed to be tired, and this expressed itself in irritable behaviour. I myself was irritated when a man tried to start a conversation with me by telling me I looked tired. I told him to mind his own business. A couple of merchants in Aswan had had the temerity to tell me to smile, a similar personal attack. These aggressive approaches were revealing of Egypt's political sickness, but also of the country's Europeanized attitudes – a Peninsula Arab would never accuse a stranger of face crime, an unthinkable rudeness. Later on, a fight broke out in the carriage. A middle-aged man took issue with a younger man's behaviour, something to do with the younger man's female companion. The older man displayed an enormous amount of aggression, but was restrained by some other male passengers, the whole outburst an example of acting up. But one could feel the frustration. This was a country where everyone was at the end of their tether, heroically hanging on for the sake of their families.

In the twilight, I could just about see the landscape of Lower Egypt, an ever more densely populated and built-up area. There were more and larger apartment blocks visible by the railway line; cheap housing thrown up to house Egypt's bursting population. And then darkness fell. As if by mutual consent, the carriage fell quiet. I was in agony from sitting so long and strolled about in an attempt to get my circulation going, not without difficulty as the train was full and the aisles cluttered with bags and limply hanging limbs. The train then stopped and we were delayed for what seemed like an eternity. I went out onto the platform to stretch my legs, and almost got left there when the train suddenly restarted. I attempted to sleep during the final leg of the journey, but only succeeded in resting my eyes. Then at long last, at ten o'clock in the evening, we arrived in Cairo.

8

MISR

Cairo was half way between Arabia and England, at least psychologically speaking if not exactly in measured distance or culturally. In one of his books, V.S. Naipaul remarked that Egypt was where Europe ended, a misconception because though they have a symbiotic and interconnected relationship, Europe and Egypt are in fact quite different. The "City of a Thousand Minarets" was definitely more eastern than western in spirit. All of Cairo's western aspects, as expressed in its architecture, fashions and food, were superficial compared to its deeper sociological and cultural make-up. Egypt's capital, with its innumerable crowded neighbourhoods, and strained infrastructure, was entirely of the undeveloped world economically, and was only liveable because Egyptians stuck together and helped each other out. Cairenes also drew succour from their long heritage and recognized importance as a centre of learning in the Arab world. The city muddled on come what may, and carried on functioning in the face of so many indignities.

It felt good, at first, to be walking around a noisy, cosmopolitan city. After checking into a hotel on Talaat Harb Street, I immediately went out to enjoy one of Cairo's principal shopping areas, only to find it wanting in some respects. One store was well stocked with Arabic religious texts, but they were of no use to me; what I wanted was a map of the country next to Egypt. Other stores displayed odd items like 20-year old manual typewriters and out of date toys. What really threw me were the numerous women's lingerie stores with skimpy underwear on full display, and this on a street where women were obliged to wear head scarves. In Egypt, women were sexually oppressed and this was ironically expressed in the way they were encouraged to be sexually attractive, without actually being allowed to be independently sexually active – the house of a Muslim is a religious space, and its sanctity is linked to the reputation of its female occupants whose sexuality is rigorously controlled by the patriarchal family. This was as true in Egypt as it was in Saudi Arabia. It was also noticeable how prostitution and drinking was very low key downtown, in contrast to the decades of the early 20th century when Europeans dominated Cairo's social scene. Failing to get the map I wanted, I bought an ice cream and craned my neck to get a good look at all the colonial era architecture, a real mix of styles. But when I tried to photograph one curvilinear art-deco residential block, a security guard appeared from nowhere and started shouting at me hysterically. He was acting up, like the middle-aged man on the train; I lowered my camera and slowly walked away.

Since it was in the neighbourhood, and since it was the thing to do, I went along to the Egyptian Museum the next day. I intended to sketch some artefacts there, like a real pro, but when I got inside the building, after going through a thorough security screening, I found a dozen people drawing, which put me off. In fact, the whole museum, which I personally and perhaps inevitably found rather disappointing, was packed out with visitors who, like me, felt they had to go there. The problem with the Egyptian Museum, and indeed with all Egypt's sites of antiquity, was that they were full of people who should *not* have been there at all. We knew next to nothing about Egyptology, and our obsessive interest was borrowed from popular archaeologists who had a narrow and specialized interest in the past. The thing that struck me most about the museum was how little there was to show for the 3000 years of history it supposedly covered, Egypt's treasures having been previously looted and dispersed throughout the world. There were some mummies, of course, tombs and statues and the like, but they all seemed monochrome and dull, having been taken out of context and dumped in the museum building at random. Meanwhile, blond-haired Scandinavian female tourists strode about the museum's staircases like modern-day goddesses – they were infinitely more interesting to me, and to the museum's security detail, than the stylized granite figures that adorned the hallways. I feigned an interest in this or that artefact, all the while keeping one eye on the north European nymphs, only to lose track of them somewhere in the Greek statues section. On the upper floor of the museum, I stumbled across the Tutankhamun room, which displayed the young pharaoh's funeral mask and associated regalia. This exhibit was the only truly impressive thing in the museum, the star of the show. Standing in front of the iconic mask in the surprisingly relaxed room, I felt tiny bomblets of recognition go off in my mind: the mask was exactly as I had seen it expertly photographed in so many encyclopaedias and magazines. Seeing it for real was almost superfluous if you had seen the photographs, but together with all the other funeral paraphernalia it really added up to something extraordinary and unblemished, and I almost expected Elizabeth Taylor suddenly to turn up. Howard Carter's discovery of Tutankhamun's tomb led to the consumerization of archaeology; the beautiful mask energized Egypt's tourist industry, a gold rush.

———

AT THE AMERICAN UNIVERSITY BOOKSHOP, near Tahrir Square, I was finally able to purchase a decent map of Libya. In the modern bookshop I met Nasser, an English instructor at one of Cairo's private language institutes. He was looking for a suitable English language textbook to buy for some of his students and had asked my advice when he saw me browsing books nearby. I told him to write his own book, which seemed to strike a chord with him. Upon discovering I was British, and a sometime English teacher, he invited me to a café for a coffee. It was the best offer I had had all day, and it was with relief that I tossed a book on scuba diving aside, mentally ditching a vague plan I had to go snorkelling in the Red Sea. My Libyan visa was taking a bit of time to arrange, but while it was in process I was not going anywhere, and certainly not going on any tomb raids, I decided. It was my intention to get to know Cairo better, if that was at all possible in the limited time I would be there.

Nasser and I went to a back street café where a man was sucking on a hookah pipe like the caterpillar in *Alice in Wonderland*. Other men sipped their coffees, killing time socially. Nasser was unusual in that he was western educated but chose to wear Arab dress. He was wearing a winter Arab long shirt. Made of wool, these shirts are warm and fantastically comfortable. They were not really practical for me though, not with all the things I carried in my pockets and had slung off my belt. Nasser wanted to know what I was doing in Cairo and his face lit up when I said I was on a *rihla fi talab al-ilm*. The Islamic reference set him off on a long religious treatise; he was, evidently, a fundamentalist of sorts, a born-again Muslim. And so I got a long, unsolicited explanation of what the Hajj pilgrimage was all about. I explained to Nasser, as diplomatically as I could, that as a non-Muslim I had no right to enter Mecca or Medina, and consequently had little interest in the Hajj, or anything related to it; and I really couldn't fathom why people would want to gather in such numbers, as if at an over-subscribed rock festival. The Hajj was desperately important to Muslims though, all of whom are obligated to try and make the pilgrimage at least once in their lifetime.

The equalitarian appeal of Islam was something I could discern anyway, partly from Nasser's remarks – "But Garee, it is great to be with everyone, and everyone is equal" – but also from observation. Our coffee arrived. It was another warm day, so we sat in the shade outside. The man smoking the hookah had a collar around his neck to support a whiplash injury, and it was this that made him appear caterpillar-like. Nasser continued to wax lyrical about the Hajj, and I felt the need to steer him onto another topic.

I had read that morning in a local English-language paper that twelve Egyptian television satellite channels had been suspended for not toeing the government line; seventy Islamists had been rounded up and thrown into detention. They were "democratic" Islamists, the ones who planned to win power through the ballot box, and then turn Egypt into a model Islamic state. Hosni Mubarak, Egypt's president since 1981, had other ideas: he had no intention of letting the Islamists gain power, and periodically suppressed them, along with anyone else that threatened him politically.

I said, "So, Nasser, tell me about Egypt. What's going on?"

"This country is corrupt. There is nothing we can do about it, but there will be another revolution. At the present, those who rule us take everything. They control land and rent or sell it to anyone they like. The class of bureaucrats is the one that has benefited from Mubarak's rule; he is responsible for the system and for the corruption." Who did Nasser think would lead this revolution, the Islamists? "No. There will be another revolution like the one in '53 that got rid of the King Farouk and the British. People are frustrated now as they were then. But at the least the British did something for the country. They reinvested some money, and we had an efficient and honest civil service. Now you can't get anything done without a bribe. You might not think so, but what you have in Britain is not bad, let me tell you. Those MPs' expenses are nothing compared to what ministers steal from the people here."

I asked, "Nasser, who will lead this revolution, where is the leadership?" And what was going to be the role of the Islamic Brotherhood, one of the most powerful underground forces in the country, a banned organization that had tried to assassinate Mubarak several times during the former air force commander's long and turbulent presidency?

Nasser said, "Mubarak cannot hold on much longer. He's getting old. We have other good leaders but they have been neutralized by the ruling party. For example, Dr Ayman Nour, a presidential candidate, was framed and sentenced to five years' hard labour. In return for participation in the First Gulf War, $20 billion in foreign debt was forgiven, and Mubarak was given the backing he needed from the US to stay in power. But the elections have been a sham, and Mubarak cannot stay in power without US support." So far, I was impressed with Nasser's insight, but he still could not say precisely who would likely lead a revolution. Without leadership, a revolution becomes an aimless uprising, and the establishment finds a way to hold on to power after making some scapegoats. Nasser seemed to have confidence in his predictions nonetheless. He also talked quite candidly about his life.

"I work at a school, but I'm exploited by both my employer and my landlord. I'm expected to stay at the school all day, even though I only have four or five hours of classes each day. From my salary more than half goes on rent, and I barely have enough money left for food and cigarettes. There is no possibility to take a holiday, and I must make a contribution to my parents of course." Nasser spoke calmly and slowly, but was frustrated by his lack of prospects. He was very bright, and quite collected. Cairenes had seen it all, and apparently saw it coming. Egypt's first revolution had been so promising, the Agrarian Reform Law redistributing land to those who tilled it for the first time, but the country was now mired in all sorts of economic difficulties: there was high unemployment, 20 percent of the population lived below the poverty line, and oil production came nowhere near meeting domestic demand for petroleum and other oil-related products. Tourism ebbed and flowed, but in fact Egypt only ranked 23rd in the world in terms of the number of tourists visiting each year, behind 13th place Russia, for example. And Egypt was a net food importer, its weak point and source of American leverage over it.

Nasser asked me what I was doing in Cairo, and I told him

that I was on my way to Libya. He assumed I was after gold, goblets and statues; I told him that I did not value antiques in the way many people did, and had only a passing interest in visiting sites of antiquity, as an extension of my interest in living cultures. If I ever found a valuable Roman bronze bust under my feet, I'd have my photograph taken with it and then hand it over to the nearest authorities. Actually my attitude was typically oriental, and could be understood by Nasser. But my lack of interest in a monetary return did not make sense to someone who was hard up. "But many Europeans come here looking for old things. They go to the desert, and know where to look. They make a lot of money," Nasser said, explaining the phenomenon like a maths problem.

Did I want to go and see the pyramids at Giza? No thanks. But Nasser insisted I think about it, and we made an appointment to meet the following day, by which time I would have changed my mind.

THE FAÇADES of most of the buildings in Cairo were in good repair, some of the balconies and pilaster work pleasingly ornate. My own hotel, a guesthouse in fact, was situated high up in an art-deco five storey building that was, like an aging human body, slowly crumbling on the inside. An antiquated but serviceable lift whisked me silently and smoothly to the guesthouse on the fifth floor, all the lift's clockwork winding gear in view. There were many such buildings, and many such elevators, in Cairo, all stuck in time, but all occupied and used to capacity. My room in the guesthouse had polished parquet floors, twin beds, and clean linen. From the room's balcony, I watched the ant colony-like city below come to life as the sun disappeared and the lights came on. Cairo came alive at night when its population filled the streets, and when the neon lights came on making the old buildings look like drag queens. But the noise of traffic, amplified in the canyon of Talaat Harb Street, was a constant irritant that could only be got rid of by closing the windows' shutters and switching on the air-conditioning. The guesthouse was not very charming despite the fascinating ride in the lift up to it: the place was run a bit like a military camp, and young men were posted in the corridors, ostensibly to serve the guests, but actually to watch that nobody stole the chromium garbage cans. Once they realized I was not going to buy a sightseeing package tour, the staff lost interest in me.

I met Nasser at a nearby coffee house the next morning, where we had tea and Danish slices, or "Ice Danish" as everyone called them. Like many frustrated male Egyptians, Nasser took comfort in food and he was rather corpulent, a paradox in a country that could not produce enough food to feed its population. He also owned a car, something he had achieved by spending time working in Saudi Arabia. This was his weekend, and he wanted to show me around. After a leisurely coffee and chat, we duly piled into his car and drove off at high speed, a remarkable feat given the lack of room on the street. Another working day was beginning in Egypt, and the capital's taxis and private cars were out in full force, beeping and honking like mad, even when at a standstill. I had expressed an interest in visiting Coptic Cairo, part of the Old City where several Christian church buildings stood, still serving Egypt's large Christian community. Nasser knew how to get there and parked his car at a nearby market. After a security frisk, we entered the area where the churches and associated buildings were concentrated. They were active and in good repair, and many tourists floated in and out of the buildings. What interested me was the level of security: Coptic Cairo was under siege, and a large number of nervous looking security guards had been drafted in to protect the area's visitors.

After a quick walk around the Old City, we got back in Nasser's saloon car and drove slowly up the city's riverside road finally crossing the Sixth of October Bridge into Zamalek, an upmarket suburb built on an island in the Nile. The river on both sides of the island was massive, much bigger and more impressive than the Thames, with non-stop high-rise developments along its banks. In Zamalek, we stopped to browse in some English-language bookstores where I stocked up on reading material, and we then had lunch in an Italian-style restaurant. Over our meal, Nasser tried to explain what honour killings were all about, but his explanation left me confused. What kind of man would shoot his cousin in the head, or bury his daughter alive? Inexplicably, these things happened in modern Arab countries, and female circumcision was still a common practice in Egypt. It was hard to square these practices with sophisticated Cairo, where the best European literature and food was readily available. As we ate by the window of the restaurant, a tourist bus whooshed by outside. Remembering the terrorist incident of 1997, it occurred to me that grouping oneself together with other tourists on a bus was not the wisest of choices. That is what made all the security around Cairo a joke – terrorists could easily kill a bunch of Europeans on a bus without going anywhere near a museum, a hotel, or Coptic Cairo.

We took a little walk around Zamalek after lunch, and I was delighted to find a post office where the staff understood how to wrap and stamp a parcel. Near the American University Campus, there were yet more bookshops and an establishment that described itself as a "pub", which somehow seemed too good to be true. The atmosphere was a world away from the crowded tenement blocks of Cairo's suburbs, yet even here on the leafy island the residential areas were starting to show signs of advanced wear and tear; buses were overcrowded, and the roads clogged with traffic. Zamalek reminded me of Beirut: European in a louche sort of way, but becoming an increasingly thick urban jungle. The pleasant park space on the island was being strangled by the boa constrictor of development; there was no unused land anywhere. Nasser, restless, informed me that the pyramids would be quiet in the afternoon and that we should not miss this chance to see them; I therefore went there together with him, an unavoidable assignation.

Like Tutankhamun's mask, the pyramids and sphinx of Giza are usually photographed without any messy contextual details intruding. The photographs are therefore somewhat misleading, and the truly epic scale of the pyramids can only be appreciated by seeing them for the first time from the gate of the park that surrounds them. Here you get to see everything, as it was designed to be seen: a collection of pyramids guarded by a sphinx, built on high ground overlooking Cairo. What else was here in antiquity? Quite a lot one could imagine: gardens, brightly painted temple walls, and the smoothly encased giant pyramids; it must have been quite a sight. After buying our tickets, Nasser and I walked up to the sphinx, which was a lot smaller and scraggier than I had expected; it was half-buried in a pit with some scaffolding hanging off its side. Visiting tourists were over-awed, "It's probably the most well-known icon in the world," drooled one man to his bored-looking wife. After a circuit around the sphinx, I really felt I had seen all that I needed to see at Giza, the context essentially, but Nasser insisted on taking a closer look at the Great Pyramid. The significance of these pyramids lay in the fact that they required a highly centralized political authority to achieve their construction. And I wondered if the pharaohs were loved or loathed by the ancient Egyptian people. It could not have been nice to have been sealed up in a tomb after years of devoted service, the fate of some skilled craftsmen working on various tombs and pyramids around Egypt – a land called *Misr* in Arabic, a word also synonymous with Cairo.

Under no circumstances did I want to go into the underground chambers of the Great Pyramid. I did not want to inhale stale air. And then there was the curse of the pharaohs to worry about. So instead, after Nasser's suggestion, we made a circuit of the base of the structure, the four sides of the pyramid having an average error of less than six centimetres in length. The blocks of stone that were apparently emplaced at the rate of twelve an hour during the pyramid's construction were massive close up. No amount of time or weathering had reduced this internal core of masonry. As we walked, tourists galloped past in horse-drawn carriages, on donkeys, and in authorized vehicles. They appeared to be going to some point beyond the pyramids to get photos with the afternoon sun behind them. Nasser and I hailed one of the old-fashioned horse cabs and took a short ride out to the viewing spot, like Victorians. We briefly stopped at the viewing area to take in the pyramids bathed in golden sunlight, and therefore looking newer, fresher and more photogenic, and then left the park area not sticking around for the Light and Sound show.

When I pointed out to Nasser that I had seen pyramids at Meroe, which pre-dated the great pyramids of Giza, he became quite agitated. Meroe was in Sudan, and they could not possibly have invented pyramid building in that remote swamp of a land, he informed me.

"Garee, we have everything in Egypt. We have many temples and pyramids. Of course, Egyptians invented pyramid build-ing." Did it really matter who invented them? Clearly, ancient engineers borrowed ideas off one another, much like artists did. I doubt there was ever a single original inventor of the pyramid structure, though pharaohs naturally had their favourite archi-tects who they liked to talk up.

We drove back downtown through the modern suburb of Giza, a hellish place full of air pollution, crowded tenements, and impatient car drivers. An audio recording of the Koran played on Nasser's in-car stereo, a soothing and artistic recita-tion which helped keep us calm among the general hubbub of the neighbourhood. The traffic at least kept moving, albeit at a snail's pace, and we eventually re-crossed the Sixth of October Bridge and then careened across Tahrir Square into the down-town district where Nasser dropped me off. His weekend was over, and it would not be possible for us to meet again, so we exchanged information before Nasser shot off in a *Misr* flourish. Almost immediately, I was approached by a tout. Did I want a hotel, or a guide to show me the Egyptian Museum? No, and no again was my answer.

With some time on my hands, I spent the next couple of days exploring the back streets of the downtown area. Cairo was divided into village-sized neighbourhoods where everyone knew everyone else, and it was possible to see the same people in the same places on a daily basis. I got a haircut in one salon courtesy of a glamorous looking woman who asked what I wanted when I walked in, and I don't think she was talking about a haircut. I went to several cinemas and tried to watch an Egyptian melodrama all the way through once, but could never quite manage to stay longer than half an hour, even though some of the films' slapstick humour was quite well done. I sought out a night club, but timidly avoided entering when I finally found one – the dingy establishment looked like it was run by the mafia, and my journeyman clothes hardly met the dress code. At a travel agent's office, I once more toyed with the idea of making a trip to the Red Sea, and discussed the arrangements with a beautiful young Cleopatra-like female assistant; later scuppering these plans on the grounds that going to Sharm el-Sheikh would have been a detour, and a rather long one at that. On my last day in the big city, I visited Cairo University. Like everything in Egypt, the institution proved to be oversubscribed and under-resourced. It did look like a real school though, one with impressive buildings, a genuine campus atmosphere, and lots of bright-looking young people walking about. However, my theory about schools really being prisons was borne out by the fact that the university was sealed off to outsiders and guarded. Ostensibly, the guards were there to stop terrorists getting in, but actually they were there to keep an eye on the students.

What finally drove me out of Cairo was the noise on a Friday, the Islamic holy day. It was simply unbearable to wake up to honking traffic on this day, as on the other six. A pocket guide-book on Alexandria, which I had bought along with the map of Libya at the American University book shop, made the famous ancient port look very enticing. The Greco-Roman Museum and modern library were of particular interest to me, and I thought it would be better to spend the rest of my remaining time in Egypt there rather than in maddening Cairo. There were regular trains to the port, and on the Saturday I took a helter-skelter taxi ride to the train station. The taxi could get nowhere near the station's entrance, however, and I was left to haul my luggage across broken ground and over exposed pipes – the station was being renovated and had become a building site. Ducking under some scaffolding, I finally made it to the ticket office where I fought a major battle to get a second-class seat on the train, the clerk at first saying there were none available in the hope of getting a bribe. But I caught her selling a ticket to an expatriate American-Egyptian, and demanded a seat, finally getting one. There was a one hour wait before the train departed, which I spent reading the Alexandria pocket guide in the station's café, an oasis of calm amid all the chaos.

IT WAS my misfortune to get a seat on the train next to an obese man, who insisted on owning the dividing arm rest between us, and behind a young man who insisted on playing a car-racing simulation video on his laptop computer, complete with noisy sound effects. The manic video game reminded me of one of the characters in Naguib Mahfouz's novel *Miramar* who drives up and down Alexandria's *corniche* like a Formula One driver. The train carriage filled up to capacity, and there was no escape from the noise. I turned and looked out the window, the passing view my only consolation. The train ran parallel to a canal for a distance, grain silos dotted along it, and then we crossed the wide Nile once more, the last time I would do so. After crossing the river, we drifted into open fields where there was more farm machinery about than ever, the sunlight picking out the tractors and other vehicles. There were many more, and different kinds of, trees in the delta region that we now traversed, including willow trees. These familiar trees, which seemed out of place, and other visual prompts, like clouds in the sky, gave me a sense of returning home for the first time.

Housing estates, mosques and electricity pylons announced the outskirts of Alexandria. By now the sky was full of bruised clouds hanging motionless like UFOs. It took me a while to remember the connection between these flying saucers and possible rain, a weather condition I had not experienced since leaving Asmara, but in the end it remained dry for the rest of the journey. We duly arrived at Alexandria station after a trip that had taken a little over two hours. The crowded port station was, like Cairo's, being renovated; a shopping centre about to engulf the place. I was forced into a funnel of disembarking passengers and pushed along like a bit of flotsam. We reached the end of the platform where exiting involved walking across the rail tracks; the railway line symbolically dividing my trip back to England into two halves: mentally, I was now on Part II of my journey. A ride in a decrepit yellow taxi then got me to a hotel in Midan Square, near Alexandria's historic waterfront.

Alexandria's ancient history has largely been buried or built upon, only hints and shadows remaining. The lighthouse, of course, was destroyed by an earthquake hundreds of years ago. Parts of its ruins were later incorporated into the more recently built Qaitbay Fort in the Eastern Harbour. There was the Roman Odeum, the only existing example in Egypt of this type of Greco-Roman theatre which once hosted music and poetry competitions. Located in the middle of town, the ruins were crawling with tourists. They were nonetheless impressive, the theatre perfectly proportioned. As for the Greco-Roman museum, a long and frustrating search got me to a museum, but the no photography rule kept me out of it. That was as far as I got with Alexandria's ancient history, and I spent most of the rest of my time in the city sipping coffee, or a beer if I could find one, in hotel cafés watching the world go by in a place that no longer had any living connection to its namesake, or Greco-Roman culture.

It was in Alexandria, apparently more liberal than any other city in Egypt, where I came face to face with the country's economic and political failure. Again like Cairo, the city was a crowded mess lacking good public amenities and sensible town planning. Grand hotels had been neglected, while the renovated ones were scandalously overpriced. Public transport still ran – the tramway was a comic-like marvel – but where was the investment? How was it that there was money to develop holiday resorts, but none to buy new buses or improve roads and public buildings? Alexandria's new library was finished in 2000. The library did represent a significant investment, but the money came from overseas, as did the design idea. I went to the leviathan library out of curiosity early one morning only to discover that it did not open until 10.30 a.m. Frustrated by the late opening, I killed time in an expensive café before paying US $2 for a ticket to enter what had become a tourist attraction. One could take photos inside the main building, but bags had to be left in a cloakroom, and visitors were obliged to pass through a metal-detector scan, which was sad. The new library, designed like a Roman amphitheatre on the inside, was fabulous, although a cursory glance at the English and French book collection revealed them to be not much better than what one might find at a low ranking university in the UK. I could not judge the quality of the Arabic collection, which may have been very good, and the library did have a good reference section that included the Coptic Encyclopaedia, a goldmine of information on Christianity in the Middle East past and present. I was also surprised to find a copy of Salman Rushdie's *The Satanic Verses* on the English literature shelves; no wonder security had been so tight. It was noticeable that there were more tourists than readers at the library, and I wondered if the money lavished on this huge building could not have been better spent constructing several smaller libraries, but then it was not my money at stake, and politicians must have their prestige projects.

There was no western expatriate scene in the Egyptian port city, and anyone looking for Lawrence Durrell's Alexandria will only find it in his Quartet. The food available in restaurants was dreadful, and the service even worse; single people on their own were ignored, a kind of castigation for not being sociable. My feelings for the inhabitants of this workaday port were mixed. I sympathized with them having to put up with a dead-end government. But their bad driving and boorish manners tried my patience on more than one occasion. Overall, Alexandria was not my beat, and I resolved to leave as soon as my Libyan visa came through. Meanwhile, I drifted in and out of dreary bars and restaurants looking for John Mills, the star of the classic film *Ice-Cold in Alex*, but was left chasing a ghost, my own ghost probably. Alexandria, a shadow of its former self, disorientated me at every turn as I wandered around it like a lost boy. It would have taken a hardy type of outsider to remain in Alexandria after Egypt became independent, someone like the Greek-Egyptian poet Constantine Cavafy, a person who relied on his internal mental resources to make something out of nothing, his poem *The City* a critique of those restless discontents who think they might find happiness elsewhere, but who won't find peace anywhere.

A cold front blew in off the Mediterranean, the first cool weather I had encountered thus far on my trip, and I found it revivifying. Standing on the balcony of my hotel room I took long draughts of the moisture-laden sea air. It was time to move out and begin the long haul westwards across North Africa. The next day, I packed, checked my luggage, and then took a taxi through Alexandria's interminable traffic out to the bus station – it would not be possible to travel by train again until Tunisia. The taxi driver finally dropped me in a grubby pot-holed bus park in a nondescript neighbourhood on the outskirts of town. Just as I arrived there, it started to rain, a few drops at first and then a great deluge. I had packed a raincoat for exactly just such an occasion, and donned the plastic cape with satisfaction at my foresight; though it would be the last time I would ever wear it. A few passengers sat huddled in a shelter near the ticket office, and I joined them after booking a seat on a bus headed to Marsa Matrouh. The rain intensified, and water started flooding the ground where we sat; it leaked through holes in the corrugated iron roof. A miserable wait ensued, but then the bus came and we all made our escape.

Sitting near the front of the coach, I managed to get a good view out onto the outskirts of Alexandria, an apocalyptic landscape, something like the suburbs of a Soviet industrial town. The rain eased off, but the sky remained moody and cast dark shadows over a polluted lake and endless kilometres of poor tenements. The bus was filthy, too, and this lack of responsibility also disappointed me. It was as if people had decided to give up, to not try and improve things. And I knew why: because the social-political system did not reward initiative; quite the opposite. Again, this was as true in Egypt as it had been in Saudi Arabia. Farther from Alexandria, maybe at the 15-kilometre mark, I was amazed to see a brand new swanky hotel built by the road. What was that all about? Was it a film set? Either side of the hotel were half-finished apartment blocks with no windows and almost certainly no amenities that appeared to be inhabited. The incongruous hotel heralded a whole series of resorts full of chalets unfinished to one degree or another. The holiday camps had enticing names like "Caribiano," "Granada," and "La Jolie Place." I suppose the "Maadi" was reserved for Islamists, even fundamentalists needing a vacation. The weirdly empty resorts looked like they had been prepared to take an enforced population transfer. After 20 kilometres the road became deserted again, in both senses, but instead of going all the way to Marsa, I got off near the village of Alamein and, on the 68th anniversary of the start of the landmark World War II battle, walked the short distance from the coastal road to the El Alamein Military Museum.

THE AFTERNOON SUN lit up the Western Desert, a wide expanse of which could be clearly seen from the museum's approach road. This desert area contains an estimated four million unexploded mines, and millions more unexploded artillery shells. The Europeans fought their war in Egypt, Libya, and Tunisia, and left behind this deadly legacy – every year Bedouins are killed after tripping over live mines or unexploded shells. There was no question of going on a tour of desert battle sites, and one was left with the road side museum that contained an odd and aging collection of military hardware, uniforms and artefacts. The building was state-owned and, like everything else in Egypt, had not been touched since it had been set up, belatedly in 1965 in the case of the Alamein Military Museum. It is an interesting fact that war museums and war memorials are often created long after the events they commemorate. This is because the participants in a war generally want to forget about it afterwards, only later taking an interest in returning to the sites where they once fought. By the 1960s, there was obviously a momentum to create a museum at El Alamein, by which time much of the battlefield hardware had already been salvaged for scrap or lost in the desert. Thus in the forecourt of the museum I found a motley collection of light tanks, artillery pieces and trucks, although what was there was pretty good. I was delighted to get a good look at a British 25 pounder field gun, and a German 88 flak gun together, toy versions of which I owned in my fanatically militarist childhood. Without its armoured apron, and emplaced in a semi-buried pit, the 88 looked forlorn, hardly the deadly weapon of yore; the freshly painted 25 pounder, however, appeared like it was ready to be fired in anger at a moment's notice, and this seemed to symbolize all the merits of a weapon universally recognized as the best general-purpose field gun of the war. There were no German Panzers at the museum, a disappointment, and only one Matilda, one Sherman and a couple of other diminutive tanks, not exactly the land ironclads imagined by H.G. Wells. The American Sherman, perhaps one of those rushed to North Africa just before the El Alamein battle, at least had some presence.

Idiosyncratically arranged – a model of a dashing Wehrmacht motorcyclist and outrider distastefully sat behind a bust of Field

Marshal Bernard Montgomery – the inside of the museum was actually fascinating both in what it displayed, and overall as a fossilized interpretation of events. The Egyptians had with a disinterested equanimity treated all sides involved in the battle as equals, and images of allied soldiers in uniform were mixed up with their axis counterparts, a break with normal conventions. Uniforms, medals, flags, personal weapons and other artefacts from the conflict were placed according to nationality, however, a room each for the Germans, Italians and the British, the latter together with their Indian, South African, New Zealand and Greek allies. Much of what I saw was strangely familiar to me; I had used a British army surplus desert rucksack as a schoolboy; I had seen many of the photos before. But what was obvious to me from my visit to the El Alamein Museum, which survives on tourist traffic in the winter high season, was that after one more generation the memory of the Second Battle of El Alamein will start to fade, like the memory of so many great battles before it, and the museum will close down having served its purpose. Indeed part of the museum, a command bunker once used by Field Marshal Erwin Rommel, had already closed. The lights on a charmingly old-fashioned war gaming board that showed the location of all the World War II North African battle sites were dead, and you felt it was only a matter of time before someone chopped it up for firewood.

The rain earlier in the day, the hunt for the museum, and then my slow examination of everything on show there, had rather tired me out and so the museum's small but operational café came as a welcome haven. At first the café assistant's eagerness to please raised my suspicions. Why was he being so nice? What did he want? It turned out he wanted to give the customer good service, which was sort of startling. I had been used to surly, inefficient service everywhere in Egypt, and here was this polite, well-spoken young man, not in the least bit obsequious, giving me just the right amount of attention, no more and no less. Within a few minutes I realized he was an intelligent person, and probably on the lookout for contacts. Since I was the only customer in the café, I invited him for a coffee and we sat and chatted. Where was I headed, he asked, and I told him Marsa Matrouh and then on to Libya: I had received confirmation that my Libyan visa was ready from the travel agent and it now only remained to get up to the Egyptian-Libyan border where I would be met by an escort. I still had a couple of days in hand before my date of entry, hence my visit to the museum.

Muath said, "It's very far to the border, why don't you have something to eat? I can order and have it delivered." It was a thoughtful suggestion, but I was happy with my snacks and a coffee.

"What are you doing in Libya?"

"Nothing much", I said, "Just passing through." Was I a treasure hunter? Nope. Muath, like many people, could not understand why I would want to spend my own time and money rambling through North Africa when I could be back home earning a living. My reasons for travelling were at once simple and complex. Firstly, I was privileged; I had choices, and I chose to travel, not for fun but to learn something, which put me apart from the crowd perhaps, but there were plenty of like-minded travellers from rich countries out there. It was an imbalance of power that allowed people like me to travel to Egypt, and other poorer countries, and then go home and describe those places on my own terms, without sanction or permission, an act that would not be reciprocated. Travel writing is implicated in colonialism, one had to admit.

Muath pointedly asked, "Why do you travel?"

I answered, "Because I can; because I want to find something out for myself first hand and not rely on others' reports. Take Islam, for example. When people talk about "Islam" in the West they only see one colour; however, Islam is perhaps a dozen colours. You have to travel to see the differences."

"Hundreds of shades," Muath interjected. My interlocutor was from Upper Egypt; he belonged to a large Bedouin family and had ten siblings. This background perhaps accounted for his responsible attitude and good verbal communication skills, the latter trait something I had noticed about Bedouins whenever I had interacted with them, along with their good manners and upright body posture. Muath smoked and sipped a Turkish coffee, his only pleasures in life. He frankly and without embarrassment told me that as a young, single Muslim man his opportunities for sexual activity were non-existent, yet another frustration for this business graduate who could not find suitable employment in Alexandria. It was his ambition to become a father so he could have a son to love, and to love him. I wished him luck with that. Why couldn't he find a job?

"There are not enough jobs. Egypt is poor because all the money was stolen by government officials. Without *wasta*, there is no way to get a good job here. They are reserved for those in government and their families and connections. We need factories, not just tourism. I worked in an office in Alexandria, but my employer forced me to work twelve hours a day, and after paying for rent and expenses I had no money left, there was no point in doing it. My brother helped me get this job and I use my time to study Italian." I admired Muath for using his down time to learn another language, which showed he had determination, but his story was similar to Nasser's: only by going abroad would he be able to get out of a dead-end existence.

Like many Egyptians, Muath had a low opinion of Mubarak. "Most of the country's wealth is held by ten percent of the population, everyone else is just making ends meet. The key to getting on is to get property or land and then play the speculation game. This is what Egypt is all about." The young graduate went on to describe how the seaside resorts were as much a product of speculation as of genuine demand. There was no level playing field: government officials held all the advantages since they could approve or reject planning applications at will. As a social class, they gave one another favourable treatment. In other words, the whole social and economic system was rotten to the core. "Mubarak is responsible for this system," Muath coolly pointed out. Like Nasser, he felt another revolution was just around the corner, and that it would not be led by the Islamists, but by secular activists. It was certainly true that Egypt had some kind of liberal political tradition, unlike Saudi Arabia, and that the educated youth had a healthy interest in politics. Muath, for example, struck me as being very well informed, and sensibly realized that religion was not in and of itself going to resolve all that ailed contemporary Egypt.

After an hour, I reluctantly left the museum, really wanting to stay with Muath but needing to leave. Time was getting on and I still had to hitch a ride to Marsa, and so parted company with the young Egyptian man who was a credit to his country. He took my details, expressing a desire to work abroad, but in his well-mannered way did not directly ask for help. As we shook hands he urged me to have many sons. "I'll try," I said, half-heartedly, and then walked back down the access road to the coastal highway. After a short time, I managed to flag down a speeding minibus that took me 300 kilometres up the road under dramatic cloud-filled skies, one of the most enjoyable rides of my journey.

THERE IS something romantic about turning up at a seaside resort out of season, but the romance soon wears off. I arrived at Marsa Matrouh at night, and scrambled to find a hotel. Just off the *corniche* I found one, which had a name that linked it to Florida. As hotels go, it had many pretensions, but it also had two advantages: it was cheap, and the rooms had a sea view. A stiff breeze blew in off the Mediterranean, and the curtains flailed about wildly, as the concierge opened the window to my room. When the young man left, I tipped him, wanting an ally in the empty hotel, but he came right back with a bar of soap and extra toilet paper, thus fulfilling all his obligations to me. The room was rather small, but the balcony was roomy, and so I sat in it and read, and sipped beer, acting the tourist. I tried reading Albert Camus's *The Rebel*, but gave up on it, finding the book obtuse and unreadable. Fortunately, I had Ben Jelloun's *This Blinding*

Absence of Light to hand, a brilliantly imagined account of a real life story written somewhat in the manner of Truman Capote's *In Cold Blood*, except told in the first person. Anyone who wants to gain some insight into the value of Islam should read Jelloun's account of how a political prisoner survives a sadistic incarceration in Morocco by believing in God and, by inference, believing in himself. The weather over the Mediterranean had permanently cooled, but I sat and read in my shorts enjoying the refreshing cold front air. Marsa Matrouh was completely empty save for a few barmy Europeans sunning themselves on the sands. Alas the Rommel Beach bunker museum was closed when I dropped by one morning, bored to death and looking for a diversion. Then an email from Libya confirmed my travel arrangements, and I packed and hurriedly journeyed westwards on another flying minibus, my dash across Libya beginning in Marsa; *Sturm, Schwung, Wucht.*

9

THE SIX-DAY DASH

To open a map of Libya in the morning and stare at it was to immerse oneself in a wondrous dreamscape. My colourful map of this enormous country, which I studied daily in Egypt, was particularly conducive to armchair travelling: sand seas, rock deserts, high plateaus, depressions, oases, mountain ranges, dried out wadis, swamps and salt marshes all combined in a fantastically rugged interior. Cultural references glossed "Prehistoric Rock Art", "Tuareg Mosque", "Tombs of the Bani Khattah Rulers", and "Camel Market", were equally intriguing. Clearly, there was a whole world out there in Libya's back yard, one little known or reported on, yet a rich world; a social world like that described in Ibrahim Al-Koni's dreamy, elliptical novels; a world full of sages, diviners, prophesies, demons, curses and vengeance, but also of love, passion and heroism. The desert was not really empty; it was full of the past, and present, and it had a future. Modern Libya was covered in oil wells, the new oases, and these settlements were linked to the coast by aqueducts and asphalt roads. It was true, however, that the majority of Libya's relatively small population lived along the country's long coastline, as has been the case since the primacy of the Phoenicians, and it was along this coastline that I intended to travel from

Egypt to Tunisia, a journey that could be done in four days, but which I planned to do in six, allowing for a full day's rest en route.

<hr>

It took a while to find the bus station on the west side of Marsa Matrouh; most traffic heading out of town moved eastwards, as did the tourist flow – travelling east to west in North Africa was against the grain, but quite possible if one did it in short bursts, like the short burst from Marsa to the Egyptian border town of Soloum, my next destination. The station, when I found it, was quiet, and business slow. I quickly found a ride in a shared minibus, but I had to negotiate the price. The driver was a Bedouin who shouted rather than talked: "THALATHEEN!!" He wanted 30 Egyptian pounds to take me up the road. I knew that was over the odds, but instead of going crazy, as Stefanie might have, I put in an offer which I knew to be about right: *ashreen*, 20, I said. The driver shouted, "KHAMSASHREEN!!" He said 25 pounds in a way that settled it, and I did not mind paying considering I had three pieces of luggage, all of which had to be loaded up onto the roof rack; I was all too pleased to be getting out of Marsa, and away from the *Psycho* atmosphere of the empty hotel. My luggage was loaded up and we waited for more passengers. Everything was handled in the usual Arab way, without fuss or undue haste, and when the minibus was full off we went. The driver, who chain-smoked, handled the vehicle confidently, his large tattooed hand shifting the sheepskin-covered gear stick with consummate skill. A road sign indicated Soloum was 225 kilometres distant. The road we travelled on was in good repair, and the distance was slashed away as we hurtled westwards, a dozen local passengers, the experienced driver, and I. There were a surprising number of dwellings along the highway in this faraway stretch of Egyptian territory, and there were even a few public bus shelters, but the only off-road transport to be seen was the donkey and cart. The villagers had a marginal existence, having nothing but a few goats and fruit trees to live by. The patches of cultivated trees were the only trees in this parched landscape, however, which was to all intents and purposes a desert. Small whorls of dust chased us along.

We stopped for lunch at a roadside cafeteria, the driver shrewdly collecting our fares before parking. In the large, well-run cafeteria I ordered beans, salad and bread. The beans, prepared in tomato sauce with some fatty mutton added for flavour, were excellent. The others all ate, too, and this set everyone up nicely for the second stage of the drive. The road, hitherto flat, started to undulate. About 20 kilometres from Soloum one could see the Libyan Plateau, an immense land form that marked the end of Egypt and the beginning of Cyrenaica. Traditionally, the only way through was at the Halfaya Pass, but here at Soloum a hairpin road had been built up the side of the plateau, a more direct route for the big cargo trucks that plied between Libya and Egypt. It was only when we arrived in town that this zigzagging road, and the slow-moving transports on it, became visible. Soloum was, predictably, a one-street town; a ribbon of development by the highway. The driver of the minibus dropped me off at a small square where there was three guesthouses to choose from; I chose the "ElGezer", for its name, and took a three-bed room rather than stay in the dingy dormitory. The El-Gezer was a dump, but the concierge was civil enough and I was able to get a discount on the room. There was nowhere to go and nothing to do in town, so I puffed on a hookah pipe and chatted with the concierge, who spoke a little English, in the evening. As the night wore on, more transients drifted into the guesthouse, all of us awaiting the morning when we would head to the border.

ANTICIPATION WOKE me up early the next day, but there was absolutely no point in actually getting up; this much I had learnt. Instead, I forced myself to stay in bed until I heard activity outside in the street whereupon I dressed and went for a coffee. Sitting with me at the café was a Libyan man, who seemed keen to make friends and get my information. We agreed to share a taxi to the border and left after a while in an estate car driven by a local who could have done the trip blindfolded. The Libyan kept asking me for this and that bit of information, and constantly sought to reassure me about the border crossing, because in fact I had no idea where I was going or how one was supposed to enter Libya. In theory, my escort would be waiting with the paperwork, but where exactly would he be waiting? I had merely been told that he would be on the "other side." We climbed up the hairpin road slowly and then quickly covered the remaining few kilometres to the border, a barren, windswept place. Our passports were checked thrice even before we got to the immigration proper – the Egyptians were nervous about something. At the first gate I got out of the taxi, thinking it would be unwise to go on without first hearing from my contact. I then got a text message from Mahjub, the escort and driver, informing me that he was waiting for me and that I should proceed through Egyptian immigration. I did so, but leaving Egypt was not straightforward, and involved a long round of inspections, security checks, luggage searches and, a last little slap, payment for an exit stamp. A company of Egyptian soldiers were guarding the road between the Egyptian and Libyan checkpoints, their guns bristling. I later learned they were there to stop an aid convoy that was on its way from Britain to Gaza; so much for Arab solidarity.

I sat on my suitcase just before the Libyan checkpoint and enjoyed the afternoon sun, sipping a coffee bought at a kiosk, and joshed a bit with the Libyan border guards, who were more relaxed than their Egyptian counterparts. One by one people came up to me, asked me what I was doing, placed phone calls on my behalf, and finally asked me if I wanted to pay $50 for a visa. Making such a bribe would have got me into Libya, but there was the problem of getting out – tourists had to exit the country accompanied by their escort. Besides, the agreement with the Libyan travel agent had been made orally and everything was based on trust: it would not have been right to leave my escort in the lurch; he had, after all, come a long way to meet me. I waited and waited as a steady stream of vehicles and trucks trundled past into the all-green flag nation, and then at last my escort turned up.

"Meester Garee…"

I said, "Yes, that's me old boy, good to see you," or words to that effect.

A gentle giant of a Tuareg tribesman, dressed in jeans and a T-shirt, and with sunglasses pushed up over his knitted forehead, greeted me warmly, and then told me to wait. I was slightly agitated, not caring to hang about any longer and wondering where my escort's vehicle was: we were on my coin now, and I wanted action. Inevitably, complications had to be dealt with and paperwork processed, and so further patience was required. Finally, we got the all-clear and we walked into Libya, Mahjub and his sidekick Akil carrying two of my three pieces of luggage. It had taken the best part of a day to go less than ten kilometres.

***

In Mahjub's resplendent sports utility vehicle, we drove away from the border. I sat in the roomy front passenger seat and arranged myself for the road trip ahead, finding a spot each for my map, camera and notebook. At first, I was unhappy about Akil's presence, but it was, from a local point of view, common sense for a driver to take a companion with him on such a long journey, for reasons of security as much as for the company. Akil was young, and generally useless, but his English was a bit better than Mahjub's, and he also had a slightly better knowledge of our route, the good-hearted driver clueless about everything – this job was an apprenticeship for him. So, there we were: three amigos on the road to Tripoli.

There was no excitement, merely relief, now that I was actually in Libya. The road trip ahead I regarded as a bit of time off almost; I would not have to think much over the next six days, and could sit back and enjoy the ride. Certainly Libya was a different kettle of fish compared to Egypt: the road was better, the sky seemed bigger, and settlements were less populated. However, there were the familiar paraphernalia of a North African police state: road blocks, edgy and abusive guardsmen, and a suspicion of anyone waving a camera about. We quickly passed through Qasr al Jady, Kambut and Al Qa'rah, stopping only briefly so I could change some money at a bank, where my US dollars were readily welcomed even though the Euro was now the foreign currency of choice in much of North Africa. We stopped again to eat lunch at a roadside cafeteria, the food a cut above that of Egypt and very filling; the border crossing had been very stressful, and this translated itself into a ravenous hunger. My escorts were also hungry having not eaten during the day. By observing the way people were dressed, and the leisurely way they ate large meals, it was obvious to me that Libya was much better off than Egypt; the people less poor. The generalization held pretty much across the board, except in the quality of housing, which was almost equally bad in both countries.

After lunch, we carried on driving westwards towards Tobruk, which is where I would spend my first night in Libya, but not before visiting the Commonwealth War Cemetery on the outskirts of town, which was located just off the highway we were driving on. Under a moody late afternoon sky, I let my escort go off for an hour and entered The Tobruk War Cemetery, resting place of 2479 allied servicemen, by myself. There was very little nearby to indicate the fierceness of the battle that raged around the port city for 240 days from April 1941 onwards; some barbed wire and rusting tin cans nearby were not necessarily from World War II. But the cemetery itself, and a

German one not far away that contained over 6000 graves, spoke volumes. Tobruk eventually fell to Rommel's Afrika Korps, testament to the German field marshal's professionalism. But it was in the fire and brimstone of the siege of Tobruk that the British army got the measure of their German counterparts, developing new tactics and testing new weapons for future reference. The fact that Tobruk held out so long sent a strong message to Berlin, something along the lines of, "This war is not going to be the pushover you thought it was going to be, and in fact you now have a fight on your hands." The cost of sending that message was of course evident in the neatly landscaped cemetery that I walked around, a few appropriate words engraved on every marble gravestone. The first one I examined read, "Signalman F.W. Coombs, Royal Signals, 19th December 1942, Age 31...In Memory of a Loving Husband and Daddy...Sleep My Darling."

Coombs may have died in the battle to retake Tobruk, or at some other skirmish. On and on the graves bore witness to the fallen; I counted 18 graves belonging to soldiers of the Sudan Defence Force, among the many Muslim graves of the British Imperial Indian and African regiments. A large part of the cemetery was dedicated to men of the Australian Imperial Force, the soldiers who heroically beat back the initial assaults on Tobruk; another special section of the cemetery had been reserved for officers and men of the Polish Independent Brigade, and I was glad to see the Poles, who fought with such valour alongside the British, especially honoured here in the Libyan desert. Lengthening shadows thrown from the gravestones symbolized the backbone of those defenders of Tobruk.

My escort later returned, and we immediately drove away from the cemetery and into town, a nondescript sort of place as it turned out, but without the squalor of an average Egyptian town. There was a lot of haphazard construction all over the place though, a sign of a lack of proper planning, and many unfinished apartments were unoccupied. Downtown proved to be a kind of socialist version of Saudi Arabia; it had everything one might need, but in scarce supply. I found a suitable hotel and booked in; Mahjub and Akil went off to I knew not where. They assured me they would be back at eight the next morning. The hotel was simple, but adequate in every respect. Actually I had wanted to camp out in the desert, but my escort did not think this was a good idea; they were responsible for me, and preferred to have me locked up in a hotel where I could be easily found. In the evening, I went for a walk around the pleasant and fairly quiet streets near the hotel, and almost immediately discovered Tobruk Church. The sanctuary, a backdrop of many a British serviceman's souvenir photo, appeared to be disused. The church was guarded by two World War II-vintage anti-tank cannons, which made it look like a temporary military head-quarters. The stores in town by the church were mostly shut, and so I settled for an espresso coffee at a local café, Italian tastes popping up for the first time. The young men of the town were altogether more western fashion-conscious than their Egyptian counterparts, and one could buy a decent western-style suit in Tobruk, not that I was in the market for one. From the rooftop of the hotel, I watched the sun go down on the minarets of Tobruk; a blood-red sky that had at one time silhouetted British and Australian soldiers as they went out on their aggressive night patrols.

There were few guests at the hotel, and it was not until I had breakfast the next morning that I bumped into an Englishman, the first I had spoken to since Saudi Arabia. He had been part of the convoy delivering aid to the emasculated Gaza Strip. The Egyptians had turned his group back at the border and, having parted company with the convoy my breakfast companion was now at a loose end and without an escort. He wanted to tag along with me, but I did not think this was a good idea and, remembering Stefanie, cruelly sent him in the direction of the local bus station.

It was I who was left alone in the hotel though, the other two amigos apparently taking the opportunity to catch up on lost sleep; to my intense annoyance they did not arrive to pick me up until eleven o'clock. In view of this tardy performance, I took Mahjub, the eldest and therefore the responsible party, to one side and gave him a very quiet and calm dressing down, which he took good-naturedly, almost not taking me seriously since I had not displayed any anger. This is one of the unfortunate things about the Middle East: politicians and leaders believe, with some justification, that in order to get instructions followed it is necessary to make people fear them, which creates a self-reinforcing cycle of abuse. I needed to keep Mahjub and Akil on my side, without alienating them or becoming too familiar with them, a delicate balancing act. A little tardiness may seem trivial, and they had certainly thought so, but it badly delayed us, and the time would be hard to make up, as I tried to explain to Mahjub, who clearly had not thought of half of the things I had been thinking of, like the position of the sun at different times of the day, for example. We eventually got underway, driving out of Tobruk at high speed westwards, and the fun of the drive soon made me forget the morning's frustration.

We drove along at a steady clip, the Mediterranean to our right, and either the desert or an escarpment to our left. It was the road trip I had dreamed of when watching videos of Libya in advance of my travels; the sea was pretty, the sky big; there was sunshine, and there were clouds. Old telegraph poles cut across the empty landscape, one of the few signs of modern life in a rapeseed yellow desert. Early in the afternoon we passed through the coastal town of Derna, a place that was hard to assess from a speeding car, but it looked like a busy enough little port with its warehouses and lines of imported German cars. On the way through town I noticed a young boy crossing the road, looking every inch the dignified Arab in his smartly pressed long shirt. The sight of this boy in his shirt represented a direct cultural connection to Arabia, a connection that I would see and apprehend again and again in North Africa, an important thread to my journey. Near Derna, Mahjub made a brief diversion and drove us into the mountains to some prehistoric cave or other. In order to save time, I told him that we would give it a miss, and he happily drove us back to the coast, sharing my indifference to this particular tourist attraction.

Cyrene, an ancient city founded by the Greeks in the foothills above the Mediterranean, and after which Cyrenaica was named, was of more interest to me, and I wanted to get there before it got dark, something we achieved. The ruins were announced by protruding bits of walls and foundations here and there as we drove up into the hills from the coastal plain. At Cyrene proper, I again left my escort and quietly stepped into the quite open and unpatrolled ruins by myself. The site was magical for the lack of tourist infrastructure; a lone ticket office was closed. The afternoon sky clouded over, and the diffused light lit the Roman columns and walls evenly. Many headless statues stood about like mannequins, paradoxically adding considerable movement to the ruins by their presence. The statues, some of which had been removed and placed in a nearby museum, fascinated me; in their poses and attitudes we come close to feeling the ancient world, a world that cannot be intellectually reconstructed despite all our best imaginative efforts. That ancient world was not unchanging, and the Greek city was later conquered by the Phoenicians and then the Romans, the latter building their characteristically impressive structures, including a huge amphitheatre and two enormous temples, on top of the original city. But the statuary was Greek, in spirit if not materially, and much of it mesmerised in its grace, smoothness, and lack of shame or self-consciousness. I ranged about the amphitheatre and the walls and the slopes of Cyrene, revelling in the unpackaged and unguided freedom of the moment, the coastal plain stretching away below me like an ancient Greek orchard.

Satisfied with my brief visit to Cyrene, I returned to the car where I woke up the sleepy pair.

"Tired Meester Garee?" Akil asked, and I was slightly, but I insisted that we get to Benghazi that evening.

Akil protested, "Benghazi is very far, maybe three hours..." Quite true, I replied, and this was of course the three hours he had spent in bed that morning. Mahjub smiled at my riposte, and he smartly drove down the hill to the coast where we picked up the main highway. The road veered inland, over a brown, rusty soil, and then ran down by the sea again. We passed through an area of greenness which appeared to include fruit trees, so I was not completely imagining the orchard, and then over a river into a gorgeous sunset, tail lights of other cars guiding us westwards, my escort not bothering with prayers. We got to Benghazi late, found accommodation for the night, and retired without further exploring the town, the sight of Colonel Gaddafi dressed in a fancy European military uniform on a billboard enough to let me know this town was probably a dull sort of place, completely under the dictator's thumb.

Day three of the road trip began on time. We planned to drive from Benghazi around the Gulf of Sirte to Misratah, more than 800 kilometres distant. Dispensing with breakfast, and munching on a few dates instead, Mahjub donned his sunglasses and hit the gas. We sped past some unimaginative revolutionary monument, a new football stadium, and over a new bridge into the desert on a tree-lined dual carriageway. The trees had obviously been planted as a beautification effort, and considerable money must also have been put into the development of agriculture, of which there was some evidence by the roadside. In one parched field a tractor was active, though doing exactly what was hard to say. Probably the driver was on his way home. It seemed to me that if you ploughed this type of ground the soil would blow away. Trees dotted about on the horizon shimmered like a mirage; maybe they were an illusion. Electrical pylons stretched down the sides of the road like columns of soldiers, there being no other practical way to design the electricity grid, and they soon became the only landmarks in a featureless landscape. We hurtled along at 140 kilometres per hour, at first in a southerly direction, and then north-westwards after passing through Al Uqaylah. I was cut off from the outside world in the car, and at times wondered why I was bothering with this trip at all, but it was better than flying, and at least I had got to see Cyrene. There was not much to be seen before Misratah, at least not from the highway. In places the road was as straight as a Roman road, quite possibly because it was one, and a cloudless sky made the drive more monotonous than it might have been otherwise. Mahjub never let up, pounding his heart with his fist and sighing in some emotional gesture that seemed to say, "This is killing me." I knew he had not had enough sleep the night before, and watched him in case he dropped off at the wheel, which would have been unfortunate considering he was not slowing for bends in the road, but in the end we were fine. Around the Gulf of Sirte near the road I noticed unoccupied residences, perhaps a failed attempt to settle Bedouins. Salt flats added to a desolation only broken up by a fenced-off oil refinery. Free-range camels interrupted our mad dash, forcing us to reduce speed to a crawl as they lazily strolled across the highway, but mostly it was a pell-mell drive. A road sign indicated Misratah was still 300 kilometres away, and on seeing this sign I sighed and banged my chest, which Mahjub thought was funny. We stopped for lunch in Sirte, Colonel Gaddafi's home town, eating a scratch lunch at a roadside café, and followed this with a short nap before the home straight 249-kilometre run into Misratah along a new dual carriageway. We made it in good time, and after a lengthy search for suitable accommodation, I ended up staying in a state-run hotel next to the local airport.

The surly staff at the Soviet-style hotel put me on the third floor where all the decrepit rooms used by airline staff were found. My room had witnessed a few debauched parties judging by the cigarette burns and casual damage to the furnishings. To get one of the better rooms on the first or second floors one had to pay a premium. I forget how much the premium was, but on principle I was not going to pay it, and so took the insult instead. The room was not that bad, probably state of the art in 1970; it was the bait and switch tactics that so irritated. It was too late to go anywhere else though as my escort had disappeared. It seemed Mahjub and Akil were sleeping in our large vehicle, which could be converted into mobile sleeping quarters, a much better option than staying in a hotel in my view, though a slightly less secure one. After a hot shower, something not available in the car, I slept like a Siberian log behind sun-reflecting curtains. In the morning, I walked about the Stalinesque corridors of the hotel in search of breakfast, eventually finding the bread, boiled eggs and jam *ménage-à-trois* sitting on buffet tables in a large, underused dining room. A few business types were loading up on the tuck, and I forcefed myself thinking we might have a long day ahead. The hotel was a miserable place, and when Mahjub arrived to pick me up, a bit late naturally, I almost gave him a hug. Onward to Tripoli at a pace was the day's agenda; Akil had dressed in a suit and winkle pickers for the occasion.

<hr>

ON THE WAY TO TRIPOLI, there was another "big city" for us to visit: Leptis Magna. The Romans colonized Africa long before the Arabs, and like all imperialists, built on a scale and grandeur that almost outdid their home metropolis. Leptis, located on the Libyan coast 130 kilometres east of Tripoli (not be confused with Lebanon's port city of the same name), was en route and I saw no reason not to drop by. By lunchtime we were in the vicinity and after a decent meal at a roadside café we found the entrance to the ruins, a huge site only partly excavated. Mahjub and Akil waited for me in the car while I went off on a quick exploration. There were a scattering of European tourists at Leptis, all of whom had come in a tour group. Some of these tourists were having their bags searched, just in case they were kleptomaniac treasure hunters, or so I was informed by Salman, my English-fluent tour guide. Unfortunately, romping about Leptis Magna alone was not allowed.

"Yes, we open the tourists' bags. Some of them don't like it; and then we find they have taken something." How excruciatingly embarrassing! As if colonizing Libya and ripping off their resources had not been bad enough, some Europeans engaged in petty theft when they were on holiday there. I assured Salman that I had no interest in whipping away any "treasure." In fact, my purpose in visiting the ruins was to meet someone like him, someone I could chat to other than my escort.

Salman spoke English with the intonations of an Oxford don; he was one of those people who had never stepped outside their country but who listened to BBC broadcasts regularly and could imitate Received Pronunciation very well. We walked into a city founded by the Phoenicians, adopted by the Romans, and then conquered in turn by the Vandals and the Berbers, the latter ransacking it. The city was re-taken by the Byzantines, but fell into disuse by the time of the Arab conquest. There really was not much more I needed to know. Salman thought otherwise and launched into a running commentary.

"Ah, here we have Severus's Arch, a fine example of…" A fine example of an arch; okay got it. Nice carvings of nymphs there, but what about Gaddafi? We walked down the old main street of the city, dead straight walls either side concealing unearthed dwellings.

"That is where the horses were tied and watered…"

"Amazing…so, tell me Salman, what you think of Gaddafi?" Salman frowned and walked on briskly.

"This market was built by the Phoenicians and is over 3000 years old…"

Muammar Mohammed al-Gaddafi had ruled Libya since a military coup d'état brought him to power in 1969. Considered a troublemaker in the West, he had indeed got up to all kinds of mischief over the years, but his real sin was not to accept subservience to western interests; he had been an independent operator in the Cold War, relying on the Soviets for weapons; he would not play US-ball. A sometimes buffoonish eccentric, Gaddafi was actually extremely adept at the political game; he had certainly succeeded in making everyone in Libya fear him. Over the years, the "Brother Leader" had had no compunction about having political opponents bumped off. Gaddafi had clung on to power in recent times by cultivating the Italians, and by quietly dropping his nuclear weapons programme; by starting to play ball in other words. However, a mass killing of an estimated 1200 political prisoners at the government's Abu Salim prison in 1996 was hard to cover up, and one felt that Gaddafi, or someone closely associated with him, had gone way too far, and that it was only a matter of time before he was toppled, a political dynasty ending with the wily, ruthless Bedouin who had created it. The Libyans most likely to stand up to Gaddafi were either dead or in exile and this lack of political opposition meant Gaddafi still continued to call the shots domestically, sometimes quite literally, at least for the moment.

"I mean do you think one of his sons is going to become the next president, or leader, of Libya?" I asked, directly.

"And over here is the frigidarium…one of the best examples…in summer the people would bathe here…" Salman was not paying much attention to my questions, and continued with his commentary. I took some photographs to give myself something to do. We had gone on a quick circuit of the forum, which must have been a huge and splendid building in its day. What impressed me the most were fragments of fallen lintels that had inscribed lettering on them. The Latin, when complete, spelled out the names of various emperors. This language seemed shockingly modern, as if it had been written yesterday. One fragment read "Britannic", which obviously formed a part of one emperor's formal title, a link to Britain.

I tried a slightly different tack. "Do you think Gaddafi is a good president, Salman?"

"To us, he is a brother; someone who is there to help the people." At least I now had him on-topic.

"What about the Abu Salim killings? Who was responsible for that?" This time, and perhaps surprisingly, Salman did not try to evade my question.

"Yes, I know about that. It was a mistake. Gaddafi said so, and had those responsible punished."

"But wasn't Gaddafi ultimately responsible? I do not believe such a pre-meditated massacre would have been carried out on an official's initiative. The order must have come from the top." When I said the top, I meant Gaddafi, or possibly someone in his family; one of Gaddafi's sons in particular has a reputation for thuggish behaviour. Salman did not disagree with my analysis. Overall, he thought the incident regrettable, but he did not care to dwell on it. He was a devout Muslim, and chose to bury his head in prayers rather than confront the dictator lording it over his country, which in the circumstances was not unwise.

"We have problems here. But we solve our problems our way, among the families. In Britain, you have social problems and high crime. We do not have these kinds of problems in Libya; our country is peaceful." Salman was putting a brave face on things. I knew that you did not kill 1200 people in an Arab country and get away with it. Gaddafi, a fifth-rate political thinker and blame-shifter, would indeed have to face the families of the 1200 sooner or later; the law of the desert demanded retribution, and I was reminded of something Gaddafi had written in his political treatise, *The Green Book:* "The code of ethics enforced by the tribe on its members is a kind of social education better and nobler than any school education."

Our lightning tour over, Salman and I shared a snack meal. The guide now relaxed knowing that I was not going to ask him any more awkward questions: eating together obliged me to cease serious-minded conversation. Salman recommended the nearby museum where all the statues found at the site had been placed, and after saying our goodbyes I went there to round off my tour. The statues all stood there, lifeless, among a huge mural of Gaddafi pumping both his arms in the air, the massed statues apparently cheering him on.

In Tripoli, I enjoyed 24 hours without my escort. After getting into town, and booking into a back street hotel, I gave Mahjub and Akil the day off and proceeded to explore the city alone on foot. Libya's capital was small compared to Cairo, and relatively undeveloped compared to any city in Saudi Arabia. Gaddafi, whose uniformed picture graced the main square downtown, had wasted a great deal of money on foreign military adventures, despite stating his objection on principle to such adventures in *The Green Book*, and Tripoli was still in recovery after years of isolation and UN-backed sanctions. There was then a curious mixture of poverty and wealth in a city that had been largely built with oil money. There were A-grade shops and hotels in Tripoli, but on average the place seemed to be in a condition of arrested development. The larger hotels, offices and banks did not seem to function very well; staff had a surliness about them that suggested they could not be fired. Out on the street, people were reasonably civil, and I noticed that the women were less rabbit-like than in Egypt and Arabia; they walked about with some confidence and were not afraid to talk to men, though of course they refrained from talking to strangers. At the downtown National Museum – lots more statues – I saw many European tourists. Libya was open to package tourism, obviously because the rake-off could be maximised and concentrated. These tourists took an exaggerated interest in the Roman sculptures and mosaics on display. I thought the less-visited exhibits on Bedouin culture and desert fauna more interesting insofar as they were deemed worthy of display at all; many modern Libyans had clearly lost contact with desert culture, and someone had thought it would be a good idea to remind them of where they came from. There were also all kinds of "revolutionary-era" documents from the 1970s on display, including a photograph of a younger Gaddafi opening the museum. More recent photographs showed The Brother Leader shaking hands with Silvio Berlusconi, Italy's Prime Minister. That left most of Gaddafi's intervening radical history unreported.

On the outskirts of Tripoli, I had noticed some nice gated villas with well-tended gardens, but downtown by the city's harbour the quality of the housing was generally poor, and the Italian-era colonial architecture had not been renovated since independence. Restaurants offered average food, although it was consistently better than what I had come across in Egypt. There was the usual lack of condiments, and lack of imagination in the cooking, though. In the same way I had found it difficult to purchase a map of Libya in Cairo, I found it difficult, impossible in fact, to buy a map of Tunisia in Tripoli. I did come across a book store that had an impressive collection of classic travel books on North Africa written by Europeans though, which only went to prove that my project was hardly original. Those Europeans had gone out into Libya's back yard; intrepid adventurers that they were. The change in the relative value of currencies, and travel restrictions, meant that such exploring was not really practical these days, not to someone like me anyway. Over lunch in the hotel restaurant, I perused the local English-language daily newspaper, searching for some juicy titbit. On the back page was a feature article about a visit to town by the computer software mogul Bill Gates. He was there with his wife Melinda. Only they were staying on his yacht, which was moored in the harbour. Bill had flown to Leptis Magna and Sabratha, another set of Roman ruins further up the coast, in a helicopter, while his wife had done some shopping in town. Apparently, the couple had "expressed their satisfaction and joy at visiting the Jamahiriya." Gates was impressed with Libya's "nice beaches", which he had viewed from the helicopter, the weather being too rough to voyage about in a yacht. If I had thought myself a superficial traveller, then at least I was in good company.

Akil came by my hotel that evening; he didn't know what to do in the city, and also wanted to check up on me. I sent him away not fancying a homosocial evening with him, which was rude of me. He had relatives in the neighbourhood; let him go to them, I reasoned. I paid for this unfriendliness the next day when Mahjub and Akil once more arrived late for our scheduled departure. This time, I did not really care – the Tunisian border was not that far away and by the end of the afternoon I would be in another country, goodbye Libya. We hurriedly loaded my bags into the car. The back streets of Tripoli were jammed with traffic, and it took some nifty manoeuvring to get our large vehicle out of the morass. Finally, we got underway on the main road driving westwards into a light sandstorm. About half way to the border, we stopped at the Roman ruins of Sabratha, the centrepiece of which was a huge re-constructed theatre. We took a quick walk around the terraced seating and stage of this impressive and quite modern looking building, ancestor to so many London and Broadway theatres. With a roof, and lit by torches, the setting would have really been something. An on-site museum contained some mosaics, and a striking bust of Jupiter, hair flowing wildly. Meanwhile, outside, the dust was starting to blow wildly, and so we left precipitously not bothering with the rest of the site that appeared to be made up of unreconstructed ruins.

The sandstorm added a touch of drama to the last leg of my dash across Libya, which took me up to the Tunisian border. There was not much to see along the road on the way: some abandoned residential developments; the occasional unused bus stop; the odd stand of limp looking trees. Nearer to the border, there were no settlements at all, which put Tripoli's importance as a population centre into some sort of perspective. Then, just beyond a newly-built service station that also appeared to be unused, we came to the border. There were some vehicles there, a few cafés and some police buildings, and that was all. In the swirling dust, a convoy of ultra-well-equipped four-wheel drive vehicles manned by a group of nattily dressed Austrians waited patiently to make the border crossing. I saw one of the Austrians hand all their passports to a Libyan immigration official, and then walk away, a trusting thing to do – I had no intention of letting my passport out of my sight. After a little snack, Mahjub and Akil helped me take my bags up to the Libyan border post where I carefully watched as two border officials casually manhandled my travel document, desperately trying to catch me out on something, and perplexed at the fact that my paperwork was in order. With no reason to detain me any further, and after the most perfunctory of searches, I was given permission to continue on foot to the Tunisian border. There was barely time to say goodbye to my escort, but we shook hands, and I slipped Mahjub my fee which he had not as yet asked for. He beamed a big smile after counting out the money I gave him, and for the first time in six days seemed to breathe easily.

10

FRANCOPHONE AFRICA

With a Tintin-like neckerchief over my nose, I scampered along in the dust storm, a bag in each hand and one on my back, in search of officialdom. The Tunisian side of the border proved to be a lot less formal than what I had experienced on the Libyan side, and when I did find the low key border post a smartly dressed gendarme waved me to the front of a queue of workers having their passports stamped. I did not especially want to jump the queue but, with authority on my side, was easily corrupted. Throwing an apologetic smile to the bundle wielding plebeians, I nuzzled up to the kiosk and waited for the entry stamp to be thumped in my burgundy travel document – Her Majesty, "Requests and requires." Did you read that bit, Freddie: *requires.* The immigration official asked me where I was staying, and this time I mentioned the name of a well-known international hotel chain to avoid further questions. Kachink. I was in, for up to 30 days.

The border crossing had been a memorable one, and I now found myself at the southern extremity of Tunisia, a remote sort of place. I passed through a gate and into a car park that reminded me of Khartoum in its crudeness. A large number of yellow French-made cars in varying states of decrepitude, but still working, languished on the dusty asphalt, and before long a pack of taxi drivers fell upon me like sharks swarming a bloodied prey. Hammerhead would take me into town, but wanted an exorbitant fee. Tiger and Bull got in on the act, and assured me that they could get me to nearby Ben Guerdane for half of what Hammerhead was quoting. A host of white-tips offered similar. I listened to the bids trying to guess the real price of the ride because there was no public transport to be had. I decided to try my hand at hitch-hiking, but that did not work; although one man kindly stopped, he was not going the same way as me, which seemed odd because there was only one road to Ben Guerdane. Eventually, I got into a small shared taxi paying a lot less than I had at first been quoted for the ride.

There were five of us crammed into the taxi, all males. I sat squeezed up against the window in a back seat. The 40-minute ride was interesting for all its discomfort, effectively my intro-duction to Tunisia, part of Francophone Africa. There was an immediate change in the landscape and in the mental atmosphere. Curiously, compared to Libya, Tunisia here in the south looked tatty, and the landscape rugged and bushy; it was littered with junk and car wrecks strewn over a vast open space. But the really significant difference was psychological, and I found my fellow passengers were not interested in me at all, perhaps sensing my low social status as evidenced by the fact I was travelling in a crowded taxi; the attitude was European. Actually, I was relived to not be the centre of attention, and glad of my new-found anonymity; I was back "on the road", escort-less.

At Ben Guerdane, I staggered out of the taxi, stiff as a board, and tried to get my bearings. The town was quite small, but had a couple of guesthouses, and I ruminated on staying there. However, the crappy restaurants, all of which only served some variant of *poulet*, were discouraging. There were some taxi agents near where I had been dropped off, and I asked about transport to Medenine. The response I got, a ridiculously inflated quote, became a pattern in Tunisia, and was probably a result of the large number of gullible European tourists that visited these

African shores every year, tourists I would bump up against very soon. Disappointed, and somewhat exasperated not to have been able to arrange transport out of town, I killed time eating a lollipop outside a general store. A woman came by. She was unveiled and wore her hair openly. I asked her, using my pigeon French for the first time in a long while, where I could find a shared taxi. She pointed out where the local *louage* station could be found, and then proceeded to flirt with me in a way that was disconcerting at first, but which quickly became pleasant. Where was I staying? Hmm, a good question. Not in Ben Guerdane, I finally decided after wavering a little. At the shared taxi rank, I asked around for a ride, and again encountered sharks, indeed some of them I recognized from the border. In the end, I got a ride with a driver for what I thought was a reasonable price, but which was in fact only a third of what the last passenger to board the taxi paid. With this last bit of gleaned intelligence I finally ascertained the going rate for a hired ride.

We drove off into a dry landscape, whorls of loose dust once more snaking across the road in front of us as if over a sand dune. We stopped to buy gas, a process that to my surprise involved jerry cans and not a pump. Still, the road was quite good. Still in the far reaches of provincial Tunisia, whitewashed settlements and olive groves came into view, some of the latter enormous in size. Elsewhere, trees had been planted in an obvious attempt to prevent desertification. Unlike the farm dwellings, the residential housing looked to be of poor quality, a sign of social class distinctions of the European type; Tunisia did not become Africa's most open economy by giving handouts out to the poor, and its "free market" economic policies had led to chronic unemployment, something evident in the shabby boon-docks we were driving through. After a couple of hours, we arrived in Medenine, a market town where I booked into the nearest hotel, a multi-storey concrete block that was something between a youth hostel and a Catholic seminary.

In Medenine, I gave myself a makeover getting my hair cut and my beard trimmed; amongst all the clean-shaven men, I had become a little self-conscious and did not want to be mistaken for an Islamist. In the barber's shop, where I waited my turn, a television was showing a British-made travel programme. The intrepid presenter impressed me at first, his location somewhere in a remote desert in South America, but when he described his car as his "teddy bear", I winced. Meanwhile, the barber nattered away like a Frenchman to his buddies who drifted in and out of his shop casually. Walking about town later that evening, I was shocked by the Frenchiness of it all: amorous couples canoodled openly, women dressed in fashionable jeans and Tshirts; two trousered women passed me by, one of them holding an authentically large just-baked baguette; store fronts were more often than not glossed in French: *Parfumerie, Pharmacie, Centre Public de Télécommunications, Librairie*, and so on. The French influence also expressed itself in a certain civility: car drivers in town did not necessarily assume they were participating in a race every time they went on a trip. I went for a *café au lait* and actually got some swift service from the *garçon*, and a decent *café*; modish leather jackets, mopeds and powerfully carcinogenic cigarettes all evoked France. None of these things should have surprised me, I suppose, since Tunisia had been a French protectorate for 75 years, only becoming independent after World War II. Medenine was rather poor, however; the infrastructure was dated; the road vehicles dilapidated.

The next leg of my journey, taken in a *louage* after several long and tedious attempts to negotiate a reasonable price, took me up to Gabès on the Mediterranean coast. We passed through more dry countryside dotted with farms and villas, and yet more extended olive groves. This time the vehicle was new and very comfortable; I had a proper amount of space, and the highly professional driver had managed to get my entire *bagages* in the rear boot, along with a dozen boxes of agricultural produce belonging to one of the other passengers. The sandstorm of the previous day had more or less subsided, and visibility was very good; the sky was blue, but there was no severe heat, a great relief. The other passengers, mostly young men, wore jackets considering the weather wintry. We got to Gabès in less than two hours and, not wanting to stay there, I immediately booked an onward ticket at the local train station. I was headed northwards towards Tunis, but wanted to stop somewhere en route, eventually choosing the seaside resort of Sousse on the basis of a rather enticing photograph that adorned a map that I had picked up in Medenine. The train would not leave until three that afternoon, which left me a couple of hours to take a look around town.

The first thing I noticed in Gabès, as in Medenine, was the profusion of national flags up all over the place, as if it were Independence Day every day here. Never far away from a flag, one would find a Big Brother type of image of the country's president Zine El Abidine Ben Ali, the man who crushed an Islamist movement and went on to become president of Tunisia in 1987. At first quite liberal, Ben Ali went on to become a dictator, a little-censured one since he played US ball very satisfactorily, although even George Bush once found it necessary to upbraid Ben Ali in public. But Ben Ali was a stubborn man who did not see the need to take advice from a junior, even if that junior was the president of the most powerful country in the world. The Tunisian president's personality cult was disturbing in its ubiquitousness; no one who had their photograph plastered up everywhere like this could possibly be a psychologically secure person, it was just absurd. I went to a local restaurant to try the food, and ate something forgettable. It was nice to see couples and friends enjoying one another, however, despite Ben Ali's totalitarianism. Back out in the street some schoolgirls said hello to me, showing a lot of self-confidence, and lack of regard for "honour." I said hello back, and then tried the park, which was not exactly inspiring, but at least there was a park, one with operational public toilets. A couple were sharing a romantic moment by a pond, but it was one of those self-conscious moments, and when the young woman saw me she walked away from her date, no doubt wanting to be chased. Leaving the park, I went back to the station an hour early, and found myself a spot to lie down on the platform, to the consternation of the stationmaster whose sense of order I upset.

The train arrived, and I got on it happy to be leaving the rather dull provincial city. On departure, the carriage was almost empty, and the windows could be opened, which made for a relaxing journey. Sousse was 263 kilometres to the north, so we were in for a lengthy ride. The railway line followed the coastline a short distance, at one point almost on top of a beach, but then swerved inland taking a direct route north; scenes of the beach were quickly replaced by that of an oil refinery, a scrap yard and an industrial complex of some kind. It was a balmy 30 degrees Celsius on the train, or so my pocket thermometer read. The other passengers were all wrapped up in woolly sweaters thinking it to be rather cool. We crossed a couple of small rivers and then ploughed on through open farmland, a bit greener here than in the south but still looking like it might become a desert in a year or two. Night fell, and I flipped out a book to read, enjoying the pleasure of travelling for the sake of it. A well-dressed conductor came along and punctiliously examined my ticket before punching a clean, neat hole through it. The conductor asked me where I was headed, and nodded his head approvingly when I said Sousse.

A German woman and her daughter walked stiffly out of the dining room and into the hotel's back yard area, chose some recliner chairs on the grass, and prepared themselves for a day by the pool. It seemed odd, because it was really rather cool outdoors, or at least it felt that way to a semi-acclimatized desert rat. I sat on the balcony of my room overlooking the pool, observing the young woman through my binoculars. It was my only distraction in the mind-blowingly boring resort. The girl read a fat paperback book, and then put it down, stretching out to catch some sun rays, an act of lunacy by local standards. She was never more than a foot away from her mother, the iron chaperone. I left the hotel in search of food, finally buying a beans and camel bones concoction from a local café. Outside on the street, the resort's main tourist drag was lightly populated by pasty-faced Europeans. Two Dutchman, dressed in skimpy shorts, were buying postcards, oblivious to the impropriety of their dress. Clearly, Tunisians were used to Europeans' strange behaviour and attire. I returned to the four-star hotel – four stars meant it was neither five star, nor three-star, and that is all – and nibbled the contents of the polystyrene box takeaway back on my balcony, my roving binoculars looking for the young German woman, only to see her march into lunch with her mum; I would not see them again.

After arriving in Sousse late, I had quickly found the main tourist quarter by the sea, and booked into the first decent hotel that presented itself, which turned out to be a sprawling four-star, high-rise pile of concrete, a sort of battery hen farm for sun-seeking Europeans on a budget. The place, as I discovered the next day, was full of German and French tourists having a late-season break. Some of them were deliriously happy, barking warm morning greetings to the hotel staff, who reciprocated with equal warmth. I suppose they counted as the ideal tourists. Others, especially singletons, appeared to be quite miserable, suffering from the classic I-don't-know-what-to-do-here syndrome. From the first minute, I felt I did not fit in to the scheme of things, and I almost left the next day, but stayed two nights wanting to observe a full day's cycle at the holiday camp, and take a short break; I had been travelling non-stop since leaving Tripoli. The hotel served up a reasonable breakfast, adding cereals and some scrambled eggs and sausages to the usual boiled eggs and bread fare. It was at breakfast that I took a good look at all the greying people, wondering if the countries of economically advanced Europe would be able to support state pensions in the future. Overall, I could not help feeling like a patient in a lunatic asylum; everyone was so dissociated from the real world around them.

A morning walk around town revealed it to be a typical

tourist centre in every way, full of restaurants, bars and souvenir shops. Ben Ali's face was all over the place and the beach front had Tunisian national flags planted every ten metres, a scene redolent of a Nuremberg rally. I did not get far enough out of town to see Sousse's non-tourist neighbourhoods, but I did take a stroll through the medina, or old town, located opposite the port. The medina, with its crenelated walls, palm trees, and narrow streets was every inch the average European's vision of what North Africa was about, all it lacked was a few French legionnaires. Every five paces, someone tried to sell me something: jewellery, a leather jacket, some traditional clothing, brass plates and fez hats were among the proffered items. It amazed me anybody would buy this stuff, but buy it tourists did, in their droves. Seeking an escape from the hoopla, I darted down a back alleyway eventually finding an exit from the maze. By the harbour, more tourists ambled about, clearly out of their element as the dust started to stir once more. In the harbour, an imitation Barbary Coast pirate ship sat unoccupied. I assumed it was some kind of floating restaurant, but later spied it edging up and down the coast out to sea, by far the most impressive sight of the day. On my second evening in town I went out in search of a consolation prize, and found it in the form of a litre-glass of beer, ice-cold in Sousse.

As I had arrived in town, so I left it, boarding a midday train bound for the capital at the local railway station. On the way to the station, and up and down the whole *corniche* the previous day in fact, I noticed a lot of unemployed young men sitting about nursing coffees. Most tourists did not "see" these "invisible" people, but I was very aware of their presence, representing a kind of parallel world to the hotel from which they were firmly excluded. About this, I wrote in my notebook, "It's the same story right across North Africa. It's surprising there is not more social discontent." Prescient words in hindsight. The train was packed with people heading back to the Tunisia's capital after enjoying a weekend getaway; here were the more affluent and well-educated Tunisians, some of them French-speaking. The way I was ignored was definitely French. Most of the females in the carriage were unveiled, and some of them rather coquettish, dangling shoes from their toes. As we travelled northwards, after departing Sousse, the countryside whizzed past, a more dwelling-dense version of what I had seen in the south, but featuring the same olive groves and whitewashed buildings. Flowers, hills and the occasional bit of woodland added variety to the scene, however. I had actually bought a first-class ticket, but there seemed to be very little difference between first and second class, as there was little difference between the variously starred hotels. The carriage soon filled up, and one or two people even had to stand the remaining distance to Tunis. On-train services came by, and I bought a chicken sandwich, which was perfectly made and included a little red chilli, a Moroccan touch.

Further north, the passing landscape became more picturesque and somewhat European with garden walls and neat paths scattered about, perhaps the legacy of long-gone French settlers. Conical cypresses pointed skywards, as if out of a Van Gogh painting. The mountains got higher and more dramatic with rain clouds over them. Stopping at Enfidha, I stuck my nose out of the open carriage door, and it felt decidedly fresh. We stopped at a couple more stations after that, before arriving at the bustling capital.

Tunis railway station, which could have passed for any French provincial station, was full of activity when we arrived in the middle of the afternoon. Beyond the station's forecourt it was even more crowded, manic even, between rows of very elegant colonial buildings. The density of people walking about seemed about equal in every street, and for a while this totally disorientated me. It is always the case that you can find a cheap hotel near a railway station though, and so I kept the station in view as I walked up and down the crowded streets, eventually finding a suitable place to stay on *Rue De Yougoslavie*, a street named after a state that no longer existed, an irony obviously lost on the city's civil administration.

Over the next few days, I roamed about Tunis on foot, a city that was still quite enchanting if seemingly overpopulated. The unemployed walked the streets together with the employed in a constant search for amusement and distraction. Avenue Habib Bourguiba, the main shopping thoroughfare, was a fine Parisian-style wide boulevard and had a fairly wide range of shops stocking the usual consumer goods. However, as in Libya, as soon as you moved away from the main road you entered a zone of scarcity, partly disguised by the grandeur of Tunis's fine architecture. On Bourguiba there were several cinemas offering a choice of films, decent if expensive restaurants, and modern fashion outlets. In a shopping arcade, I sat in a café and sipped a coffee. Hardly anyone was spending money in the arcade. At an international hotel, I drank a beer in the bar, enjoying the decadent atmosphere, emphasized by the orientalist paintings on the walls. Two Frenchman were chatting up a young Tunisian girl, negotiating some kind of debauchery. The girl smoked, smiled and then shook her head. An older woman dressed in a glamorous fluffy collared outfit came in by herself and sat near me, flashing a smile in my direction, a cue I did not take up. Such a gathering of strangers, entirely public, was unthinkable in Saudi Arabia, and I momentarily relished it before getting bored and leaving to explore more of the city. I soon found a café near a cinema full of men heartily swilling beers in an entirely civilized way. A lone female sat with three male friends, outnumbered about 100 to one. In the evening, *bon vivants* caroused around the back streets near the hotel, yelling loudly to vent their youthful frustrations. Tunisia was anomalous in many ways; outwardly "liberal" – 21 women sat in Tunisia's rubber stamp parliament, and polygamy was banned by law – there was yet zero political freedom in the country: all newspapers and magazines were rigorously censored, and non-governmental political activity barely existed. A popular online video-sharing website had been banned since November 1997, an almost pointless prohibition since denizens of the Internet soon learn how to access censored websites. Once held up as a paragon of virtue in Africa, Tunisia ranked near the bottom in democracy surveys, along with Saudi Arabia, Sudan and Eritrea. You sort of wondered what was going on behind the presidential palace gates.

Not wanting to hang around in Tunis too long, I soon set about trying to secure a tourist visa for onward travel through Algeria, a country that was the joker in the pack in my mind. Just finding the Algerian Consulate was a major job in itself. I set out to find it one morning in what passed for the diplomatic quarter. I had already booked a hotel in Algiers and had had the reservation emailed to me, a required document when applying for the visa. With this document in hand, I felt I had a 50-50 chance of getting what I wanted, though information I had read online indicated otherwise. After a long walk, I finally found the original location of the consulate, but the building had since been handed over to the Palestinian Liberation Organization. Asking about, I got the name of the street where the Algerian Consulate could be found, and hurried there in a taxi. I arrived just as the place was closing its gates, necessitating a return trip the next morning. On my second visit, I was ushered in to a waiting room after passing through some reinforced outer metal gates. Sitting in the room alone, I realized I was doing something non-routine, and I knew I would need to be very persuasive to get a visa. Unfortunately, the lady sent out to get rid of me insisted on speaking French, even though she understood English. We therefore entered a two-language argument, me pleading in English, her rejecting my pleas in French. It was hopeless; I was getting a firm brush off: *monsieur*, if you want a visa, get one in London not here in Tunisia, was the gist of the message being conveyed to me. Five minutes later I left the fortified consulate despondent. I was left with two options: either fly to Morocco, or pay for a travel agent to get me into Algeria. I did not want to repeat the Libyan escort experience in Algeria, so I booked a flight to Casablanca, and went off to a bar in a big huff.

MY MASTER PLAN TO travel the length of North Africa overland had been blown out of the water by a French-speaking apparatchik. And Algeria was such an interesting case too; it was the most French influenced country west of Arabia; the native Algerians had fought a thoroughly modern and thoroughly unpleasant war in order to gain independence, and then suffered a thoroughly nasty civil war beginning in 1990 when native Islamists won an election only to be denied power. Algeria was a country in recovery after that civil war, which still erupted now and again like a dormant volcano coming back to life. Like Saudi Arabia, Algeria was a vast country, a place I knew little about, but one generally thought of as being dangerous to travel to; you certainly would not have wanted to go anywhere near the place in the 1990s. I was therefore circumspect from the start, and always knew the difficult part would be getting in, but my starting point in Saudi Arabia had precluded getting the required visa in advance. I knew there were ways around the problem, but the effort involved in getting into Sudan and Libya had exhausted me, and I was simply not prepared to sit it out in Tunis waiting for paperwork to be processed. Algeria was out.

My failure to obtain a visa for Algeria meant I would have to break my no-fly rule for the third time. Resigned to flying again, I decided to exit Tunis as soon as possible without going anywhere near ancient Carthage just up the road. I booked my flight accordingly, and this left just one more day in town, which I spent wandering around the city's old medina. In the morning, it was dead quiet outside in the street and I surmised the day was a national holiday of some kind. Only when I saw lambs tied up to lamp posts awaiting slaughter did I twig that this was *Eid al Fitr*, the end of the Hajj, a time when Muslim families gathered for a feast. So, my last day in Tunis was spent walking around largely empty streets. Hoping to catch the zoo open, I walked some distance to the city park where the animal prison was located. Of course, it was closed. I snatched some glimpses of caged birds from the perimeter fence of the park; they were an unfortunate metaphor for the people of Tunisia: dignified and exotic, but trapped. The city was pleasingly tidy and free of litter near the zoo; warm lambs' blood flowed down street gutters as I walked past villas on my way back to the downtown area. A couple of police officers drove along the empty streets on large motorbikes, the type you see cameramen riding in the Tour de France every year. Nearer the town centre, the neighbourhoods became poorer and grimier, the sort of place Mohammed Bouazizi, who would trigger a major rebellion two months later by immolating himself, lived. In these neighbourhoods, with their broken and dilapidated houses, one could see, or apprehend, unemployment, near-desperation, and a lot of suppressed anger. On guard outside closed government buildings smartly dressed guardsmen toted ultra-modern French-made rifles.

On my last evening in Tunis, I went to the international hotel once more for dinner, drearily eating alone in a setting made for couples and families. But the few couples and families eating there seemed to be as miserable as me; it felt like we were attending the last supper in Hitler's bunker, and after paying the bill I left and returned directly to my hotel on *Rue De Yougoslavie* to get some rest, the evening not disturbed by carousing drunks on this religious night.

GROUND SPEED: 485 miles per hour, distance to destination 968 miles, altitude: 27,300 feet, Temperature outside: -36°F. It was so nice to know all these details of the near-empty flight I was on, but what did 485 miles per hour really mean? It meant something beyond my comprehension; the world of modern science required you to understand things that were not understandable in a tangible way. Of more interest to me was our route, as displayed on the overhead screen above my seat, which I cross-referenced with the expensive, but now redundant, hard copy map of Algeria sitting in my lap. The first recognizable place name was Annaba, an Algerian town not far from the Tunisian border. The flight path then slipped between Bizerte, Dougga and Béja, before arcing across Algeria's long, green coastal crescent. The flight statistics were given in both metric and imperial, or American customary measurements, and flashed on and off between a graphic of a plane edging its way along a line. We were soon over Béja headed to Constantine, a city of major historical importance in Algeria. After seeing this glorious place name my heart sank, and I suddenly lost interest in following our route, in the same way a child suddenly tires of playing with a toy. The in-flight atmosphere gradually sent me into a near-coma, and I remained inert and bored for the rest of the speeded-up journey to the westernmost end of Arab culture.

ANOTHER DAY ON THE ROAD, and I found myself at another airport that could have been anywhere, but was in fact in Casablanca, or close to it. The few passengers on the plane soon dispersed inside arrivals. I felt totally disorientated and unmotivated on arrival, and after picking up my suitcase from the surprisingly efficient baggage reclaim area, I sat at a café table and tried to collect myself. The first noticeable thing about Morocco was that it was rather expensive compared to the other countries I had visited, and it took a moment for me to accept the price asked for a sandwich and a soda. The airport had a slightly seedy air about it, filled with little gangs of men who seemed to be plotting a bank robbery, or some other mischief. It was almost certainly my imagination, but I thought I could smell the briny odour of the Atlantic; there were certainly molecules of unfamiliar perfumes and foods in the air. How to get into town was something of a mystery – I had again failed to do any research about this in advance, and there was no information counter inside the airport. Eventually I went there by train; a branch railway line conveniently began downstairs under the arrivals hall. The airport, I discovered, was located some distance from

the city, and before arriving in town we passed through an intermediate zone of wintry brown fields, an interlude that broke the
caravanserai spell of the airport. The first settlements in this land
as viewed from the train looked European with their garden
walls, hedgerows, and fruit trees. Kids played soccer here and
there on scratch pitches, as they did everywhere west of Arabia,
football being the great social leveller. Lots of green grass, ironically not to be found on the soccer pitch, indicated rain had
fallen in these parts recently. Within 20 minutes, the train arrived
at the Casa Voyageurs station, which meant we were in
Casablanca; this lack of concurrence between place name and
station name was to be my undoing later on.

Casablanca disappointed me, to put it mildly. Of course, the
city's name, like Khartoum's, was redolent, to a European or
American ear, of the colonial era, and was closely associated
with both a well-known Hollywood film, and a wartime allied
strategy conference. However, the city had a long history as a
port going back to Phoenician times, not gaining its present
name until the 18th century when Sultan Mohammed Ben
Abdallah constructed the first buildings of a town that would
later be expanded by the French. The Casa Voyageurs station, a
rather nasty modern pastiche design something between a
mosque and a cuckoo clock, did not reflect this long and illustrious history. It was a perfectly reasonable building, just not as
grand or as old as I had expected, and the cheap apartment
blocks, reflecting architecture from the 1969-89 period, were of a
progressively nastier look the newer they were. It was astound-
ingly quiet around the station, and then I remembered – the Hajj
week holiday. Everything was closed, which was just great: from
one shutdown city to another.

There were two accommodation options located either side of
the station: a classic cheap hotel, where the sheets are changed
twice a year, or a new-age "budget" hotel that felt like a tele-
phone exchange and was as cut off from reality as it was possible
to be. I took a room in the classic cheap hotel, a price quickly
agreed upon with the major-domo, who was having a major nap

when I walked in. Sheepskins strewn over chairs suggested a fairly cold winter was just around the corner. In Casablanca, the temperature was a few notches cooler than in Tunis, and blustery wet weather later in the evening was a major departure from what I had been used to on the trip thus far; it definitely felt like Europe was not far away now.

Taking advantage of the emptiness of the streets, I took a long hike around town in the morning. At first, I was completely lost, relying on the gravitational pull of the city centre to orientate me. Compared to Tunis, Casablanca's streets were grubby; the air was dirty, even without all the usual honking traffic; the residential buildings were up to date, but not exactly elegant. However, I felt Morocco was more authentically French than Tunisia, the latter exaggeratedly French. As I got closer to the port, a familiar sound assailed my ears, the cry of a seagull. It was feasting on sheep remains left at a street corner, of which there were quite a few strewn about that morning. Eventually, I found the town centre, which did indeed have the white houses and terraced buildings that gave the city its name, but many of the older buildings were in poor repair, and were gradually being replaced by taller, modern structures. It started to rain, and I did not have my rain cape with me, so I dived into the lobby of one high-rise, an international hotel. The place was another Captain Nemo space: cut off from the world and completely psychologically self-contained. Some French tourists were sitting in the lounge sipping mineral water and watching an inane programme on television; they were tired after a big round of sightseeing, and in need of the Great Third Eye. I asked at reception for a map of the city, and they told me to go buy one at a book store; so much for service! Less than 50 metres away, the rain tipped down on parked trailer trucks and a building site. I scooted past covering my head with a bit of cardboard after leaving the hotel, glad to be in the contingent world once more.

Determined to make the most of clearer weather, I went out early the next day. I retraced my steps into town, hoping to catch a glimpse of romance somewhere, but this was hard to find. For one thing, Casablanca, like many cities, had been surrendered to the motor car, even though it had not been built for car use. The result was traffic bottlenecks and pedestrian kill-zones. I walked down a tree-lined boulevard to the King Hassan II Mosque, a monumental house of worship built on reclaimed land. The mosque was not romantic; rather it was imposing: big and powerful looking. Symbolically, the huge mosque marked the western boundary of Islam, though of course the influence of that religion is global these days. The great mosque was closed, so I was left admiring it from the outside, which to a large degree was the way it was supposed to be admired, deliberately built as it was in the sea to reflect God's omnipotence over all. A walk around the sea wall to the harbour brought me to a dead end. The sea front had not been beautified at all and this reflected rather poorly on the city, a town of contrasts with upmarket areas besides neglected working class neighbour hoods. I walked through one of the latter quarters, pushing my way past men carting sheepskins away by the dozen. Children played football happily in a rough and ready playground, oblivious to the injustice of their circumstances.

On the way back to the station, I bought a little food at a small supermarket, since all the restaurants in town were closed for the holiday. There was nothing unusual about the store, except for a whole skinned sheep in someone's shopping basket, which struck a dissonant note in my brain. A child pawed one hoofed leg of the deceased lamb, a macabre touch. Also, the piles of spices lying on a table were unnaturally abundant, who would ever need so much chilli powder? The citizens of Casablanca did, obviously. The book store, when I found it, was closed, but a man was selling French-language magazines on the sidewalk outside. No maps. What was interesting was that there was not one single Spanish title among the journals and magazines; apparently no one had much interest in Spanish culture in Casablanca. At a large café, a host of men sat avidly watching a football game on television. It was impossible for me to find a seat, and so I took my coffee outside. By now, the sun had come out and the birds were singing, as if it were spring, when in fact the northern hemisphere was moving into winter. My internal season meter was thrown into confusion once again, and, feeling sort of frisky, I wondered if I should go on a side trip, perhaps south to Marrakech. Instead, the next morning, I headed northwards towards the Rif Mountains, thinking to put my tent and walking poles, which I had hauled across Africa, to some use.

IN MOROCCO, I got to enjoy train travel once more. The day started well, and after paying off the Adams-family hoteliers, I strode out into a city that was slowly coming back to life after the public holiday. At the local post office, I posted some papers back to England, paying through the nose for the service. So much did I pay, in fact, that I almost took the parcel back to throw away, only the prospect of losing some useful maps preventing me from taking this rash action. The postage in Morocco cost about ten times what it cost in Sudan and Libya, probably comparable to the rates in most European countries. But here was not Europe! If anyone thinks the privatization of postal services will result in anything good, they'd better think again, because private mail services, which my parcel had been sent by, cost the earth. A strong espresso at the station café did not help calm me down after this episode. Neither did a pretty French female tourist walking about on her own in the station's newsagents. She was going to Marrakech, I surmised, but when I saw her buy one of those turgid economics magazines, beloved of Eurocrats, I looked the other way and checked the clock on the wall: it was time to catch the train.

The train on the platform facing me, liveried in cream and orange, was an antique, but a solid one, and its promising presence put me in a good mood, especially when I got what used to count as a first-class compartment to myself, complete with a window that opened. It was the best possible start to the day, and I sat back to enjoy what would be a long ride, in the end somewhat longer than originally intended. Soon after pulling out of Casablanca, a couple of local men came and sat in my compartment. They were not very communicative, but they were polite and well-mannered, a contrast to two other fellows who would join me much later. After what seemed like a long time, as if the train had been watering, we pulled out of Casablanca and began the long run up Morocco's north-eastern seaboard.

My plan was to stop at Moulay El Mehdi station, 237 kilometres distant, and then hook up with a mountain road which traversed the Rif Mountain range. The idea was to get to Chefchaouen, a well-known mountain resort town, and then do a bit of hiking in the area. It was a good plan, the sort you dream up after studying maps, but everything depended on getting off the train in the right place. This was difficult because place names and station names did not match, and the stations along the line were not clearly marked in any case. The journey northwards below grey skies, via Morocco's capital Rabat, thus took on the character of a mystery ride. The urban areas we passed through, including the capital, were a mess, and the smell of rotting cabbage wafted through the carriage as the train trundled through poor-looking neighbourhoods. The countryside, wide open and green, was more encouraging, and its huge expanse surprising. In this vast emptiness, settlements were small and much of the land under-utilized. At Kenitra, a lot of local people gathered outside the train, including women colourfully dressed in traditional clothing, their hands hennaed for *Eid al Fitr*. But tons of trash were casually strewn about on the ground nearby, an unpleasant sight that clashed with one's expectations of what Morocco would be like. The further north we went, the richer the countryside appeared to become, climaxing in a stretch that was almost Oregon-like in its fertility and frontier feel. Yet a donkey and cart, seen here as seen all across North Africa, reminded me of where I was; prickly pear bushes an echo of faraway Asmara. The air blowing in through the window here was fresh and pleasant compared to the towns. Suddenly, in the middle of nowhere, the train stopped and we were delayed for over an hour. The wait, in warm afternoon sun, dragged on, and then just as suddenly we began moving again, in an easterly direction according to my compass.

Moulay El Mehdi must be near by now, I reasoned, but we were spending an inordinate amount of time heading eastwards. A branch of the railway line did in fact go due eastwards to Moulay-Idriss, and then continued on to Fez, the well-known northern cultural centre popular with tourists. Were we headed to Fez? Was I on the wrong train? Feeling a little tired, I stretched out on the seat and took a catnap, one of the best ways to deal with a stressful situation. After a while, I opened my resting eyes and glanced at the compass. The needle still pointed eastwards. This was ridiculous. I placed the compass in different places, seeing if the reading would change, but it did not. At that moment, the conductor came by and told me, in a mixture of Arabic and French that I had missed my stop, and we were now well on our way to Tangiers. So much for my brilliant mountain road linkup plan, and so much for my pocket compass! Another man, a resident of Chefchaouen who spoke some English, informed that it would not have been easy to find transport on the mountain road anyway, an obvious point, but in my experience where there is a road there is a way. All was speculation now, and I let it go.

The train clattered on, sometimes quite fast and at other times slowing to a crawl. The Atlantic, which had been out of sight for much of the ride, re-appeared like a trusty, reliable friend; tankers sailed up and down its majestic, authoritative waters reflecting the light fantastic as they ploughed through the water like aircraft carriers. A grassy rolling countryside rolled by. A group of cheerful young men, probably farm hands, waved to the train from atop a pickup truck as we shot past, an innocent gesture. But the settlements by the railroad soon became boxy and ugly, laundry hung out to dry and randomly placed electricity pylons now a familiar part of the landscape.

Not far out from Tangiers, near some Atlantic seaside resort or other, two men got on the train. They were American tourists.

I had been standing in the corridor outside my compartment when they bundled past me into the compartment. One of them, the younger one, promptly sat down on the seat I had been sitting on. He then stretched out and fell asleep. I was a bit annoyed to lose my seat to this interloper. But it was my fault I had lost the seat. It was no major loss, however, and I simply sat opposite, facing the direction the train was moving in for the first time, and rearranged my notebook, in which I had only scribbled desultory notes that afternoon. The second man, older and more diffident than the youthful slob who had not bothered to take his shoes off, asked me where I was from by way of starting a conversation. How was I to answer that question? Americans always reply immediately and with great gusto, something along the lines of "Upstate New Jersey, sir." Should I say Saudi Arabia, Tunisia, Casablanca or England? I told him I had grown up on the south-east coast of Britain, but had been around a bit since then. This started him off on a long monologue about all the places he had been. Apparently, together with his dear friend, he had been on two round the world trips – "RTWs" as he called them – and was in the middle of a third orbit.

"Morocco is amazing isn't it," the middle-aged American said, without any supporting evidence. It was all right, I suppose. I hadn't really seen all that much of it, I confessed. Had I seen the pyramids in Egypt? Yes.

"Oh, they were amazing weren't they?" I suppose they were. He was surprised by my lack of enthusiasm.

"But Cairo is amazing, isn't it?" Here I could not agree with my interlocutor.

"No, actually, not if you mean that in a positive way; I thought it was noisy, polluted, overcrowded and generally unpleasant. Compared to other crowded cities, like Hong Kong, it's a dump." The American looked at me like an impatient teacher might look at a student who couldn't grasp something simple.

"Oh, yeah? Your observations are about as profound as

noting that Mexico City isn't as slick as Los Angeles. You need to get out more buddy."

I said, "Well, I wasn't trying to be profound; I was just giving you my opinion. Remember that Hong Kong started from a lower economic position than Cairo, but has developed over the years. Cairo has, it appears, stood still. I'm sure there are myriad reasons for this, but the place bored me stiff after about four days…" I didn't get a chance to finish what I wanted to say.

"What! You were bored after four days?! My God, we stayed a fortnight and we couldn't get enough of it. We went to Islamic Cairo and visited the Al Azhar mosque, Ibn Tulun mosque, Sultan Hassan mosque, Beit Harrawi house, Beit Suleymani houses, and Bab Zuweila. Didn't you see the show of the turning dervishes at Tannoura?!" He came out with a long list of "exciting" things he and his partner had done in Cairo, and that was how he saw the place: as a list of things to do and to be ticked off.

I coolly replied, "The pyramids and the museum can be done in one day. That leaves you trying to get a handle on Greater Cairo. I found the people nervous and cloying, if not exactly unpleasant, and the city impossible to walk about in. By day four I was pulling my hair out…" Again he cut me off, now agitated.

"You ran out of things to do in four days, in a city of 14 million people with a 5,000-year history, a mix of cultures, an interesting nightlife, a vibrant intellectual scene, remarkable shopping for those who want it, one of the premier museums of the world, the existing Ancient Wonder and its fellow monuments, and one of the world's great rivers, covered with a variety of watercraft you can sail on day and night. Now, you want me to take you seriously? Listen bud, if you can't occupy your mind profitably for four days in any city of over five million, say nothing about Cairo, it doesn't mean the city is slow and dull. It means you are!" It wasn't what the American said that shocked me, but the way he was talking, so dismissive of my opinions, so aggressively self-righteous, and this after having only just met me. The tourist took no interest in having a dialogue; he was talking at me and not with me. He had not even listened to me properly: I had not said Cairo was slow and dull; merely that it had bored me after four days, which is a different assertion altogether.

I caught another glimpse of the Atlantic, waves crashing on a beach, and felt resentment at this obsessed tourist's intrusion into my private, meditative world.

"I didn't think Alexandria was up to that much either," I countered, knowing it would exasperate the American. He stared at me coldly, hunched his shoulders, and then buried his head in a guidebook. I went back to staring out of the window, glad to have ended the parallel monologues. The rest of the journey into Tangiers took about 20 minutes, a long time in the circumstances. Finally, after a six-hour haul, I was able to get off the train. The sleeping gaucho awoke as we pulled into the station, got up without paying me the slightest attention, got off the train and walked away holding the hand of his friend, RTW 3 in progress.

At first sight, Tangiers looked like a harridan, and the new and modern train station did not really hide the ugliness. Outside the station the architecture was a really nasty mix of modern high-rise developments and concrete residential blocks that stretched up and down the long *corniche* road. Inland, one glimpsed more commodious villas, and simple, traditional low-rise houses, but most of this older type of housing nearer the sea had been cleared out in favour of making a buck. It was a very warm afternoon, and I sweated profusely as I dragged my luggage about looking for a bus. But there was no public transport of any kind, only taxis. I therefore walked to the coastal road, where I ate something at a fast food outlet, before eventually locating a cheap hotel down by the port and near the old medina.

Over the years, quite a few European and American artists have sojourned in Tangiers, and the place acquired a reputation for raffishness and sexual licentiousness. Like any port town, it was a bit seedy, and I do believe someone tried to sell me drugs at one point. But on the whole it was obvious that Tangiers, like punk rock, had been quickly commercialized to cash in on its reputation and today it stands as a monument to venture capitalism and the domination of the motor car. In the same way that the tourists, of whom there were a quite few in town, did not "see" the local people, I did not really see them, and concentrated on the city and its people. On my first walk around town the next day, I was struck by how completely culturally Arabic the place was: bars and cafés were very homosocial; women only went about with a male guardian. The medina was thoroughly Arabic, a very tight-knit community despite the constant flow of transients that came to it from the outside. In the medina, I once more found the cultural thread that stretched all the way back to the Arabian Peninsula: the language, foremost. I stopped at a small store and spoke a little Arabic, fluently, which was perfectly understood and had been understood everywhere in North Africa; there were the same manners and cool long shirts; there were the same strong shared values. For example, an underage girl strolled about in her pyjamas in the medina, not seen as a sexual object but as community-protected child. If anyone had tried to molest her that person would have been very swiftly dealt with by the neighbours, and this was implicitly understood. But no one would think of bothering her anyway, since reputation was everything in an Arab community. In general, people here had the time of day for one another; greetings were warm and friendly, especially for children who were loved and appreciated with a genuine, sincere and deep warmth, and this it seemed to me was where the real beauty of Arab culture lay. A culturally-Arab father could be brutal towards his child if disobeyed, but his love for his offspring was unswerving and unconditional; and children were given space to grow.

Plotting my exit from Africa, I hunted about for a passage to Gibraltar, finally buying an open-ended ticket from a travel agent. I had, in my mind at least, come to the end of Arabia, and it was time to return to Europe sooner rather than later. There was not much else for me to do in Tangiers, a city that came alive at night, but which lacked an open social scene. This was confirmed when I went to one of the old hotels in the medina, thinking there might be a nice little bar to repair to. But the lobby of the hotel was empty, despite a sign up that claimed the establishment was fully booked, a piano standing forlorn under a sweeping staircase. I glanced up and looked at a framed news clipping on the wall, taken from a British tabloid newspaper, probably sent to the owner of the hotel by the author, entitled, "Tangiers in 24 hours". The general drift of the article, aimed at British holidaymakers headed to southern Spain, was that one should not miss the chance to go to Africa for the day and engage in some "bargain-hunting." Bargain hunting? What on earth was our illustrious correspondent on about? There was nothing worth buying in Tangiers except the local wine so far as I could see. For all its apparent glitz, Morocco was really quite poor; there was chronic unemployment and a scarcity of resources. Tangiers reflected these facts of national life clearly to anyone who chose to look. Down in the old medina, I came across two obese, aging European cannons, which sat in their mounts, an as yet unexploited tourist attraction. Several men and a boy stood there with nothing to do; they were unemployed. It was hard to gauge their mood, but hopefully melancholic may have summed it up best. The boy was wearing a torn jacket. He stared out at Spain intently, probably dreaming of working there one day, as so many Moroccans did.

I decided to leave on the next boat to Gibraltar, wrapping up the North African segment of my trip. The travel agent had informed me that a boat departed daily at midday, and so after a hearty breakfast of beans flavoured with cayenne, salt and cumin the following day, I packed and went to find the shuttle bus that would take me to the ferry terminal, located a few kilometres away. The bus station was open, but things were slow first thing in the morning, which came as no surprise at all. Two men were charging unwitting tourists a fee to have their luggage "secured." One young Japanese man, also headed to the ferry terminal, informed me that I "must" pay. I didn't think so, and scoffed at the local man when he asked me for some money; at which he very politely informed me that payment was not obligatory. This shocked the young Japanese tourist who up to then didn't realize he was being scammed; but in the perverse logic of a victim, his opinion of me immediately went down when I refused to pay. He would not see me later slip the local man a bill, as a reward for his non-pushiness – again, my psychology had been rather well read. With a friendly pat on the back from this poor Moroccan, I boarded the bus that would take me out of the Arabic cultural zone and to my appointment with Europe. Like many endings, leaving Tangiers was a bit of an anti-climax, a bus ride through a landscape scarred by random development. We drove on a new road past half-built villas, abandoned swimming pools and cement mixers warming up for the next instalment of the new Morocco. It took 45 minutes to get to the ferry terminal, but I had arrived in good time only to discover that there was no ship to Gibraltar until the evening because it was a Sunday. Not wanting to wait in the terminal until evening, I switched my ticket and got on an Algeciras-bound catamaran.

III

EUROPE

11

FORTRESS EUROPE

A COUPLE OF WELL-SCRUBBED EUROPEANS LOUNGED ON THE SHIP. They had been over in Tangiers for the day, bargain-hunting no doubt. The other few dozen passengers were Moroccans returning to jobs in Spain, mostly scruffily-dressed men. Sporting desert pants and a white shirt, I was the demi-explorer prematurely on his way home. The catamaran closed the distance between Africa and Spain in no time, but culturally speaking it was a wide gap that we crossed. The first signs of Western Europe came in the form of the duty free shop on the ship, staffed by perky Spaniards. The goods on sale in the shop, including oversized bars of chocolate, overpriced perfume, and a bog standard array of booze, which interested me even less than the trinkets in Tangiers's old medina. I bought a beer at the bar, for the novelty of it, somewhat regretting the high price. No one batted an eyelid. The Spanish women at duty free laughed loudly at their own stories. The European mainland then quickly loomed large in the lounge's slanted deck windows, a bird jolting across the scene, and I took my beer outside to watch our arrival in the port of Algeciras. Our ship glided into the large harbour effortlessly, on a clear day over the Mediterranean, a smooth entry into the Eurozone.

Formalities were remarkably light at Spanish immigration. I

had expected guard dogs and armed police, but instead there was a lone female official holding the European fort. Power she had aplenty though. She scrutinized everyone's paperwork carefully, not letting one couple enter without referring the case to higher authority. My turn to step up to the glass booth came and, after my passport was swiped through a code reader, I was permitted entry with a cheery "monsieur" from the steely gatekeeper. That was a relief because for a moment there I had felt like an illegal migrant trying to con their way into the Promised Land.

Sunday was not the ideal day to turn up in Spain, and there was no possibility of changing money in the port. I could have taken the train to Madrid that afternoon, but the lack of cash obliged me to stay at a hotel on the *corniche* instead. The concierge at the hotel spoke passable English and I got the room at a reasonable rate. It was the first half-decent place I had lodged in for weeks, and there were signs of good functionality all over the room: neat electric switches, proper wiring, and rolling shutters on the windows that rolled. A windowless bathroom that flooded every time I used it harkened back to Africa though. And Spanish TV programming was pretty awful; a bit like British television without the flashiness. I watched a Spanish movie that was so artless it was a joke. Later, I strolled down by the harbour and tried every place possible to change money, but entering Europe was like jumping into the proverbial shark pool; no less than six money-changers tried to fleece me. Clearly one had to be careful where one did business in the euro-pool because evidently no one had any shame.

My quest to change money continued the next day. The morning was a bit slow, which I was used to, but local businesses opened reasonably early, and on time. Algeciras's town centre was a neat toy land compared to Africa, and I bounced along like a child staring at the fantasy-like window dressing. The people around me all looked unreal, too, sort of like puppets. It was the tailored clothes and make-up that momentarily threw my recognition system out of kilter. I went to one bank, and grappled with the door for a while before realizing you had to press a button and wait for the door to be opened for you. Inside, I queued at a counter and eventually got some service, but held off on changing money in the hope of finding a better rate elsewhere. A long peregrination later I found myself back at the same bank, grateful for what I could get. When I finally changed my dollars for Euros, at what I felt was an unfavourable rate, I had to wait for the bank clerk to photocopy my passport, an almost unbelievably silly formality given the small amount of money involved. The transaction was done, eventually. Flush with Euros, I then went to the railway station to book a ticket to Madrid. This done, I had the afternoon free, and so I jumped on a bus to La Linea, thinking to make a quickie visit to the Rock of Gibraltar.

IT TOOK 30 minutes to get over to La Linea, from where it was but a short walk over to the border, surely one of the most anomalous and artificial in the world. British immigration was again informal, but quite proper for all that, and the lone official looked at my passport carefully if briefly. And then I was inside the Crown Colony, under the massive limestone outcrop that Britain has occupied since 1713. Although only a tiny territory, Gibraltar, even 20 metres in, had a British vibrancy about it. Land use was maximised and the roads cordoned off with safety barriers; the traffic zoomed about in that no-nonsense, no-slowing-down British way. A motorcyclist drove past, fully and properly kitted out in leathers, like something out of the Australian cult film *Mad Max*. I crossed the aerodrome where during World War II two squadrons of Spitfires were based. And then I was more or less in the high street, window shopping along with all the other tourists.

Free-wheeling Gibraltar felt like a Chinatown, and it seemed odd to me that I did not see any Chinese people there, although a few Indians worked in the money-changing outlets. The colony is actually populated by a large number of British expatriates, and English-speaking Spaniards. If there was no visible military presence to speak of, it was obvious that the token garrison could be reinforced at short notice, and that had always been understood by the Spanish government, which has so far resisted the temptation to retake Gibraltar by force, not least because Spain has two tiny Gibraltar-like colonies in Morocco and does not want to set a precedent. And besides, everyone wants access to duty-free liquor. After changing some Euros I proceeded to spend 37 Sterling pounds without really trying, my first purchase a small bottle of Scotch. After an "al fresco" fish 'n' chips, I went in search of the cable car that glided up the sloping side of Gibraltar's steep rock, finding it after passing the grave-yard where some casualties from the battle of Trafalgar were buried, "…here lay buried those glorious dead…[they] died for the British Empire", read a sign.

A middle-aged Englishwoman, an expatriate, was chatting with the cable car guard, whom she knew, "A nice day for it…" She was headed to the peak, together with an American-Japanese family, and I. The ride up was spectacular and well worth the ticket, although I kept my eyes on the rock most of the way because I am afraid of heights, or more precisely, afraid of sheer drops. The Englishwoman had no such qualms and stared out the rear window of the car as we ascended with Swiss efficiency. She had done the ride many times, and was on her way to do a "delivery", whatever that meant. When we got to the top of the rock, the woman disappeared; the Americans and I wandered around the cable car station and took in the terrific views out over Algeciras Bay, and the Mediterranean.

"Hey, is this where the Germans put the guns of Navarone?" The American man had watched too many movies, and was confusing myth with reality. I didn't want to say that though because he was just being friendly.

I said, "Yeah, it was somewhere in the Mediterranean." The couple's two daughters jumped in the air, their mother freezing the action photographically. I left the Americans and walked about, admiring the resident Barbary macaques that slunk about like drunks, walking purposefully on a wall one moment, suddenly falling over its side the next second, only to make a nonchalant recovery on some tree branch. With no predators, the macaques owned the peak. Having done The Rock, I returned to the town below, and then made my way back to the border, re-entering Spain as the sun set over the British Empire.

———

THE RAILWAY STATION seemed very quiet considering the first of the day's two Madrid-bound trains was, in theory, about to leave. I shuffled into the station café taking a coffee and toast standing at the bar in the Spanish manner. But nothing was going on; no passengers were arriving. I checked at the ticket office, and then checked my watch: Spain was one hour ahead of Morocco, and I had not adjusted my watch, and so I had missed the morning train. Exchanging my ticket for the afternoon train obliged me to pay a hefty fee for the transfer, something I resented since it was a same-day departure, and neither train could possibly have been full. Being Europe, there was no arguing the toss, and I paid the money. They were surprised to see me back at the hotel. I dumped my luggage and, at my wits' end, went for another walkabout.

In a bad mood, I plodded around the town's streets aimlessly. Most of the action, such as it was, was going on around the market. But fruit and vegetables, the only things worth buying at the market, were of no immediate interest to me. I tried to kill time at a café, but found it impossible to get service. In Spain, they expected you to speak Spanish, which was perfectly reason-able, only I had never learnt Spanish, and speaking Arabic only put you in an ignored underclass. A cold front had blown in over southern Spain, the first real blast of winter, and I put on a coat for the first time. With my arms folded across my chest to keep warm, I plodded about in and out of shopping precincts, reading and trying to translate Spanish signs. At a zebra crossing I waited for a car to go past, but the driver actually stopped his vehicle. That definitely threw me; no motorist ever stops for a pedestrian in the Middle East or Africa. I should have been pleased, but strangely I felt irritated by the driver's timidity; I was still adjusting to the rules-based approach to life. In one street, two women walked past me trying to attract my attention. This also seemed like odd behaviour: I didn't know them at all, why would they do that? In a café I frequented, poster-sized pictures of Marilyn Monroe adorned the walls, an example of a woman being crudely exploited long after her tragic death. In another street, residents were having a boot fair and selling every piece of junk imaginable: old toys, paperweights, lamp shades, and even old shoes. A self-respecting Arab – and all Arabs are self-respecting – would not have touched any of this rubbish with a barge pole. Meanwhile, everyone in Algeciras was doing something; everyone was on the move and purposeful, there were few loafers about. I really didn't know what to do, and so I went back to the hotel to take a nap, sleeping on the couch in reception, a loafer. It was not long before the concierge woke me up.

"Non monsieur..." This is a hotel...I got my bags and went back to the railway station where I waited for the Madrid train. In the railway station café a man of ethnic Chinese origin was sinking coins into the greedy mechanism of a slot machine. I ordered a beer and sat comatose at a table. At last, the station started to fill with people, and they were a bright, hopeful and well-equipped bunch. Everyone looked so young, making me feel old. The demographic of Europe had surely changed in the two years I had been away, but actually the comparison I was making in my mind was with the late 1980s, when it had been my turn to be young. A train arrived at the station and we were duly summoned to board it. Nothing symbolized Europe's fortress-like character more than the highly controlled manner in which we were ushered onto the train, after our bags had been scanned. At every step of this process we were carefully watched by officers of the Spanish Civil Guard, alert to any potential threats. I thought it was very sad that the romance of train travel had gone here in Spain, at least on the inter-city trains, the result of terrorism. As if to match the mood, the sky above us clouded over and it was threatening to rain. I sat in my appointed carriage seat, having been micro-managed every inch of the way from the station waiting room.

The train was not crowded, but then train travel here was about ten times as expensive as in Morocco. My fingers found an ashtray on the seat arm, but it had been soldered down: paranoia and Puritanism on the *Red Nacional de los Ferrocarriles Españoles*, or RENFE, as the state-owned Spanish railway company is known. It was, however, good to be on a train and once again moving towards my final destination. The landscape outside was unremarkable in every respect, almost planned tedium. A road ran parallel to the railway track in many places, which in Spain often meant an accompanying cycle path, too. Such purpose-built tracks marked the end of peaceful co-existence between cyclists and motor car drivers; each now had their own territory, at the cost of more lost countryside. Graffiti idiots, as opposed to artists, had sprayed many concrete road barriers with meaningless signatures, an abject display of narcissism. The sky darkened even more, and then I could no longer make out anything except the vague outline of hills, probably pretty in the summer, but now a gloomy presence. It was raining over some of these hills, and the atmosphere seemed to cool all round, a monochrome mood. I sat back and read my Madrid pocket guidebook, purchased in Gibraltar, determined not to turn up in Spain's capital totally clueless. The train ground on at a deceptively fast speed, and rain hit the window. I stared in wonder at the streaming rivulets of water on the glass, like a Tuareg tribesman might have. It was quite a long ride to the capital, lengthened by an excruciating one-hour delay somewhere. Luckily, there was an oasis on the train where I was able to water myself.

12

MADRID SOJOURN

Having travelled almost non-stop since leaving Eritrea, I decided to pause in Madrid. I wanted to spend some time at the art galleries there, and generally soak up the atmosphere of the city. The place was rather atmosphere-less, or artificial, I felt, but there was no shortage of public art in the city, which had been carefully selected, purchased, and put on display; and there would be plenty of famous paintings that I would see live for the first time, a counterpoint to the rather austere Saudi visual environment I had lived in for two years. I therefore soon found myself falling head first into an extended session of art viewing, starting at the Fundación Caja; in conjunction with the Thyssen Bornemisza museum, a special exhibition of impressionist work on the theme of "Gardens" was being held there, and I went to see it on my first full day in town.

The Impressionists: wonderful, never boring. Within a minute of entering the exhibition space, a converted public building, I was face to face with Van Gogh's *Trees and Undergrowth*. A very simple idea it was to go and paint the undergrowth in the woods, but not so simple a subject to paint in practice; the lighting contrast in such an environment is a nightmare and extremely difficult to translate accurately into correct tonal values. Van Gogh pulled it off brilliantly in this painting and returned to the subject more than once, finding it both romantic and melancholy, always interpreting the trees and foliage with different values according to the season. Van Gogh, strictly speaking a post-impressionist painter, featured alongside other post-impressionists at the exhibition including Klimt, Vuillard, Bonnard and Toulouse-Lautrec, and some others. I liked pretty much everything I saw; I found it moving and inspiring that people had dedicated themselves so whole-heartedly to creating such beautiful paintings, such individualized visions of the world.

"Shoossshhh…" A human shoosh-machine standing by the entrance to the hall attempted to quieten the talking heads visiting the museum, mostly respectable, middle-class, mature adults. It seemed like a joke, or a Gilbert and George installation perhaps?

Claude Monet: utterly brilliant, and not a stroke out of place anywhere in his work. His paintings, mimicking nature, actually changed colour as you looked at them, a rather clever trick. Ernest Quost's *Morning Flowers*: outstanding. And if the purple flower in the foreground was starting to fade, so what? Even the great pyramids will return to dust eventually… Two birds in flight animated the painting, a conventional device, but one perfectly done in Quost's beautifully rendered scene. It was also interesting to see paintings by Camille Pissarro, the influential artist's artist, his *Kensington Gardens* a master class in using colour suggestively, the brain completing the picture from the subtle prompts; on closer inspection, however, I found his brushwork to be very detailed. The exhibition also introduced me to the works of artists I was not familiar with such as Marie Egner, Johann Victor Kramer, Lovis Corinth, Wilhelm Trübner, Fritz von Uhde, Max Liebermann, and John Lavery, the latter whose *Garden in Morocco* harkened back to the colonial era in North Africa. After absorbing as much of the exhibition as I could, I headed out into the street and took dinner in a clean and well-lit restaurant, among jolly groups of Spaniards and the odd singleton tourist.

Suzanne Lacy's various mixed media works highlighting gender based violence, exhibited at the Reina Sofía art museum, were a wakeup call, one from 30 years ago in fact but sadly still relevant – a demonstration against male chauvinism in Sol Square that I witnessed whilst in Madrid confirmed this. Lacy's powerful work was classified feminist, and it made me realize that we must all be feminists; really it's a case of if you are not with us you are against us. An American artist, Lacy had once gone around Los Angeles stamping "rape" on municipal maps in an attempt to highlight the violence women faced in that city on a daily basis, and her thought-provoking work was confrontational to one degree or another. I admired her work, which was by far the most engaging I would see at the Reina Sofía, where great works of modern art had essentially been put out to pasture. I had gone there on a cool morning, free of charge on the museum's 20th anniversary. The building itself, part new and part old, was difficult to navigate and I gave up looking for Francis Bacon's stuff. I enjoyed Hans-Peter Feldmann's works, mostly photo collages, but in retrospect they looked a bit tame.

The Reina Sofía contained many works by Pablo Picasso and Joan Miró, the two titans of 20th century art. I was eyeballing one of Picasso's typically bold and imaginative sketches when a Japanese tour group walked by, led by a guide who introduced the great artist plainly by name.

"Ahhh, Picasso, ne…" The small tour group nodded, grunted and giggled – to them Picasso was a dirty old man, not much more than a pornographer. Meanwhile, Picasso's *Guernica* had reverently been placed in a hall to itself, and was well guarded. Although it is undoubtedly a masterpiece, one wonders at the irony of it being revered in this way, a form of neutralization. I think *Guernica* should be sent to the White House and left on the grass there regardless of what happens to it. Nearby, one of Miró's portraits, superficially playful and innocent, was actually intensely intellectual to a degree that made Picasso's numerous portraits seem realist by comparison. The oeuvres of Picasso and Miró made a galaxy that no art gallery could contain – one was left staring at star remnants at the Reina. Together with *Guernica* was a section that dealt with the Spanish Civil War. The propaganda posters, paintings and sketches showed Republican sympathies, and it was one of the paradoxes of modern Spain that their work was admired and displayed at the same time as its central message – the need to end the monarchy and replace it with a republic – was ignored, or neutralized.

On another day, at the Thyssen-Bornemisza museum proper, I caught the rest of the Impressionist exhibition and then walked around the permanent collection, a vast privately-donated hoard containing a bit, and sometimes quite a lot, of everything. The collectors were promiscuous, but they had taste, and they had money, and the collection was an astonishing assemblage of artworks spanning centuries, very nicely presented, and arranged in chronological order. I dived in at the "Italian Primitives" section. It soon became apparent that there was really nothing primitive about the work of mediaeval artists, their paintings subtly sophisticated in composition and colour if locked onto one subject: the crucifixion. Faces were beautifully and freshly rendered on these old canvasses, and the devotion and feeling could be very affecting. Paolo Uccello's *Christ on the Cross, the Virgin and Three Mourning Saints*, for example, was utterly modern in its use of luminescent paint for the cross, set against an almost surrealist landscape. Later, I tried to find a print of this painting at the museum gift shop, only to find they had a print of everything bar this masterpiece. From the Italian Primitives, I followed the history of western art through the collection's representative samples, an exhilarating if exhausting experience. I was alert to some interesting titbits: an appearance of the famous Kiki of Montparnasse in a painting by Kees van Dongen, for example. Works from the avant-garde and surrealist movements piqued my interest when I was flagging; Francis Picabia's *Predicament* was a small slice of this artist's amazing brain. Alas, it was around Mondrian that I started to burn out, and by the time I got to the Expressionists I was completely unable to appreciate their messy daubs. No one shooshed us at the Thyssen, but the body language of the staff let it be known that anyone who laid so much as a little finger on any of the exalted works of art could expect to be swiftly karate chopped.

Most people visit Madrid's botanical gardens to cool off after a circuit of the city's premier national art museum, the Prado; I went there to cool off *before* visiting it, a daunting prospect. On a cold autumnal day, golden leaves covered the garden's pathways, and I stealthily trod about them like a Cold War-era spy. Again, I was struck by the artificiality of everything, the obsessive neatness of the flower borders; the fussy rearranging of nature. The gardens reminded me of what I would see at home when I finally got back there. Suitably cooled off, I hit the Prado with an illicit bottle of water tucked in one pocket. In the end, it was a productive visit. Deciding to give the special Renoir exhibition a miss, I initially focused on the Prado's extensive collection of Peter Paul Rubens's work. No fewer than 90 paintings credited to Rubens were on display in large adjoining rooms at the Prado, with plenty of space to view them properly. One of my favourites, *The Birth of the Milky Way*, depicting the Greek myth at the moment when Juno pushes the suckling Hercules away, milk spurting up to form the stars, was also not available as a print at the museum gift shop, perhaps due to its popularity. To spend an hour or two studying these 90 paintings was probably enough for one day, but I ploughed on not wanting to miss the works of Velázquez. The museum was quite crowded by the time I got to the Spanish master's *Las Meninas*, which I was obliged, perhaps appropriately, to view through a throng of schoolchildren. After that, I called it a day, unable to digest any more brilliance, and walked back to my pension in Sol Square in the rain.

THE ROOM I had rented at a fourth-floor pension was small but just so in every way. It had an en suite bathroom, with a little bathtub and bidet, a deceptively spacious combined closet and storage space, a comfortable bed and a wall-mounted television. There was even central heating, which worked perfectly and kept the space cosy at all hours. A window looked out over an inner sinkhole of a courtyard, but I seldom opened the window's shutters preferring cavernous privacy. The other floors of the building were occupied by private residences and the whole place, with its polished wooden staircase, was rather homey. The pension was managed by an elusive woman who spoke English quite well. Her direct manner had attracted me when I had first spoken to her through the building's intercom shortly after arriving in Madrid from the south of Spain.

After that first night, Carmen largely avoided me, and the pension had few other visitors. Television did not interest me that much, but with no one to talk to, I thought I'd try a few channels out; but I needed the manageress's assistance to get the television working. She lived in the pension, and so I called her name out in reception one afternoon. A few minutes later she was in my room, fiddling with the remote control. I suppose if I ever had a chance in Madrid, this was it. Carmen was about my age and pretty; perhaps she was an underappreciated wife. Getting a picture on the screen, she said something about a "blue" channel, smiled for the first time, and then moved her hips closer to mine. I don't know why I failed to take advantage of the situation, but there was something odd about Carmen; she had hidden away from me and not wanted to talk for several days. I sensed, rightly or wrongly, that her sudden eroticism had an ulterior motive, and I instinctively held back. She never forgave me for this, giving my room a ruthless clean every afternoon thereafter, even making me wait in reception to let the floor dry each time.

Carmen reminded me of an artwork I had seen in the Reina Sofía, a photomontage by the Spanish artist and political activist Josep Renau. The work was a simple contrast: two portraits of Spanish women, one traditional and one liberated. What made the work powerful was its life size, and the total contrast between a woman swathed in emasculating clothes, crucifixes and a shawl, and a woman dressed in uniform like a man, her hair flowing and mouth open as if barking an order or shouting a revolutionary slogan. At the bottom right of the montage, under the portrait of the liberated woman, the artist had glossed, "Shedding her outer Layer of Superstition and Misery, from the Immemorial Slave there Emerged THE WOMAN Capable of Active Participation in the Making of the Future." Carmen, in her actions, attitude and demeanour was the equivalent of the traditional woman. She may have worn tight-fitting pants, but the net around her mind was equally tight. I later came to think that many Spanish women, and perhaps also men, had a conflict within them between the conservative and the modern, and that appearances could be deceiving.

In between museum visits, I ate out at tourist restaurants where one could order by number, a practical solution; it got me what I wanted instead of what a waiter or waitress thought I wanted. I liked one café in particular, which was small, simple and organized like a bar. Entering the bistro one day at lunchtime, I was assailed by a dog. I shooed the animal away.

The dog owner, a late-middle aged man with grey hair and a beard, who was sitting at the bar, addressed me, neutrally it seemed, "You no like dog meester?"

My facetious sense of humour came to the fore; I said, "I hate them. I think they should all be killed."

"And kill you after," the Spaniard's even reply. It suddenly occurred to me that Spaniards would not find jokes about killing funny, not after the Spanish Civil War. To my relief, the man understood I was joking; he had some familiarity with Anglo-Saxons. He was having a coffee with a buddy; I had my lunch, as usual out of sync with local mealtimes. Having started a conversation, we continued it in a desultory way. Then a man came in with his wife. I stupidly changed stools to give them some room at the bar. The haughty man almost punched me, throwing my just vacated stool aside as he summoned the waiter. The small contretemps was nothing, and I continued my meal at a nearby high table, leaving the silly old duffer to wave his dignity about at the bar. My reintegration to Europe via Spanish culture was hitting a few sandbanks though; I understood Spaniards less than I understood Arabs. The dog lover, who had seen the little incident, left with his pal. Did I want to take the dog home with me, he asked on the way out?

I said, "*You* take the dog home," and he smiled, and then left, irrevocably and for ever.

Donde esta oficina de correos? A wave from the man at the kiosk in the direction of Madrid's main post office was most encouraging: my Spanish was coming along. In fact, the gaudy architectural encrustation, from where I intended to post a parcel to Mikhail, was just across the road – Mikhail had requested I send anything I no longer wanted to him, something I was happy to do. Little did I know that this apparently simple task would be so time-consuming. The post office was an imposing burlesque building on the outside, a starship on the inside. I entered it and took a counter ticket, and then wandered about the long, curvilinear black and yellow counter, looking to get my parcel posted. After filling out some paperwork, I was obliged to cover the box in brown paper for some odd reason – the box was perfectly brown already, why brown it any more? Eyeing a section where boxes could be machine-sealed with plastic tapes, I guessed I could get the assistance I was looking for there. I fumbled for the right words to explain I needed to wrap my box in brown paper, but the section chief understood and, after purchasing a little pack that contained paper and tape, we got to work. Only the sheet of paper was not really big enough, so we had to wrap the box twice. It was just insane because the box looked exactly the same wrapped as it did before. I went back to the original position on the counter and proudly delivered my parcel, which now resembled a Christo and Jeanne-Claude artwork. The woman at the counter looked at me in a bemused manner. What's wrong now? I was so busy wrapping the parcel up, I hadn't paid. So, I paid. The parcel was reverently placed on a trolley, which looked like a medical gurney, and I was done. Were all post offices in Spain so hopelessly inefficient?

A ticket system was also in operation at the Atocha Railway Station, one of Madrid's major transport hubs. I went there one day to book my onward ticket to Paris; something I thought might take an hour or so to accomplish. Having taken my ticket, I sauntered off into the main hall of the station, the centre of which had been converted into a tropical garden complete with humidifiers, ponds and tall palm trees. This was all very relaxing, and I strolled around the garden enjoying the twittering of exotic birds and insects. How long would it take for my number to come up? I went back to the ticket office to check the progress of the ticket counter, and calculated I would be there about two or three hours. I went off to do a bit shopping, buying a new clasp knife and compass, and then had lunch at one of the station's restaurants. It was very civilized at Atocha, after the bombing, and a huge improvement on Cairo station it must be said. But the basic task, that of booking a ticket, was taking an inordinate amount of time to achieve. After lunch, I sat and waited, and waited. My number was still about 16 places away, so I thought it safe to go and take five minutes to admire the croaking frogs in the garden pond. When I went back to the ticket office soon afterwards I noticed my number had just passed. I rushed to the counter, and explained I had been waiting for three hours, and sorry for missing my number. I was told to get another ticket and wait again. Well, Manuel, I don't think so. I pleaded with the counter assistant, and then shouted at him, an act that attracted the attention of an armed policewoman; station security thinking I was about to start a one-person riot. Not getting any satisfaction, I left the ticket office and went to "Customer Services," located in a plush office near ticketing. I spoke to a man there, a sort of clean-shaven android, who did not really listen to me so much as look in my direction, and who told me I had to get another ticket and wait again.

A group of females in the back office came out when I got angry at the android – "What kind of 'service' is this?!" – and gave me motherly, sympathetic looks, as they might give to a distressed child. Really angry, but still in control of my temper, I strode back into the ticket office and went back to the international counter.

When all else fails, lie: "Customer Services have authorized you to sell me a ticket, now", I said. The assistant, perhaps grateful that he had not yet been punched, relented and served me after making a point of nobly serving a pregnant woman first. The pregnant woman waltzed off with her tickets, and I did likewise after deciding on a date for taking the overnight train to Paris. In the end, it could not have been simpler.

<hr>

On a surprisingly cold morning, I darted out of the pension on a mission to break out of Madrid and see a bit of the surrounding countryside. Admittedly, this was detouring, but I had a week left before departing for Paris and, having walked around the downtown area incessantly, I felt the need to go somewhere else. I wanted to touch base with the real Spain, which I guessed might not be far away. Although out of town was of course a little different from the capital, it was not quite what I expected.

At Atocha Station, I bought a five-day travel pass from a machine, which while a bit impersonal was a lot easier to deal with than the staff at the main ticket office. Madrid City's transport system was integrated with that of the Municipal Region, a fairly large area that included a number of towns, villages, nature parks and mountain resorts. My ticket gave me access to this whole region, and not really knowing where to start I headed to Alcalá de Henares, a town about 30 kilometres north-east of the capital. Alcalá de Henares, an old university town similar to Oxford, was a pleasant enough little place. A walk through the town brought me face to face with the venerable university, an old town square and a shopping arcade where a lot of pesky school kids on an outing roamed. We all wandered about the charming, almost empty, and very clean streets, lost and bored. It rained. I went back to Madrid.

On another day, gravitating towards the Guadarrama Mountain Range, I took the train out to Escorial, the Royal Monastery. Several RENFE transport networks converged at Atocha, including local, inter-regional and international trains. It confused me that there were no security checks on local trains. In 2004, the Madrid bombers had after all utilized local trains for their heinous attacks. Why bother with security checks at all if they are not going to be comprehensive? Such thoughts were going through my mind on a chilly morning as I waited for the local train to Escorial, the first one of which I managed to miss, distracted as I was by a Japanese tourist. Another double-decker behemoth came along in no time, and soon I was comfortably transported through a countryside dotted with trees and broom scrubs. In the distance, the tops of the mountains, although not especially high, were snow-capped, making them very picturesque. I spotted a few cows in amongst electricity pylons and small industrial estates. At Escorial Station, I got off the train, along with a handful of tourists, and took a shuttle bus up to the imposing 16th century stone pile, a building as solid as the mountains on which it stood. I actually went in the great edifice, entrance being free of charge to EU passport-holders on the day of my visit, but left in frustration after being told I should leave my bag and camera in a locker. And this on top of a sign that read, "No Mobile Phones, No Cameras, No Smoking, Do Not Touch."

Dramatic dark clouds hung over the mountains as I boarded a train in the early afternoon at Escorial, but instead of returning to Madrid, I travelled in the other direction, closer to the snow-capped Guadarrama. Working from some maps and timetables I had picked up at tourist information, I calculated I could get to Cercedilla and from there transfer to the mountain line. It was touch and go with the timings, but when I got out at Cercedilla the last mountain train of the day was yet to depart. My travel pass entitled me to ride on the two-carriage workhorse, and so I jumped on the waiting train as sleet started to fall. Very soon we were off on a magical ride through the ice and the snow, climbing inexorably and inexhaustibly up to Cotos, a snowed-in mountain station, a 40-minute ride. And what a ride it was, like a spin in Father Christmas's sleigh. The weather worsened as we climbed up the mountain. At Cotos, a regular blizzard was blowing and there was nothing to do other than get a bite to eat in the small railway station café, which was doing a roaring trade since none of us could really go anywhere. We all returned down the mountain after an hour, on the same train, glad of the warmth of the carriage in cold-season Spain. On the way back, we passed the ski resort of Navacerrada, where two perfectly-equipped hikers got on the train, dusting snow off their high-tech boots as they did so. The Spaniards all seemed superbly well equipped for outdoor activities.

A desert anorak and a couple of walking poles was all I needed, I felt – bearing in mind the US Marines' motto, "Time to Improvise, Adapt, and Overcome" – to explore the nether regions of the Pedriza Nature Park, a popular hiking and climbing area north of Madrid City. I went out to the park one sunny morning by bus. We stopped outside Manzanares Castle, and I stepped out onto snow and ice, which was slowly melting in the sun. The snow was certainly novel to me, and I made slow progress up the side of the Manzanares River, after which the town was named, towards the park entrance, a simple gate at the head of a mountain path. The Pedriza featured knobbly granite outcrops with smooth slopes, the latter being the devil to walk on in the icy conditions. In the end, I only walked, very tentatively, a few kilometres into this semi-wilderness, stopping at a mountain hut to eat a sandwich before returning the way I had come. The park was popular, and a dozen people passed me on the path, most of them dealing with the conditions much better than I. One man descending the trail actually ran past me, an extraordinary feat. The mountain runner didn't seem to care at all about the ice. Meanwhile, and despite using two walking poles, I managed to slip twice, once completely tipping over backwards. Failing, in general, to adapt to the icy conditions, I beat a retreat: "We

Improvise, Adapt and Overcome, Except When We Fall Flat on Our Bum."

The Pedriza Park in winter had a strange quality to it. The whole place looked like it had been made out of plastic: there were no rough edges anywhere. In the snow, it was essentially a child's playground, with wolves, litter and any dangerous obstacles completely expurgated. In other words, it was the city slicker's perfect getaway. That's why people climbed and ran in the park instead of just walking: it was a way of upping the personal challenge, of getting a thrill. Ultimately, the park was a highly degraded natural environment, albeit a very pretty and clean one; no foxes or other wildlife were to be seen anywhere. I stared at Manzanares Castle as I waited for the bus that would take me back to Madrid. Standing proudly and immaculately in the sun, the fortification resembled a toy castle from my childhood.

THERE WAS NOT MUCH ELSE to keep me in Madrid, though I lingered there a while, catching more street life. I bought wine and pork in the rather good local department store, and other small gifts for my family at the Rastro street market. Carmen booted me out of the pension just before Constitution Day, a national holiday in Spain that ran into Immaculate Conception Day, a long weekend effectively. This left me temporarily homeless, but eventually I found another pension, taking a tiny room there. One of Ernest Hemingway's old watering holes, the Alemana, was next door and I drifted in there one night for a beer. The spit and sawdust bar was authentic enough; the drinkers, a youngish yuppie crowd, stuck to their cliques and dates, leaving me to make intense observations, so intense I think my eyeballs almost dropped out. An Irish bar, not far away, was a bit livelier, and I did not get out of the place sober – a group of Spaniards took me under their wing, plying me with drinks in exchange for a bit of English conversation.

The national holiday brought thousands of people into town,

all of whom did the same things at the same time: a lay-in, a late breakfast, shopping in the afternoon, a siesta, followed by a bit more shopping, and then a late dinner, in that order. It was literally impossible to walk through the tide of people on the streets in the afternoon, and you felt like screaming "Why?" Indeed, why were there young people holding posters of Stalin up in Sol Square at a socialist rally? If they had been holding pictures of Trotsky, I might have understood it, but Stalin? The Georgian lunatic, who had turned on his own, and on everyone else in sight including the heroic Spanish anarchists, was apparently revered by these silly skin-headed leftists. It was misguided people like these latter-day Stalinists who had given Franco his opening in the first place. Other demonstrators, mournful and silent, demanded to know the whereabouts of buried loved ones, victims of the fascist dictator's repressive rule. The Spanish Civil War was clearly still a sensitive issue in Spain despite the country's impressive economic and democratic progress since Franco's death. You felt people kept quiet about it to avoid an argument, but the terrible war was never far away from a Spaniard's consciousness.

There would be no new life for me in Spain, even though I felt drawn to the country and its great culture. What would I do in Madrid? Teach English? No, I had to get back to England. The weather changed again, a warm front bringing rain to the city, and I packed my bags. Over the holiday, I chatted with the pension staff, who hailed from Manzanares. But they had no time for tales of North Africa or Arab culture. I found this resistance, or impermeability, to the cultures of the Maghreb quite interesting. Much more than forts and guns, Europe was a fortress by dint of the mentality of its populace, who failed to see any value or utility in the Islamic cultures, so near and yet so far from them. As Siham says in Tahar Ben Jelloun's novel *Leaving Tangier*, "The Spanish don't see us, they don't give a damn, they've no use for our country."

Before leaving Madrid, I took the opportunity to make a brief visit to the Museum of America. I did so with one eye on the future. It took a little while for me to locate the museum, almost getting jumped on by two soldiers as I mistakenly tried to enter the nation's Air Force headquarters (perhaps my beard and rucksack had caused their concern). The Museo de América, a tasteful, purpose-built brick edifice, was actually to be found around the corner about five minutes' walk away.

The museum contained a good selection of artefacts from the Americas, including all manner of indigenous jewellery, pottery and statuary. The various artefacts were presented as if they were handbags in one of Madrid's swanky upmarket stores. But nowhere in a modern shop would you see such artistry put into the making of clothes, headdresses and everyday ornaments. The range of indigenous cultures was, and is, astonishing, each one specifically adapted to its physical environment. Two artefacts exhibited at the museum that particularly impressed me were a hollowed-out canoe, and a wigwam, both from North America. The latter, adapted to the wind and extreme climate of the plains, was perfect in every way, to the extent that it made you want to order one and live in it somewhere. The former item, a crude but effective vessel, somehow had the power and presence of a nuclear submarine. The owners must have been very proud of this canoe, and not a few fish would have been hauled up into it once upon a time.

At Moncloa, where the museum was located, I took Madrid's new, clean and sparky metro for the first time. Although it was all clinically clean inside the subterranean system, the passengers on the underground train were no happier or bubblier than their counterparts in London, where travelling in a confined space made everyone feel embarrassed. Later on, I took a last stroll around town, taking in the Parque del Retiro, where young ones walked about wrapped up in scarves and ski jackets, suffering in what for them constituted cold weather. On the way back to the pension, I also passed by Madrid's Ritz hotel, where a man dressed in a grey uniform and top hat blew a whistle at a departing taxi, an act that a beautiful woman dressed in a mink coat and I shared a little laugh at. Dusk fell over the city centre, and I navigated my way through Madrid's back streets, which by now had become familiar to me, guided by the streaming lights of cars that shined like powerful flashlights in a tunnel.

Madrid, site of ferocious fighting during the Civil War, did seem a bit artificial and fairy-tale-like. I generally admired the elegance, vitality and shininess of this small European capital city. But as in a children's film, the dirt and the loonies had been edited out, and what was left was a stage on which people acted; acted Spanish, naturally enough, which seemed to involve exercising a studied *joie de vivre*; a regulated and moderated enjoyment of life: people ate, drank and were merry at certain times, in certain places, and with selected friends. There were social conventions to be followed, almost Japanese in their prescriptive nature; the apparently lively and ubiquitous café and bar life was exclusive in nature. There was no drunkenness, bad behaviour or obvious danger on the downtown streets, by day or night; a kind of bourgeois conformity prevailed.

13

A JOURNEY HOME

The final leg of my journey turned out to be another dash, albeit one made by train, the most civilized, if not necessarily the best, way to travel. I got to the train station early fearing I might miss the ride home. Although "home" did not exist for me in reality; rather it was a legend, a sort of Ithaca in my mind. Practically speaking, it meant Britain, specifically the southeast corner of England, which I could travel to overland from Madrid. The European rail network would take me to within a short distance of Thanet, a one-time island and gateway to the misty land hanging off the rump of north-western Europe. All I had to do was keep going north, and I would eventually find myself in the green fields of Kent, no flight required. As I waited for the train, I checked the route over and over again on the map, it seemed like such a neat end to a somewhat difficult trip, and I was pleased with myself for having spotted it, even though it was obvious.

At Chamartín, Madrid's northern travel hub, I was once again confronted by the consumerization of public space, a phenomenon that left travellers in cramped and over-stimulating waiting areas. The station was busy, not overly so, but the easy access to overpriced food and drinks was an uncomfortable reminder of the hyper-consumerism that I could expect to find in

England. I calmly waited for the call to board the train; I had been knocking about the station for the best part of two hours, and had even gone on a walk around the neighbourhood discovering, among other things, a transit hotel, some shops and a left luggage office with fortified lockers. Watching a security official scan luggage in that office was my last impression of Spain; the station's interior could have been anywhere. The train eventually arrived and we were invited to board it, and I left the waiting area under the glow of a Christmas tree's fairy lights.

Fortunately, I am not obese, because if I had been I would never have got down the train's aisles; such was the super-compact design of the Spanish train carriage, suitable only for the slim and trim. Nonetheless, it was a major struggle to get my luggage onto the train and down the carriage. I found my four-person compartment, made out of moulded plastic, and squeezed in. I then remembered that Spaniards were rather short compared to north Europeans, and that for most of them the amount of space available was probably perfectly acceptable. After surveying my allotted space, I wondered who might join me for the overnight journey to Paris, and whether they had any luggage, because if they had anything like as much stuff as me then we would have a problem. The train, possibly due to the high cost of train travel relative to flying, was mercifully half empty, and the chirpy Englishman who joined me in my compartment merely carried a small backpack – a professional tourist. He wisely tried to avoid helping me heft my suitcase into the overhead storage space, but relented when I asked for a hand.

"Blimey mate, what you got in there, lead pipes?" he quipped, taking one end of my suitcase.

Jonathan, a lean Englishman who hailed from the British Midlands, was the first Briton I had come across since Libya. Like most lone travellers who are not eager to have their travel fantasies interrupted by a compatriot, he resented sharing a compartment with me; our forced intimacy was like arriving home too early for both of us. But we soon resolved to make the best of it, and in fact Jonathan was good company. I rattled off stories about Saudi Arabia, and about my career as an English teacher going back over a number of years, "telling all", knowing full well I would never see this amiable Brummy again once our journey had ended; he in turn told me about his extraordinary adventures in Guatemala where he almost got shot one night. Of the two of us, his stories were the more sensational; mine were didactic: I was trying to warn Jonathan away from English teaching. A young Spaniard joined us, and talked away in his rapid-fire Madrilene dialect, which Jonathan affected to comprehend. Actually, as I soon discovered, Jonathan barely understood a word, but evidently thought if he listened hard enough he might catch something. The young man finally realized that neither of the pink-faced Englishmen understood what he was saying and, slightly miffed, ceased talking. By now we were under way in the darkness, a crew of submariners sweating in a confined space. Bored and hot, Jonathan and I went off in search of the on-board cafeteria.

We found the train's buffet car soon enough, and ordered beers at the stand-up bar. A small group of young Spanish girls, most likely students, ate soup and bread as we swigged our cold *cerveza* down, two hawks among doves. The girls took photographs of one another, smiling and gay, invaluable content to be shared on a social networking website later.

"Jonathan, what have you been doing in Madrid?" I asked my travel companion. For all his adventurousness, the trim and well-dressed young man appeared to have done very little in the city in the two days he had been there. He had flown in from Britain, and was now taking the train back because he had a fear of flying. That seemed contradictory right away. And why fly to Madrid for the weekend? It seemed like an eccentric thing to do. Britons, desperate for a foreign thrill, evidently took these quickie trips on a regular basis, and the parachute-in Euro-trips were probably cheaper than going to Blackpool for the weekend. The well-behaved Spanish girls left and went back to their compartments, which left Johnny and me propping up the bar. We chatted to the comforting clickety-clack rhythms of the train.

I said, trying another tack, "So, how was Guatemala then?"

"Yeah, it were fookin' great man; cheap as chips, and lots to see. Dangerous though." Really, and what dangers did he encounter there?

"One night the inn keeper where I was staying was shot." Jonathan had been travelling with his girlfriend at the time, and they had been sleeping in a room above the reception area of a small guest house when the incident occurred.

"Was the man killed?" I asked. "Don't fookin' know. We heard it all: a man knocked on the door, there was this argy-bargy, and then a loud bang, a gunshot. We just froze, didn't move. The next day we grabbed our things, ran out the door, and didn't look back."

"So much for first aid then," I said, remembering the Red Crescent course I had attended in Riyadh.

As we sped north towards the Spanish-French border, Jonathan continued, "It's a rough sort of country. One day I was walking along the road in a town and this geezer comes up with a knife and threatens me..." This time, Jonathan's girlfriend came to the rescue, "...and my girlfriend went up to him and said 'No'..." This timely intervention apparently pacified the knife-wielding Latino, who then left the English couple alone and went on his merry way. Still, a hairy situation to find yourself in; I had travelled over a long swath of North Africa and was never once threatened, nor even felt threatened, in any way. There is always a first time, I suppose, and as Jonathan recounted his story I remembered a ruffian in Manila who had almost mugged me once, only stopped by my calmness, and by my keeping a good physical distance from him. Some tourists, it seems to me, invite trouble when abroad by not being alert, or by looking too innocent, or by appearing to be lost.

"Fookin' hell what's wrong with him like," said Jonathan, by way of concluding his story. We downed the last of our beers, and then retired to the plastic mould compartment.

The compartment was devilishly hot and, after wrestling the bunks down, we slept lightly, my inability to sleep also due in part to the constant prattling of the young Spaniard who, like a vampire, came alive in the middle of the night. He spoke into his hand phone in that rapid-fire way Madrilenes do, but softly and confidentially, which made it all the more annoying. Finally, he had the decency to go out into the corridor to continue his never-ending conversation with another vampire somewhere, "Si, si, seeee…" At a late hour, the conductor asked for our passports, required by immigration at the French border. I resented surrendering my travel document, but surmised nothing was going to happen to it, and so gave it to him. Our passports were returned in the morning.

A sweaty chill indicated the temperature had fallen, and I pulled my blanket, which I had prepared in advance, over me. The whole sleeper train thing was a lot less glamorous and fun than I had expected, which is pretty much the way things go when you travel: nothing is ever quite what you imagine it to be. Travelling by train at least gave me some time to make the mental adjustments necessary for what was going to be a major change of scene.

A WHITE-OUT LANDSCAPE of ice and snow faced us as we stared bleary-eyed out of the train window in the morning. It was a shocking sight: the French countryside resembled Siberia. Cars on nearby roads spewed fog from their exhausts like Russian trucks.

"Wow, that's weird," I mumbled, having forgotten what a really cold European winter's day looked like.

Jonathan summed the scene up better: "Looks fookin' cold." I knew right away that I was going to regret returning home at this time of the year, a couple of months ahead of the schedule I had set myself in Riyadh, a result of having failed to get into Algeria. Perhaps what I should have done was winter in Ibiza, but of course this would have been a detour, and by now I was rather set on getting back to England. Christmas I did not care for, but I wanted access to my belongings, my books, and my culture. And with a warming climate, how cold would it be in Britain anyway? The answer, as I was about to find out, was very cold indeed. Even here south of Paris, it was obvious that Western Europe was in the grip of a big chill.

Finally, we arrived at Paris's Austerlitz Station where I scrambled off the train with my bags. Jonathan disappeared into the mists of the uncrowded but frigid station. I stood there assembling my baggage and collecting myself. I considered a stay in Paris, but was having problems contacting a friend, and when I did hear from him he was at work and not available to meet me until later. Struggling to find the metro, I got on with the business of getting orientated, eventually finding my way into the city's subterranean mass transit network. Where should I go? I had no idea. Most of the hotels I knew were concentrated around the *Gare du Nord*, and so I made a beeline for that area. On the way, I studied the small metro map. "Picasso Station" – hmm, okay, I like that. But a station named "Stalingrad." Bit odd that, I mean Stalingrad hardly goes with Austerlitz. No station named after Jacques Cousteau. Paris whizzed past the window when the train emerged into the open, a city I associate with the surrealists, and with Henry Miller's *Tropic of Cancer*. Those days are gone of course, and Paris is no longer the great magnet for artists it once was, in part because of a shift in monetary values that now made the French capital an expensive place to live.

At the *Gare du Nord*, the station restaurant was cold, and I remembered Man Ray's comment in his memoir about the poor to non-existent central heating in Paris; the locals, originally of peasant stock, apparently prefer feeling cold to being over-heated. I sat down at a table in the restaurant and scribbled away in my notebook, having been too self-conscious, and too physi-cally cramped, to write on the train. One of the nice things about France is that someone sitting writing in a café or restaurant is discreetly left alone; no one finds the activity suspect. Outside the station, a blizzard of sorts was blowing; a youth in a thin anorak scampered across the street, shoulders hunched, his hands dug deep into trouser pockets. My trip had come to an end, no doubt, although I continued to procrastinate about definitely terminating it for a little while longer. After finishing up my notes, I took a walk outside the station, wanting to get away from the railway network in order to think, and to make a final decision on my next move. It had stopped snowing, but it was cold, and I was surprised to see a couple of ethnic Arab, or perhaps Berber, women trying to cadge a few coins from passers-by.

In a nearby café, I ordered a brandy – asking, with an ironic inflection, for a Napoleon Brandy. Glancing up at the façade of the *Gare du Nord* I noticed a copy of the bust of the long-haired Jupiter I had seen in the site museum at Sabratha. This connection to the Orient seemed quaint, almost retro, and it was easy to miss. It was the French who had first marked out the Near East with their obsessive mapmaking and categorizing, in preparation for European conquest. In the post-colonial era, the countries of North Africa are struggling to build their identities away from this colonial history. There is more, so much more, to Libya than Roman ruins, but how the Europeans focused on the ruins, how they elevated a dead culture whose main feature was its impulse to dominate and subject... The brandy warmed me up a bit, but also paralysed my will to action. The thought of the effort involved in looking for a hotel in the freezing weather was acting together with the brandy to shut me down, and by the time I left the café the decision to return to England by the quickest overland means available had already been made.

THERE WAS little romance in being frisked three times before boarding the Eurostar. The rather incompetent French security officers missed the four-inch clasp knife stuck in my belt. Not that the knife was an offensive weapon as such, but it had set the metal detector off several times, and I did not take it off, regarding it, a little in the Yemeni fashion, as a symbol of my dignity. When I finally threw my mobile phone into a proffered basket, the security team assumed that it was this item that had been setting the alarm off and waved me through. Being manhandled by a Frenchie left a slightly bitter taste in the mouth, and somewhat spoiled this final leg of my journey back to England. It should have been a relief to get on the train, but it felt more like I had been conned by a pricing system that had taken advantage of people stranded by cancelled flights. The Britons, who predominated in the Eurostar waiting area, took it all stoically – they were used to waiting, bad service, rip-offs and invasive security. I thought the train was late, but it was another case of me failing to take into account time differences, and in fact we were called to board the train on time. We shuffled onto the train as French railway workers manually shovelled snow off the platform, a scene that could have been painted by Claude Monet.

An ill-mannered French attendant tried to boss me into place, almost snatching the ticket in my hand. I was having none it and held onto the ticket coolly informing Madame that I could read and would surely find my seat among the 20 or so possibilities, thank you anyway. The interior of the business premier class carriage, in which I was travelling, propelled me back into the 21st century. I sat down and immediately the train set off into the murk of northern France. The irksome nannying continued as we were all force-fed a tray of food, as if we were babies, in the hermetically sealed train. It was obvious to me that the only good thing about the Eurostar, actually a bad thing from my point of view, was its speed. The possibility of striking up an interesting conversation with a travelling companion on this train was remote given the tense atmosphere, though some people gamely attempted this old-fashioned activity.

"Terrible weather isn't it," was the opening gambit from a young Anglo-Indian yuppie to his opposite number.

"Ya, awful; we were worried about getting stuck in Paris but managed to get out," replied the Whitehall bureaucrat, or arms dealer, or whoever he was, trying to be polite. He munched on a bit of salad, and ignored the small bottle of wine, "Don't normally drink." The three people sitting next to me were all absorbed in notebook computers. I tried to read Cavafy, but found his poetry too esoteric for the train ride and so switched to an American news magazine, suitable pap in the circumstances. But I found the news magazine too vapid – such publications only became interesting after about 20 years when they remind you of things you had completely forgotten about, like a super-power meeting in space, or a war on the Indo-Pakistan border. I knocked back my ration of wine, and stared out at a darkening landscape, a wasteland of empty, frozen fields.

"Ya, hmm, well, quite." The establishment Englishman was getting tired of the tiresome yuppie. Not getting a warm enough response from the Whitehall lizard, the Londoner called his office and gave a lengthy account of how he had come to be on the train at that moment, due to a cancelled flight obviously, a story lacking any kind of moment, merely a long and prosaic statement of facts. It gave him something to talk about, I suppose. But instead of leaving it at that, he next called one of his staff, a female evidently, and, with frequent interjections of "yes love", and "love you", and "you're right, yes, great", received her verbal report. Whitehall went back to work on his battle plans, for he too had a laptop computer, and I looked the other way, bored to distraction.

The Eurostar of course goes under the English Channel or "The Sleeve" as the French call it, through a tunnel, a novelty of sorts and something I was looking forward to experiencing. However, there was nothing to see in the darkness, and I barely noticed when we entered and exited the giant rabbit warren, and never was my arrival back in Britain so imperceptible, such an anti-climax. There came a point when it was obvious we were in England though: the fields looked neater and a lot more intensively cultivated; a more urbanized environment altogether. The train would stop at Ashford and, pushing my uneaten tray of

quite literally as we still had to drive from Ashford back to Thanet.

It was in Margate, Thanet, where I re-grouped, picked up the pieces of my life, and tried to move forward. I stayed at a friend's flat, in a house that had been divided into three, and in the afternoons sat stunned in the living room, the oblique winter sun picking me out through the bay window, its glare like an aeroplane's landing lights. The quality of the light, the empty streets and the general unfriendliness and dysfunction of the rental neighbourhood came as a huge shock, even though I had been here before. I was no longer of any interest to anyone; I was simply an unemployed English teacher. Consuming alcohol, watching television and shopping constituted the national pastimes. One of the reasons I had left England in the first place was to get away from what I felt to be a soulless and spiritually dead culture, from the stifling provincialism, and from pestiferous people. But now I discovered a huge class of plebeians "disabled" before their time, garbage all over the place, and young couples who thought nothing of having a violent quarrel in the street. As D.H. Lawrence once remarked upon returning to England after a four-year absence, "The place feels tight: one would like to smash something." And so people do. Enjoying a Margate sunset one evening, I witnessed some youngsters smash the window of their flat, climb out of the window onto a rooftop, and re-enter the apartment through another window, apparently to evade an angry landlord.

My priority was writing this book and, after a twilight zone period, I found a flat to stay and got on with this task. That left the problem of earning an income, and here I drew a blank, getting rejected left, right and centre by employers who regarded me like an out of work actor or down at heel musician – interesting, but probably not reliable. Meanwhile, my contacts in the Middle East tried to entice me back to work another contract there, but I was determined to hold out for better, and besides, I wanted to see my writing project through. Socially, I remained isolated. Without colleagues, and with my girlfriend far away, I felt lonely, too. My way of dealing with the situation was to write and to walk. With a friend I made at a local language school, I hiked around Thanet's pretty coastline, in and out of bays and inlets I knew well. Although these hikes were pleasantly distracting, something did not feel right. Again D.H. Lawrence expressed this feeling well saying, in effect, that when one went back home it was depressing because, although things may look familiar, your spirit was no longer to be found there. You know the streets and they look almost the same, but people you once knew are missing. After an absence measured not in months, but in decades (before Saudi Arabia I lived for many years in East Asia), you find your former social net holed and torn. Grandparents have passed on, a fact that you are reminded of daily because you remember where they lived. And then there are the people you wish had gone away but have not: forever young radio DJs, game show hosts and members of parliament from the 1970s and 80s still bubbling away like fumaroles. The British are forever engaged in role play, acting out routines, and reading scripts. To some extent this is true in all cultures, but it really bothered me when I found people were not listening to me, but on auto-pilot, because my expectations of what good communication entailed had changed vastly through years of varied cultural experience. Everything in England was routine. It was the setup I had rejected years ago; insular Britain, with its middle-class codes, and a clock ticking in every room.

The sorts of things people bemoaned in England were of less concern to me. I took it as axiomatic that the quality of life in the UK would continue to fall, that the country would become more crowded and less civil than before, that in short we are all doomed. To sum up: the weather is awful, the price of a pint is outrageous, and we all face more bureaucracy; education has turned into a crude money-making enterprise, and good luck to any young person who aspires to a university education – expect to be enslaved by debt during the best years of your life, debt being, as Noam Chomsky recently put it, a "disciplinary technique". I could go on, but there is no need because all this is old news in a media-mediated culture like no other. What is interesting is the way I now perceive this social and political landscape, how my own position in it as a detached observer makes me feel like I'm living inside a movie, in a place where all the values seem unreal. My cameo appearance in this film did not go unnoticed. As one of my friendly neighbours said the other day, intending for me to hear the remark, "What are you doing here?" It's probably the question of my life, and will no doubt be the title of my autobiography.

GETTING to the end of West of Arabia, twice in effect, was a salutary experience. The first conclusion to draw, implicit in everything that I have said in this book, is that the trip – and I include here my two years' residence in Saudi Arabia – was for me an educational and, to some extent, spiritual experience. It would have been quite reasonable to have flown out of Arabia, but I wanted to know more. One might say, I needed to know more, and therefore extended my Arab experience geographically. In *Racism Explained to My Daughter* Tahar Ben Jelloun eloquently states that travelling encourages a love of discovery and gives the traveller an insight into the richness and beauty of all cultures and, crucially, makes you realize that no culture is better than any other. There was much I liked and admired in the cultures I found west of the Arabian Peninsula, chief among them the warmth and sincerity of the people I met, and their sense of total filial loyalty. I make this generalization guardedly, as Ben Jelloun also points out, "Racism develops out of preconceived notions about peoples and their cultures… That's why you should never say things like: "Arabs are this way or that way." In order to say something though, a writer or speaker necessarily generalizes. I would say, and this is something I learned from my Arab friends, that one should seek to focus on the positive qualities of other people, and try to generalize about those qualities rather than focus on the negative. It's a choice.

Individual Arabs may be crooks, but this observation must not be applied to the identified group as a whole because it is defamatory. On the other hand, we might say all Arabs are hospitable, even though some rogues may try to kill you if you are in the wrong place at the wrong time (any observation needs qualifying).

We could go a little deeper and say that designations such as "Arab" and "Muslim" are rather meaningless. The incredible variety in outlook, manners and social habits of the peoples of West of Arabia belies attempts to generalize about them. Even within one small country, such as Eritrea, there is incredible diversity. But I was looking for connections, too. When I applied for my Eritrean visa in Riyadh, the Consul, a Tigrinyan-speaking Christian, read and perfectly understood a letter of introduction from my employer that had been written in Arabic. If there was a connection between the countries that I visited on this trip before arriving in Spain, there it was right at the beginning: the Arabic script, the language of Islam, and, like English, a very powerful imperial tool. Arabic is spoken and respected everywhere in North Africa, and to be versed in this language is to be introduced to another world, true of all languages of course. To have not known Arabic well to some extent blinded me on my travels, and my observations were the less for it, although – and here is something else I learned from my Arab friends – a great deal can be known about a person from their demeanour and psychological state, and even by small hints in what may appear to be undistinguished dress. Along with Arabic went Islam and many assumptions about correct behaviour, morality and proper relations between people that culturally marked the part of Africa I had travelled through. These assumptions never really shocked me, and most times they seemed quite logical within the cultural context. It was only when I returned to England that I started to be shocked by, to repeat the example mentioned above, the shameless screaming between spouses in the street, *in front of their children*.

The business of travel writing itself is problematic and raises political and philosophical issues. What right do I have to go trotting about naming and describing other countries and those that live there when they do not get a right to reply? How come I get this chance to move freely and independently when many a bright, intelligent Arabian female, who might write something interesting, does not get an opportunity to do so? The answer lies in power formations that 1) Elevate the European over the non-European, and 2) Elevate men over women. Imagine if a woman from Arabia, speaking very little English, came to England and wrote a book about travelling there. No one in Europe would take such a book seriously because it would not fit any pattern that preceded it, even though European men with little knowledge of Arabic, or of Arab culture, are considered fit to comment on Arabia ad infinitum. He – it's usually a he – may do so as long as he doesn't stray too far from elevating the European over the non-European. Ernesto Guevara stated in his *Motorcycle Diaries* that a writer was never really free and was very often, consciously or subconsciously, serving an agenda, one determined in the first instance by commercial publishing, but ultimately defined by the ruling class. I knew all of this to be true before starting to write this book. In my defence, I would say that I have not tried to conceal my ignorance, and that I did try to learn from experience. If you don't go out into the world, how can you begin to challenge domination, stereotyping and ignorance? At the end of travelling perhaps the biggest culture shock of all is to realize that the world cannot be described, only your relation to it, the latter encoded into everything you write.

15

WEST OF ARABIA REDUX

Soon after my arrival back in England, political sparks, ignited by the self-immolation of Mohammed Bouazizi, began to fly in Tunisia, which rapidly developed into a fire of protest and civil resistance. The demonstrators were provoked to act by high unemployment and a lack of political freedoms. President Zine El Abidine Ben Ali responded with a security crackdown that only served to stoke the fire of disobedience and rebellion. Whilst all this was happening, I noticed that the travel agent in Margate's main shopping street continued to offer mid-winter breaks in Tunisian resorts like Sousse where I had spent a couple of bored days lounging on a hotel room balcony. But events occurred so fast that Ben Ali was ousted from the presidency before anyone really knew what was happening. The Tunisian people, as I had vaguely discerned when I was there, were at the end of their tether, and sick and tired of their crook of a head of state. The Jasmine Revolution, as it has become known, was highly successful in deposing a corrupt leader, but real change in Tunisia remains elusive. This is not surprising because the basic state apparatus remains unchanged, and so far there has not been the kind of sweeping economic and political reform expected and demanded by the people in that country; powerful established interests still rule the roost. Ben Ali, meanwhile, was sentenced in absentia to 35 years in jail for various offences, a sentence he is unlikely ever to serve.

The Tunisian civil rebellion inspired similar uprisings across the Arab world, notably in Egypt where the protests really did have a revolutionary character to them – scenes of thousands of protesters charging over the Sixth of October Bridge, and of the vigorous and fearless occupation of Tahrir Square by the Egyptian people, were as stunning as they were exhilarating. These were the streets I had walked around only a couple of months before, finding myself enervated by the crowds and the chaos. It was obvious to me then that Egypt was not working, a fact confirmed by those whom I had met and made friends with there. Again, protesters' anger was directed at the head of state: they demanded the immediate resignation of President Hosni Mubarak. Mostly to save face, Mubarak held on, promising a transition of power. Unfortunately, and in character, he then ordered a brutal crackdown on the protesters and many were killed in the ensuing violence. The Egyptian army, not normally associated with domestic political repression, were called in and shamefully engaged in the severe abuse of civilian detainees, some of whom were held in the Egyptian Museum. The military were also tasked with clearing Tahrir Square in April, à la Tiananmen Square. The Egyptian protesters showed their mettle and held their ground in the face of the state directed assault on them. Mubarak had had a chance to move Egypt forward, but instead he had pursued economic policies that divided the people into haves and have-nots. In particular, the satellite cities and second-home holiday resorts that promised exclusivity were deeply resented by ordinary people struggling to get by in an economy that had been orientated away from the public interest. Mubarak was at last toppled, but as in Tunisia real change has yet to come to Egypt and there is widespread belief that the army, headed by Field Marshal Hussein Tantawi, has now hijacked the revolution.

The waves from the Tunisian and Egyptian uprisings rippled far and wide, and unrest followed in other Arab countries during the spring of 2011, including places I had visited on my travels, namely Saudi Arabia, Bahrain, Yemen and Sudan. When I heard of demonstrations in Saudi Arabia I knew they were not going to get as far as they had in Tunisia and Egypt. Saudi Arabia is a very different polity to the secular states of North Africa; it is a much more closed, and therefore easily controlled, society. Moreover, the protests in Saudi kingdom were initiated by minority Shia groups, widely despised by the majority Sunni population. Nonetheless, the House of Saud was spooked and King Abdullah quickly announced a welfare spending spree to placate the general populace. If throwing money at a dysfunctional social and political system was not going to deal with the root need for political reform, then at least it helped take the hunger out of the political opposition, an old and trusted tactic in Arabia, as elsewhere. The multibillion-pound spending package included the creation of 60,000 new jobs in the security forces, a low-income house building programme, and a stipend for the unemployed. Meanwhile, the Saudis were quick to send their troops in to bolster the Bahraini royal family's grip on power in the small island nation, with the United States' quiet approval. The Bahraini people, a Shia majority, showed great determination and courage in the face of this intervention, continuing to protest in the most difficult of circumstances. On streets I had caroused on during weekends away from Riyadh, barricades and a determined civilian resistance emerged. The demonstrations were suppressed in Bahrain, the protesters too small in number to challenge the combined power of the ruling house, shored up by the House of Saud, in turn supported by a superpower. Copycat protests in the Sudan, in Khartoum, were also quickly suppressed by the local security apparatus, but not before Mohammed Abd al-Rahman had fallen under police fire, yet another martyr resulting from the Sudanese government's desperate misrule, one of the great tragedies of Africa. No wonder the population of southern Sudan voted overwhelmingly for secession in January, and if the troubled history of the unified Sudan is now history, a war between the newly-independent Republic of South Sudan and North Sudan is, worryingly, a real possibility. In Yemen, one of the poorer countries of the Middle East, it was a different story. A mountainous country, the protests in Yemen ranged about and were not concentrated in the capital; but they were determined and vigorous, and protesters, aiming their wrath at the top, insisted that Abdullah Saleh resign. Stalling for time and also resorting to violence, Saleh has yet to go at the time of writing, but in his case he will have to step down eventually because the United States government has come to see him as a liability.

Sandwiched between Tunisia and Egypt, it is not surprising that Libya should be have been affected by the civil unrest in its more populous neighbours. The extent of the unrest there, and the way it quickly developed into a full-blown civil war, did take me by surprise though, and the courage shown by the rebels in the face of Gaddafi's wrath has been astonishing. Unfortunately, and for many reasons, it is much more difficult for the people of Libya to get rid of their overlord, not least because Gaddafi commands loyalty, and his loyalist forces are well-equipped and well-funded. The war began in February when Libyan security forces acted with characteristic ferocity killing hundreds of protesters in Benghazi. Such a vicious reaction, on top of all the other state-sponsored crimes in recent years, was essentially a declaration of war on the people, and the Libyan people, hero-ically, fought back. In March, the government predicted the imminent fall of Benghazi, but troops sent to retake the city were repelled. Battles then erupted in many Libyan cities as Gaddafi tried to re-impose his iron fist rule, with uneven results. Misratah, a city where we had spent a night after a long and exhausting drive along the Libyan coast road, saw some of the bitterest fighting of the war. Over 1000 people were killed there, including notable photojournalists Tim Hetherington and Chris Hondros. On the evening we had arrived in Misratah back in November 2010, our vehicle got a puncture obliging us to stop. Not needed to help with the repair, I went for a stroll around town during the ensuing hiatus and saw a city that seemed quite clean and well-ordered compared to some others in North Africa. There was no sign of the tension and resentment that must have lain not far below the surface of this orderliness, tension that would presently explode into all-out violence. It seems the British government could not resist the chance to get involved in this ugly civil war, siding half-heartedly with the rebels in a move that was cynically calculated to curry favour with any new Libyan regime, and give the RAF some shooting practice. And then the International Criminal Court stuck its oar in announcing an arrest warrant for Gaddafi and Saïf al-Islam, one of his sons. But I do not think the Libyan rebels will be handing Gaddafi over to the International Criminal Court when they get their hands on him, not after all that has passed in that beautiful, rich, and deeply corrupted desert country.

It seems west of Arabia will never quite be the same again, but whether this means there will be any meaningful political change in the countries where the dictators fell is another question. One of my problems with all these protests, and the way they were reported, was the emphasis on getting rid of the man at the top of the political system, as if this would be a panacea for all extant ills. What has transpired in the Arab world is not a revolution, in the French or Iranian sense, but a civilian rebellion against dysfunctional, corrupt governments. Unfortunately, getting rid of the man at the top will not in and of itself lead to significant social and political change, and opposition groups in places like Egypt are so widely divided ideologically speaking that no consensus exists on how to go forward. In such a fractured and particularized polity, another strongman, probably a military figure, inevitably takes over, and a new round of authoritarian government begins. This is a pattern that has repeated itself hundreds of times in states that do not have a democratic tradition or culture, i.e. in most Arab and African states. The Arab dictator's attitude was perfectly expressed by President Bashar al Assad of Syria, who in a public address to the Syrian people in June called for dialogue and reform at the same time as he described protesters in Syria as "saboteurs" and "germs" –

not the best way to start a dialogue with the opposition. Assad's days are almost certainly numbered also; although the security apparatus in Syria remains loyal to him thus far, Assad is rapidly losing credibility internationally. But what comes next?

One of the dangers of discussing recent events west of Arabia, and further afield in the Arab world, is that such a report may reinforce stereotypes about Arab culture being backward and unruly, of Arabs being emotional and incapable of logic, reason and restraint. But what I think the protests in Tunisia, Egypt, Libya, Yemen, and elsewhere have shown is the moral courage of peoples who suffered so much under their respective regimes, but who decided enough was enough and, regardless of the consequences, made the decision to take direct action. Anyone who knows how those regimes operated will know that this was a brave, but also a logical and reasoned response. Mass action was the only way to get the dictators' attention; it was the only way to see them off, and everyone intuited this in the collective uprisings. As the late Palestinian intellectual Edward Saïd pointed out in his landmark book *Culture and Imperialism*, representations of the Arab world since the 1967 Six-Day War have been crude, reductionist and coarsely racialist. What I think the Arab Spring has proved is that Arab culture has great moral depth, and that the Arabs – a vast agglomeration of cultures and peoples in actuality – are fighters who when pushed will think nothing of dying for a just cause. The one television image from this period of tumult that sticks out in my mind is that of an unarmed protester in Bahrain who stood verbally invoking God's power, refusing to run away from police gunfire; he was shot soon afterwards, luckily not fatally, perhaps a divine intervention.

A less spectacular news item in 2011 announced the release of an online interactive map showing the location of Spain's Civil War execution grave sites. In Sol Square in Madrid, I had watched as silent demonstrators walked holding the photographs of family members who had disappeared under Franco's repression. They were demanding more information about their loved ones' fates, and this map was a first step in meeting those demands. Perhaps 50,000 people, seen to be politically unreliable, were massacred during, and in the immediate aftermath of, the Civil War, a terrible retribution, epic in scale and extent, but one largely hushed up for decades. Franco's war on his own people was second only to Stalin's in Europe in the 20th century, and a full accounting of the crimes committed under his rule may never be completed to the satisfaction of the victims' families. His actions only go to show that so-called civilized Europeans are every bit as capable of acting barbarically as anyone else in this world, evidence that at a fundamental level people are basically all the same, capable of good or evil acts depending on circumstances, education, ideological outlook, and so forth. The terrorist bomb that killed British travel writer Peter Moss, one of 16 western tourists murdered at a café in Marrakech, Morocco, in April 2011, was not entirely unrelated to the bombs dropped from RAF aircraft on targets in Libya, and from US aircraft on targets in Afghanistan, the same year, though many in Europe and the US failed to make the connection, or were apt to apply a double standard when considering these equally violent acts.

It was Edward Saïd who first identified a deliberate process of selection and expression in the way that Arab/Islamic cultures were represented in the western media. What I found in the countries I visited after leaving Saudi Arabia, however, were complex and beautiful cultures in no way inferior to any other culture on this earth, and interconnected to Europe in many ways. North Africa is Europe's alter ego, and it is no accident that men in Tangiers daily stare at the European mainland with dreams of escaping their cramped, hardscrabble lives to go and live in what for them is a kind of paradise. Many Africans have died chasing the dream of emigration to Europe, a continent that has no interest in North Africa except as a holiday destination, or a source of raw materials. The most ironic television advertisement ever must be the one recently repeated endlessly on a well-known international news channel that sold Egypt as a place where one could find the sun, as if that were all that mattered. I am sure Egyptians get a lesson in relativity every time they watch this ad, coming to understand us a lot better than we understand them, if such distinctions are valid at all. In the same way that the young men of Morocco dream of Europe, so in an afternoon reverie I find myself once more in the lands where the sun never stops shining, and where they dance when it rains.